The publishers assert their right to use *Cool Camping* as a trademark of
Punk Publishing Ltd.

Cool Camping: England (3rd edition)
This edition published in the UK in 2011 by
Punk Publishing Ltd, 3 The Yard, Pegasus Place, London, SE11 5SD
www.punkpublishing.co.uk
www.coolcamping.co.uk

A catalogue record of this book is available from the British Library.

ISBN 978-1-906889-32-6
(ISBN 978-0-9552036-6-4 2nd edition)
(ISBN 978-0-9552036-1-9 1st edition)
10 9 8 7 6 5 4 3 2 1

KEY
CDP – chemical disposal point
1W, 1M – one women's, one men's (for loos and showers)
Vanners – collective term for campervans and caravans
Public Transport options are only included where viable

introduction

As this book hits the shelves, it will be five years since the first edition of *Cool Camping: England* – the first real dedicated 'tenters' guidebook – was unleashed on an unsuspecting British public. Back then it was just me, driving frantically around the countryside in a battered old Peugeot, with a pad of scribbled recommendations from friends and tip-offs from friends-of-friends. I managed to find just 40 special places. Thankfully, since then, as camping has continued to grow in popularity, so too have the quality and quantity of tenters' sites. Today, canvas campers are privy to a wide choice of cracking sites that cater for their simple needs: campfires; quiet corners, hill-top spots, or snug woodland clearings; and caravan-free zones.

There's a huge emphasis on the 'green' that has been cropping up across the land, too, with many site-owners tuning in to their gorgeous natural surroundings and turning a new eco-leaf. You won't just find recycling at these places, but beautifully crafted compost loos, coppice woods, sustainable water supplies, solar power, free-range and organic produce, and discounts for campers who come via public transport, too.

Cool Camping has also been expanding (organically, of course). As the original trailblazers of the tent-camping cause, we've made it our mission to once again travel the country, seeking out special campsites on your behalf. This time, it's not just me in my Peugeot – no less than 10 experienced reviewers (we wouldn't all have fitted in my little car anyway!) have been out and about, compiling reviews, chatting to owners and fellow campers, taking photos, and generally doing a very comprehensive and professional job.

The result is a beautiful new book – redesigned for this edition – that is positively bursting with superb little pockets of camping paradise: 150 sites in total. Practical info about each site, as well as things to see, do, and where to eat and drink in the area accompany a personal and honest write-up. And each of the 10 regional chapters comes with a handy map to help you locate these pitches. Importantly, while we have increased the campsite count, we haven't let our standards slip, so you can be sure that every site is a special place in its own unique way. And although there's not enough room to talk about our favourites here, just turn to the Top 10 (p12) or have a look at the pics on the cover to be inspired.

The other big change that's happened in the last five years has been the continuing focus on the web as a tool for people to plan their holidays. So we now have a lovely new website where you can search for the sort of campsite you want, view extra pictures and information, and read user reviews, too, for a really good idea about each site before you visit. (Call me old-fashioned, but I still think a good book can't be beat!)

It's another example of how things are moving forward relentlessly and unapologetically, making it all the more important for us to slip away to the countryside, pitch a tent, light a fire – and escape.

See you out there...

Jonathan Knight, Chief Camper

campsite locator

continued overleaf

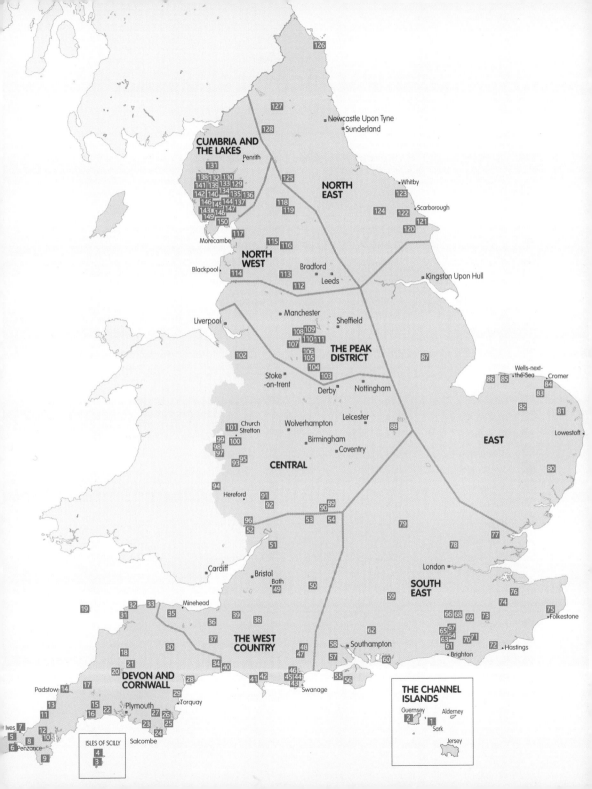

CUMBRIA AND
THE LAKES

126

127

Newcastle Upon Tyne
Sunderland

128

131
138 132 130
141 139 133 129
142 140 134 135 136
146 144 137
143 145 148 147
149 150

Penrith

125

NORTH
EAST

Whitby

123

Scarborough

124 122 121
120

118
119

117

Morecambe

115 116

NORTH
WEST

114

113

Bradford

112

Leeds

Kingston Upon Hull

Blackpool

Liverpool

Manchester

Sheffield

108 109
110 111
107

106
105
104

102

THE PEAK
DISTRICT

87

Wells-next-
the-Sea

86 85

Cromer

84
83

82

81

Lowestoft

Stoke
-on-trent

103

Derby

Nottingham

Leicester

88

EAST

80

101

Church
Stretton

99
98
97

100

Wolverhampton

Birmingham

Coventry

93 95

CENTRAL

94

Hereford

91

92

90 89

53

54

79

78

77

96

52

51

Cardiff

Bristol

Bath

49

50

London

SOUTH
EAST

76

74

75

Folkestone

19

32 33

31

35

Minehead

36

39

38

59

62

66 68
65 67
63 54
61

69 73

70 71

72

Hastings

18

21

30

37

THE WEST
COUNTRY

48
47

58

57

Southampton

60

55 56

Swanage

Brighton

Padstow

20

14

17

DEVON AND
CORNWALL

28

34 40

41 42

46
45 44
43

THE CHANNEL
ISLANDS

13

29

Torquay

Guernsey

Alderney

15

22

27 26

2

1

11

16

Plymouth

23

25

24

Sark

Ives 7

12

Salcombe

Jersey

5

10

6

8

Penzance

9

ISLES OF SCILLY

4

3

campsite locator (continued)

cool camping top 10

School league tables? Pah! Political polls? Pointless. *Strictly...* winner? Who cares... These are the big results the nation is waiting for. Try reading them out in an excited '*X Factor* announcer' voice to build the drama...

Turner Hall Farm, Cumbria **3**
If you were thinking it's impossible to find a beautiful yet quiet campsite in busy old Lakeland, you'd be wrong. Rugged, remote Turner Hall Farm is the proof. **p312**

Secret Garden, Cornwall **4**
Garden? What garden? There's no secret garden round these parts, no sir. Be on your way. And don't tell anyone else either... **p30**

ForgeWood, Kent **7**
Woodland, campfires, and beautiful countryside, less than an hour on the train from London? Who ForgeWoodn't? **p148**

Grizedale, Cumbria **8**
If *The Lord of the Rings* hadn't been filmed in New Zealand, it would surely have been shot among the green meadows and fern-splashed forestry of Grizedale. Precious. **p314**

1

histledown, Gloucestershire

eamy, roomy, rolling meadows surrounded by acres of forest makes Thistledown a place
here it's all about the space. And the fires. And the badgers. **p112**

2

Henry's, Cornwall

With a cracking coastal location, a friendly welcome, and some quirky art, this place won
top billing in the last edition, and it's just as fantastic today. **p40**

5

ole Station, Devon

ke your pick from magical woodland clearings or flower-scented meadow pitches and
t that campfire smoking. Pony-and-trap rides an optional extra... **p60**

6

Riversidelakes, Dorset

If climbing trees, jumping into lakes, and kicking back by the campfire are your sort of
pastimes, this is your sort of site. Ours too. Magical. **p104**

9

lde Garden, Suffolk

oint-sized garden campsite behind a former Suffolk pub. Choose a yurt, tipi, gypsy
ravan, or bring your own tent, and drink in the, ahem, 'intoxicating' atmosphere. **p170**

10

Dernwood Farm, East Sussex

Abandon the car and push your way through a bluebell-flooded wood to Dernwood's
peaceful clearing, for a semi-wild camping adventure in hidden Sussex **p152**

the channel islands

GUERNSEY

Vale
St Sampson
2
St Peter Port
St Saviour
St Martin
Torteval
Forest

SARK

St Anne

ALDERNEY

JERSEY

St Mary
St John
Bouley Bay
St Ouen
St Martin
Beaumont
St Brelade
St Saviour
St Helier

Site number		Page number	Cool for campfires	Stunning views	For first-time campers	Middle of nowhere	Beach within reach	Surf's up	Waterside chilling	Walk this way	Great for kids	Dog friendly	High on mountains	For car-less campers	Cool for campervans	Wet 'n' wild	Forest fun	On yer bike	Something different	A friendly welcome	Fish club
The Channel Islands																					
1	La Valette Farm	18	●		●	●	●			●		●		●		●		●		●	
2	Fauxquets Valley	22		●	●	●				●	●	●				●		●		●	

10 km

10 miles

la valette farm

La Valette Farm, Sark, Channel Islands, GY9 0SE   01481 832202   www.sercq.com

Pitch a tent in the east-facing field of La Valette Farm's campsite on the tiny isle of Sark – the smallest of the four major Channel Islands – and on a clear day, with the cliffs dropping away dramatically into the sea, you get a pristine view of the French coast, 20 miles off in the distance.

Though physically closer to France than the English mainland (which is about 80 miles to the north), Sark is a British Crown Dependency. But that's not to say it's just an extension of England, as influences from both nations have blended to produce a unique culture that was – up until 2008 – the last remaining feudal state in the western world, making it a little piece of history, too.

In 1565, after the island had been ravaged by the Black Death and become known as a place 'of pirates, thieves, brigands, murderers, and assassins', Elizabeth I granted Helier de Carteret the first Charter as Seigneur – head of the feudal government. This was based on the condition that he kept the place inhabited (with less dangerous folk), had 40 musket-wielding men as a defence force, and paid the Crown a twentieth of a knight's fee annually – two quid in today's money.

La Valette was built by those first 16th-century inhabitants and remains the only property on the island never to have been sold. Its history is etched on the stone buildings, which, though badly damaged during the Nazi occupation here – another interesting chapter in the island's chequered past – retain many of the original features. And today the whole place seems to

encapsulate Sark's appeal: history, nature, and a warm welcome.

Though the island does offer some of the essentials of 21st-century living – broadband and decent mobile phone reception – the picturesque 40-minute ferry ride from its larger sister isle, Guernsey, is essentially a journey back in time. There are no cashpoints, streetlamps, or cars here. Not that you need a car, as Sark measures just two square miles, so you can easily explore the island's unspoilt natural beauty by horse and cart, bicycle, or simply on foot. And there is plenty to discover – from wonderful flora and fauna to the secluded beaches, where more than a dozen people represents a crowded day.

La Grande Grève is the island's best sandy beach, but at the time of writing it was inaccessible due to a landslide. There are plenty of alternatives, including Dixcart Bay, which looks spectacular in the dancing morning sunlight. The island has caves too, including the Gouliot Caves, which are protected for their large population of anemones and well worth a day's exploration. The paths leading down to beaches and cave systems are steep, though, so not for the very young or old.

La Valette provides a perfect base from which to explore the island, but has plenty to offer in its own right. It is still a fully functioning farm (you may get a sideways glance or two from the resident dairy cows), and around the rear of the farmhouse you'll find the campsite proper, which is essentially a pitch-where-you-like field, but

Scenic gardens at the local bank

with breathtaking views and direct access to the cliff path and seashore below. Though the cliffs are sheer, it's only a five-minute walk down to the beach at Grève de la Ville, where you can watch the sun set and maybe take a midnight dip, then lie outside your tent in blissful silence gazing up at the stars through an unpolluted sky – the best end to a day exploring a very unique destination.

COOL FACTOR A campsite with stunning cliff-top views, and a farmhouse boasting half a century's worth of history on an island abundant in natural beauty, with unique attractions and a culture that offers a rare step back in time.

WHO'S IN Tents, responsible dog owners and their pooches – yes. Groups are happily catered for but should book in advance in summer. The island's rough tracks are not ideal for buggies or disabled access, but if you make the trip, you'll be offered a pitch. Campervans and caravans – no.

ON SITE The campsite consists of a large, gently sloping, east-facing, cliff-top field. Pitch where you like, but bear in mind it is a little exposed when windy, so it's best to hug the hedged edges of the field – more protective fencing is planned. Frame tents are available for hire if you'd prefer to leave your tent at home, and come with airbeds, table and chairs, crockery, cutlery, pots and pans, water carrier, and camping stove. The facilities block has hot metered showers (£1 for about 4 minutes); cubicle washrooms with shaver points; and a communal washing-up sink. The showers are powered by solar panels, and shower water is recycled to toilet cisterns. There's a small, slightly dated children's play area. Home-made marmalades and fresh farm produce are available to purchase. No campfires allowed, but small disposable BBQs are okay (ask permission beforehand).

OFF SITE Only 3 miles long and 1½ miles wide, but packed with beautiful natural scenery, the island is a rambler's paradise, and you're never far from a tea room if it rains. Take a boat trip with George Guille (01481 832107; www. welcometosark.com) around the island to see abundant birdlife – including puffins. For those with a head for heights, La Coupée (see www.sark.info) is a narrow isthmus joining the main part of the island (Great Sark) to the small southern peninsula known as Little Sark. It's just 3 metres wide, with a heart-quickening 80-metre drop on either side, but offers views of the most dramatic scenery in the Channel Islands. La Seigneurie (01481 832208; www.laseigneuriegardens.com) has, since 1730, been home to the Seigneur (or Lord) of Sark, and was built on the site of the 6th-century monastery of Saint Magloire. In addition to its history it has wonderful gardens.

FOOD AND DRINK La Sablonnerie (01481 832408; www.lasablonnerie.com) is the only restaurant on Little Sark. It's quite expensive, but offers romance in droves; work up an appetite in the exquisite garden, then try some locally caught seafood, followed by an unforgettable starlit carriage-ride back over La Coupée. There are only two pubs on the island – the Mermaid (01481 832022) and the Bel Air (01481 832052) – both within a 10-minute walk. The beer is very affordable and the local characters are colourful, but gastropubs these are not. Try Stocks (01481 832001; www. stockshotel.com) for a more congenial setting.

GETTING THERE Take the ferry from Guernsey (www. sarkshippingcompany.com), or Jersey (www.manche-iles-express.com), or a private charter. On arrival it's £1 well spent to get pulled up Harbour Hill. For that you get a padded seat on a quirky cart to take you up the steep dirt track (there isn't an inch of tarmac on Sark) leading into the village. From here it's a 10-minute walk to La Valette.

OPEN All year.

THE DAMAGE Adult £7 per night; child (under-11) £4. Pre-erected tents an extra £18–£45 per night (depending on size). Credit cards not accepted; no cashpoints on the island.

fauxquets valley

Fauxquets Valley Campsite, Candie Road, Castel, Guernsey, Channel Islands, GY5 7QL   01481 255460/236951   www.fauxquets.co.uk

Fauxquets is one of those places you wish you'd discovered sooner. It's a rural haven entirely in keeping with the laid-back but efficient nature of Guernsey. The campsite sits in a sheltered position overlooking the wooded Fauxquets Valley, its tranquillity enhanced by careful terracing, shrub borders, and ever-present trees. Nothing is overdone, but everything you could want is here, from roomy pitches to a small shop, efficient showers, and a swimming pool. And if you come by plane or don't fancy lugging lots of gear along with you, then pre-erected tents are available, too.

Guests can help themselves to herbs from the small herb garden, and the shop offers zero-food-mile eggs laid by the campsite chickens, as well as locally produced ice cream, cheese, and cider. The play area is small, but there are sports nets, the pool – with its large sunbathing area – and Molly the bounding campsite dog, to entertain the kids.

There's a friendly onsite atmosphere and the feeling that you're always close to nature; trees are all around, and the Terrace area overlooks the valley – a mixture of farmland and natural woods rolling down to meet the stream tinkling along the bottom.

Guernsey is easy to get around; a few minutes of walking and you're deep into its rural charms. Vazon Bay, a broad sweep of sand with more beaches either side, is a 20-minute walk away. There's also a 28-mile coastal path to wander, and bicycle exploration is a must. Hire one from the site and take to the quiet and joyously twisty lanes. No attraction is too far away on Guernsey.

COOL FACTOR Tranquil rural setting and convivial, cosmopolitan atmosphere on Guernsey.

WHO'S IN? Tents, dogs (on leads), big groups (families/ activities-based only) – yes. Campervans, caravans, young/ single-sex groups – no.

ON SITE Just over 100 pitches, all with hook-ups (£3.50) bar a small corner called Outback and the Terrace (with unmarked pitches and great views). There's a toilet block with free hot showers, washing-up area, laundry (token operated), games room with TV, swimming pool, play areas. Pre-erected tents and log cabins. The Haybarn restaurant on site has some takeaway choices. Cycle hire; small shop; free wi-fi on the reception veranda. No campfires, but BBQs okay.

OFF SITE Go to St Peter Port for the Guernsey Aquarium (01481 723301) and Victor Hugo's Hauteville House (01481 721911). Or, on a fine day, take a boat trip to the Isle of Herm (details at the quayside). Walking cards detailing routes around the area are available from the campsite.

FOOD AND DRINK The Last Post (01481 236353) is the nearest pub – a 20-minute walk inland. For foodies: Fleur du Jardin (01481 257996; www.fleurdujardin.com) for fresh, seasonal food including locally sourced meat and fish; Auberge du Val (01481 263862); or the Farmhouse Restaurant (01481 264181). Look out for boxed 'hedge veg' for honesty buys.

GETTING THERE Take a ferry or fly to the island then head for the St Andrews district. Candie Road starts near St Andrews Church. The site entrance sign is hard to spot.

PUBLIC TRANSPORT Bus no. 7 stops closest to the site, at Vazon Bay. Taxis available – mainly from St Peter Port.

OPEN May–September.

THE DAMAGE Adult £8–£10.50 per night (depending on season and pitch size); child (4 to 14) half price, under-4s free.

devon and cornwall

Devon and Cornwall

Site number		Page number	Cool for campfires	Stunning views	For first-time campers	Middle of nowhere	Beach within reach	Surf's up	Waterside chilling	Walk this way	Great for kids	Dog friendly	High on mountains	For car-less campers	Cool for campervans	Wet 'n' wild	Forest fun	On yer bike	Something different	A friendly welcome	Fish club
3	Troytown Farm	28	●	●		●	●				●	●		●							
4	Bryher	29		●		●	●							●							
5	Secret Garden	30	C		●		●	●		●					●					●	
6	Treen Farm	34					●	●		●		●			●						
7	Ayr Holiday Park	36		●	●		●	●		●	●			●	●						
8	Old Farm	38					●	●		●					●					●	
9	Henry's	40	○		●		●			●	●	●		●	●				●		
10	Carnebo Barn	42	C		●	●	●			●	●	●		●			●	●	●	●	
11	Beacon Cottage	46		●	●	●	●	●		●	●	●								●	●
12	Golden Lion Inn	50			●	●			●	●		●			●	●					●
13	Porth Joke	51			●		●	●		●	●										
14	Dennis Cove	52		●		●									●			●			
15	Botelet Farm	53			●	●				●				●					●		
16	Highertown Farm	54				●	●			●					●						
17	South Penquite	58	●		●	●				●	●				●						
18	Hole Station	60	●		●	●				●	●						●	●		●	
19	Lundy Island	64		●						●									●		
20	Roadford Lake	65							●		●				●	●		●		●	
21	South Breazle	66			●						●				●						
22	Bay View Farm	67		●			●			●		●			●					●	
23	Karrageen	68		●	●	●	●			●	●	●			●					●	
24	Maelcombe House	69	●	●		●	●			●										●	●
25	South Allington House	70	○	●	●	●	●			●	●	●			●				●	●	
26	Beryl's	71		●			●			●					●				●		
27	Old Cotmore Farm	72		●			●			●	●	●								●	
28	Prattshayes Farm	73			●		●			●					●			●		●	
29	Manor Farm	74		●	●		●			●		●								●	
30	West Middlewick Farm	76			●						●				●					●	
31	Mitchum's	78		●			●	●												●	
32	Little Meadow	80		●			●			●		●			●						
33	Sunny Lyn	81		●	●					●	●	●	●							●	
34	Trill Farm	82	C			●														●	

KEY ○ – off ground only
C – communal fire pits

10 km

10 miles

St Agnes 11
St Ives 7
Redruth
Camborne 12
St Just
Penzance A394
A394 1
5
Newlyn
8
Porthleven
Helston
6
Land's
End
Lizard 9
Lizard
Point

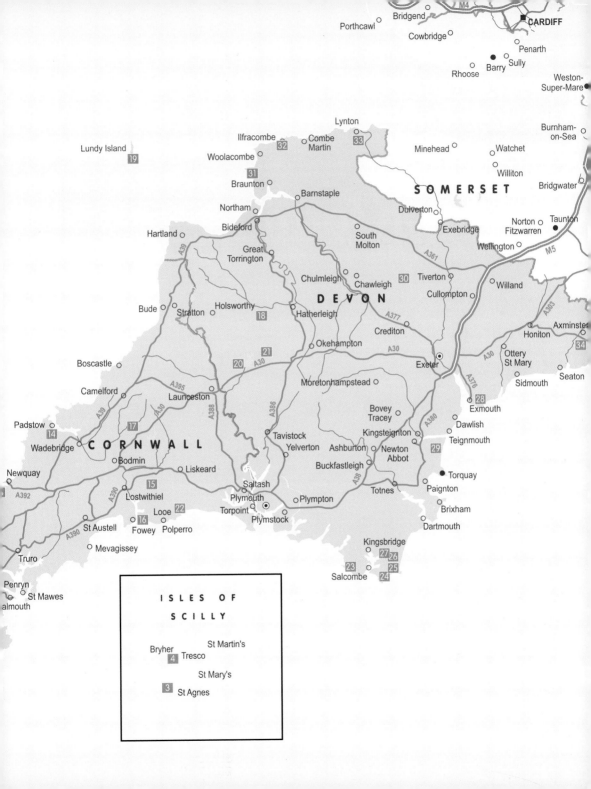

troytown farm

Troytown Farm Campsite, St Agnes, Scilly Isles, Cornwall, TR22 0PL   01720 422360   www.troytown.co.uk

Truly remote, rugged beauty lies on St Agnes, one of the smallest inhabited islands of the Scilly archipelago. Its edge-of-England Celtic scenery makes for a spectacular campsite – after a spectacular journey. Choose from a boat, plane, or helicopter to take you over the turquoise waters surrounding the islands. Then from Tresco or St Mary's (the main islands), it's just a trip on a catamaran then a tractor-ride to reach England's westernmost campsite, Troytown Farm.

This site is all about the panoramic backdrop... Atlantic waves undulating on to puzzling rock formations, heather-covered coastal landscapes, a sweeping curve of sand at nearby Pereglis Beach, and that night sky – an awe-striking bedazzlement of stars illuminating the blanket of sky above you. The downside is that you're exposed to the elements, though a couple of low walls and the odd wild-fern hedge provide some respite.

It's a simple site with just a few grassy fieldlets, but there aren't many other places in England where you can pitch as close to the sea, and watch the burning crimson sunsets from your doorstep.

COOL FACTOR Beautiful Atlantic isolation.

WHO'S IN? Tents, dogs, groups – yes. Everything else – no.

ON SITE Campfires allowed. The site comprises a few fieldlets. Clean facilities: toilets, showers (tokens required), coin-operated washing machines and tumble-dryers, shaver points, and baby-changing facilities. Onsite shop too.

OFF SITE Plenty of walking opportunities around the isle with Island Wildlife Tours (01720 422212). Snorkel with seals (Scilly Diving – 01720 422848). And with St Agnes and her views all around, you won't struggle for entertainment.

FOOD AND DRINK The Turks Head (01720 422434) in Porth Conger is the only pub on St Agnes, but it does have a gorgeous beer garden. The onsite shop also sells home-made ice cream, own-grown veg, and a small selection of meat.

GETTING THERE Contact Scilly Travel (08457 105555; www.ios-travel.co.uk) for plane and boat travel, or British International (01736 363871; www.islesofscillyhelicopter. com) for helicopter services. Contact Troytown Farm for details of transportation to the campsite.

PUBLIC TRANSPORT From Penzance train station, take a skybus, boat, or ferry to St Agnes.

OPEN March–October. (Book in advance July–August.)

THE DAMAGE £7.50–£9 per person, per night.

Bryher Campsite, Bryher, Scilly Isles, Cornwall, TR23 0PR   01720 422559   www.bryhercampsite.co.uk

The tiny Scilly Isle of Bryher has two distinct faces. To the south and east are calm blue waters filling the narrow, sheltered channel separating the island from its big sister, Tresco; while its north-western shores are a jagged jumble of weather-torn rocks, beaten and broken by the relentless Atlantic waves.

Such polar-opposite characteristics are what make this island such a special place to camp; a different landscape to suit your every mood. Look one way and you'll get sandy-beach bays ideal for sunbathing, swimming, and snorkelling (although the water can be nippy). Look the other way and you'll see prehistoric burial cairns and a heather-covered panorama that will dumbfound you.

A short climb uphill from the boat jetty, Bryher's campsite has impressive open views of the harbour, Hangman Island, and Tresco, yet occupies a sheltered spot between two high hills. Not a site for the fainthearted, it's about simple, back-to-basics camping, complementing its natural environs.

To really see the best of this island, visit in the heat of summer and enjoy your own Crusoe-like isolated island idyll.

COOL FACTOR A peaceful, natural paradise.

WHO'S IN? Tents, groups – yes. All else – no.

ON SITE Eighty pitches; clean toilets, basins, and coin-operated showers (50p). Hairdryer (20p), shaving point along with washing machine (£3 per load) and dryer (50p for 20 minutes). Freezer for ice packs. Mobile phone charging point; gas for sale. Tractor service for luggage from the quay (must be booked in advance). BBQs off the ground. No campfires.

OFF SITE See local artists' work at the Golden Eagle Studio (01720 422671); or take a boat to the larger Scilly Isles.

FOOD AND DRINK Head to Hightertown on St Martin's to sample some authentic Cornish pasties filled with locally raised beef and own-grown potatoes at St Martin's Bakery (01720 423444); or try the popular Bistro at St Martin's Hotel (01720 422090; www.stmartinshotel.co.uk).

GETTING THERE Contact Isles of Scilly Travel (08457 105555; www.ios-travel.co.uk) for plane and boat travel or British International (01736 363871) for helicopter services.

PUBLIC TRANSPORT Catch a train to Penzance and from there either a skybus, boat, or ferry to Bryher.

OPEN March–October.

THE DAMAGE £9.50 per person, per night; under-3s free. A non-refundable/transferable deposit is required on booking.

secret garden

Secret Garden, Bosavern House, St Just, Penzance, Cornwall, TR19 7RD   01736 788301   www.secretbosavern.com

The greatest difficulty this small campsite could ever encounter is living up to its name. After all, those two simple words, 'secret' and 'garden', when put together promise so much: your very own slice of Eden-like paradise full of natural pleasure.

The fact that this tiny campsite is situated on the mystical far-western edge of Cornwall, where travellers only find what they earnestly seek and don't just drop upon by mere happenstance, only adds to the anticipation and allure of this vision of your own private Eden. And the way to the Secret Garden is indeed enchanting, along the rugged coast westwards, fleeing the crowds of St Ives, or across the empty granite-strewn hills, escaping any Pirates of Penzance.

The sign outside Bosavern House – where Secret Garden hides – stating there are cream teas available, is yet another promising prospect for keen gastro-campers. But this doesn't look like a place where there is, or can be, a campsite – it's a rather grand-looking old granite mansion. 'Where's the campsite?' you ask the distinguished-looking chap who comes to the door. 'It's in the garden round the back', says he, and your little heart dares to wonder if all those wild imaginings of a secret garden can really be true.

Then reality sets in as you push past the hens, and brush off the embrace of the palm trees and other exotic plants. There it is – the Secret Garden. But what's this – other campers taking up residence in the form of two tents and two campervans? So you aren't the only Adam

or Eve to make it here after all. Drat. In fact, there are 12 spacious pitches (each equipped with a hook-up) within this lovely little oasis of vegetational tranquillity, lining the garden's hedges and edges, and quite often in high season they are all occupied. But even though it may not be solely yours, after a day or three has passed and the outside world is just a distant memory, the realisation gradually dawns that this garden campsite in all its hidden-away, intimate glory, is indeed a secret. And a perfect one at that. The onsite facilities are colourful, spotlessly maintained, and there are pleasing touches to provide a homely feel, with the lounge in the main house open for campers' use, alongside the library and bar.

The secretive feeling stays once you step outside, too, with little-trod footpaths leading off towards the coast. One such magical trail leads to Porth Nanven, through a mile of scenery that you never want to end, and this is yet another seemingly undisclosed place, despite being just a few miles from the tourist throng at Land's End, with its dramatic cliffs, breathtaking views, and attractions.

Another footpath strikes out across farmland, before burrowing its way through dark, damp, overgrown tree-tunnels to the cliffs, and to Cape Cornwall: one more well-kept secret. It's fortunate the Cape doesn't poke out into the Atlantic just a little further, or it would have been Land's End, and this beautiful, empty place might have ended up being smothered by visitors' enthusiastic footfall. As it is you can stroll here from your

Brison Rocks at Porth Nanven

Cape Cornwall

Secret Garden, enjoy a swim in the cove or tidal pool, watch the fishermen winch their boats up the steep slope from the sea, then wander back to the campsite for a cream tea in the garden… And all without encountering more than a handful of other retiring and secretive folk.

Does the Secret Garden live up to its name? As Churchill (the dog that is) would say, 'Oh Yes!'

COOL FACTOR A secret campsite, hidden away in secret Cornwall.

WHO'S IN? Tents, campervans, caravans – yes. Dogs, groups – no.

ON SITE This place is genuinely the garden of Bosavern House so, as to be expected, the ablutions block is small, providing toilets, free showers (1W, 1M), laundry, and a washing-up sink. It's a homely place, and the proprietors will even cook you breakfast if you possess the personal organisational skills to have ordered it the night before. No campfires.

OFF SITE There are many remnants of Cornwall's mining heritage scattered about on both the moors and cliffs hereabouts (see also Beacon Cottage, p46). The Levant Engine House (01736 786156; see www.nationaltrust.org.uk) – a very beautiful 4-mile walk along the coast path from the Secret Garden – contains a functioning Cornish Beam engine, which is in steam several times a week in summer. About 4 miles in the opposite direction is Sennen Cove, with its stunning beach and serious surf action, while a bit closer to the site (a mile away) is Porth Nanven, where a bracing dip awaits the adventurous. Less than a mile from the Secret Garden is Land's End Airport, where there are pleasure flights and regular flights to the Scilly Isles (08457 105555; www.ios-travel.co.uk). The Scillonian is operated by the same company as the flights, and sails to the Scilly Isles from Penzance. Between St Just and Penzance are the exotic (and slightly secretive) gardens at Trengwainton (01736 363148; see www. nationaltrust.org.uk), where plants that grow nowhere else in Britain thrive in the shelter of the walled garden.

FOOD AND DRINK For gargantuan classic Cornish cream teas look no further than the front garden where, from 2.30 until 6pm, the fat factor is put aside. The Cornish Hevva cake, with clotted cream and strawberries, is sublime. Local pubs in St Just (½ mile away) include the Commercial Hotel (01736 788455; www.commercial-hotel.co.uk), where the food is unquestionably good; the Star (01736 788767; www.thestarinn-stjust.co.uk) – an ancient, atmospheric inn with no food; and the Wellington Hotel (01736 787319; www.wellington-hotel.co.uk), which might be described as decently predictable. The Queens Arms (01736 788318; www.queensarms-botallack.co.uk) at Botallack, another mile down the road, is also fairly ordinary in the food department, but has a good selection of local ales and hosts a Beer Festival every September. For that extra-special treat, the Victoria Inn (01736 710309) at Perranuthnoe is a bit further away, but the contemporary food is as remarkable as the ancient surroundings.

GETTING THERE Follow the A30 towards Land's End, and turn right a few miles short of it, on to the B3306 after passing Crows An Wra. Bosavern House, and its Secret Garden, is on the right after 2 miles.

PUBLIC TRANSPORT The summer-only Coast Bus (no. 300, operated by First from April–October) can be boarded at Penzance (where there's a train station) and passes the site. It's also a useful means of reaching walking expeditions on the coast path.

OPEN 1 March–31 October.

THE DAMAGE Tent plus 2 people £15 per night; additional person (over 2 years) £3.20; hook-up £4.20.

treen farm

Treen Farm Campsite, Treen, St Levan, Penzance, Cornwall, TR19 6LF   01736 810273/07598 469322   www.treenfarmcampsite.co.uk

Beach babes and sun lovers, oil up and grab your flip-flops – Treen Farm's campsite, three miles shy of Land's End, is just a towel's throw from some of England's finest beaches.

During the Second World War, the army commandeered a field belonging to Treen Farm as a communications post; they constructed military buildings on the land, rendering it useless for farming – but perfect for camping. Since then, campers and cows have co-existed at Treen Farm.

The site is fantastically spacious – a field's length away from the cliff-top so it isn't overly exposed, yet you still manage to catch sea glimpses over the hedges to put your location into perspective. Being so high up does mean your shore views are slightly restricted, but you're never too far from an enviable beach.

The nearest is a 10-minute cliff-top walk and rocky scramble away: Pedn Vounder – a tiny, isolated, golden-sanded cove. The difficult position means it's never busy, but it does get cut off at high tide, so keep an eye out. At low tide, you can walk along the Pedn sands to Green Bay and the more widely known Porthcurno Beach. And if that's not enough sandy shore action, then it's just a 10-minute drive to Sennen on the north coast, where you'll find Whitesands Bay – a legendary Cornish surfing spot.

If you feel a bit beached out, nearby attractions include the Porthcurno Telegraph Museum – the first international telegraph system began here – and the unique, cliff-top, open-air Minack Theatre.

COOL FACTOR Stunning, spacious site near beaches galore.
WHO'S IN? Tents, campervans, dogs – yes. Groups – by arrangement. Mobile homes, caravans – no.
ON SITE A total of 100 pitches; no electric hook-ups. Shower blocks with 8 token-operated showers (25p), 11 toilets, disabled facilities, industrial washing machine (£3.60 per wash), and tumble dryer (20p per 5 minutes). Onsite shop/off licence supplies gas, free mobile- and camera-battery charging, and sells a range of fresh local fruit, veg, and meat. BBQs allowed off the ground. No campfires.
OFF SITE The Minack Theatre, cut into the cliffs west of Porthcurno, is on your tent-step (01736 810181; www.minack.com). Learn how to catch a bodacious wave at Sennen Cove with Smart Surf School (01736 871817; www.smartsurf.co.uk). There's also access to the epic South West Coast Path, and Land's End is just 3 miles away.
FOOD AND DRINK The Logan Rock Inn (01736 810495) in Treen is friendly, with St Austell ales and a wide choice of meals. Sweetly hidden in the fishing village of Mousehole is the Cornish Range (01736 731488; www.cornishrange.co.uk) – a seafoodie's paradise. Try the lemon sole fillets or the roast hake with crayfish risotto.
GETTING THERE Take the A30 south-west from Penzance, then the B3283 through St Buryan to Treen. The campsite reception is at the shop in the village.
PUBLIC TRANSPORT From Penzance train station catch a local bus to Land's End. Get off at the foot of the hill in Treen and it's a 5-minute walk to the campsite.
OPEN Easter/1 April–October.
THE DAMAGE Small tent plus 2 adults and a car from £11.50 per night. Extra adult £4; child (11 to 16 years) £2, (4 to 10 years) £1.50, under-4s free.

ayr holiday park

Ayr Holiday Park, St Ives, Cornwall, TR26 1EJ   01736 795855   www.ayrholidaypark.co.uk

St Ives is a delightful blend of working fishing port, holiday resort, and traditional Cornish town. Many an artist has gravitated towards its quality of light, bustling scenes, and stimulating coast and countryside since big names like Barbara Hepworth first settled here after the Second World War.

In 1993, Tate opened a substantial and impressive gallery in St Ives in recognition of resident artists and sculptors' contributions to the British art scene. The building has a view over the sandy stretches of Porthmeor – St Ives' main beach – with its super surf schools and spectacular sunsets. Also overlooking the pretty reaches of this bay is Ayr Holiday Park – best of the campsite crop here.

Everything about this campsite is organised and professional – from the facilities block and soft-landing of the children's play area to its well-placed picnic benches and outside showers for salty wetsuits. Unfortunately, the tariffs reflect all the care and attention that goes into maintaining the site and looking after its guests, so all this luxury does come at a hefty price. But when you consider Ayr's location, and peer down over that incredible vista, the cost seems justifiable.

You can also make the most of Ayr's proximity to the town and stroll down the hill to find wide-open beaches; trendy bars and cafés; any number of restaurants – from chip-cheap fish shops to contemporary fusion affairs; and, of course, the galleries. So it's fitting that Ayr, enjoying its position in the midst of a town steeped in creativity, has got the art of camping just right.

COOL FACTOR Ocean vista and prime spot in arty St Ives.

WHO'S IN? Tents, campervans, caravans, small to medium-sized dogs (not in July–August) – yes. Large dogs, huge tents, single-sex groups – no. Other groups – by arrangement.

ON SITE Eighty pitches in total, 40 with electric hook-ups, and 30 of which are hardstanding. There's a main shower and loo block with 6W, 6M magnificent showers (hot water aplenty), as well as disabled and family rooms, hairdryers, shaving points. Laundry; kids' playground; games room; wi-fi; direct access on to the coastal path. No campfires or disposable BBQs.

OFF SITE Head to the beach and try your balance at surfing; go for walks along the coastal path; or don your art-critic persona and explore the Tate St Ives (01736 796226; www.tate.org.uk/stives).

FOOD AND DRINK Blas Burgerworks (01736 797972) is a treat for meat-eaters and veggies alike. Book ahead for beachside Porthminster Café (01736 795352; www.porthminstercafe.co.uk), a friendly place serving beautifully presented, scrummy food. Stock up on provisions at the Cornish Deli (01736 795100; www.cornishdeli.com).

GETTING THERE Follow signs for St Ives from the A30, take the B3311 then B3306 to town, then follow the brown campsite signs to Ayr and Porthmeor Beach. The entrance to the campsite lies at a sharp S-bend.

PUBLIC TRANSPORT Catch a train or bus to St Ives and then taxi/bus/walk to the site. Buses from Penzance, Truro, Redruth, and Camborne travel to St Ives, too.

OPEN All year.

THE DAMAGE Caravan/campervan/tent £5.50–£13.50 (seasonal) per night; adult £4–£6.25; child £2–£3; dog £2–£3; car £2–£4; serviced pitch £4.25. Backpacker discounts.

old farm

Old Farm, Lower Pentreath, Pentreath Lane, Praa Sands, Penzance, Cornwall, TR20 9TL   01736 763221   www.theoldfarmpraasands.co.uk

In another corner of Cornwall here's another fantastic beach with another fantastic little campsite to go with it. The Old Farm site at Praa Sands is run by friendly Wendy with a lovely Cornish accent, and consists of just 14 pitches dug into a sloping garden above the farmhouse – all just a short walk away from the strip of Praa Sands.

It's said that 'praa' is an ancient Cornish word for a witch's cove, which is a bit of a worry if you're at all bothered by such things. Add in the fact that Pengersick Castle, just up the road, is supposedly one of the most haunted places in the kingdom, and you might find the place downright spooky. What's more, this little strip of Cornwall nestles between Penzance and the Lizard Peninsula, which has its own fair share of weird goings-on, with the Goonhilly Satellite Earth Station lurking there, once the largest satellite station in the world. In keeping with Cornish tradition, its dishes were named after characters in Arthurian legend, the largest, Arthur, being over 25 metres in diameter.

But you needn't worry about all that when the sun's shining and you're lounging on Praa Sands trying to finish your ice cream before it melts.

Now, before you say anything you might later regret, yes there are three large static caravans stacked up like Lego on one side of the site. They're not ideal, but in the spirit of 'you say tomayto, I say tomarto' and all that kind of love-thy-neighbour stuff, you're just going to have to accept them. After all, they're the only blemish on an otherwise cracking little campsite.

COOL FACTOR Neat and tight little site in a great location, just up the road from a marvellous sandy beach.

WHO'S IN? Tents, standard VW-sized campervans, caravans (up to 14 feet in length) – yes. Dogs, large motorhomes, big groups – no.

ON SITE Fourteen pitches spread across a garden-like area. One loo and a shower for fellas; 2 loos and a shower for gals. There are a couple of sinks for dishes and plenty of hot water. No electric hook-ups and no campfires.

OFF SITE Head down to the beach where there's a hire shop for all your watery activities, as well as plenty of sand to play with. If you fancy a bit of ghoul hunting you can sign up for a ghost night at Pengersick Castle at www.ghosthunting.org.uk.

FOOD AND DRINK Down by the shore there's a fish-and-chip shop, a café, and a pub (the Sandbar – 01736 763516). Up in the village there's a post office and garage (Newtown Services – 01736 763894) selling basic provisions. For something fancy, there's The Bay (01736 366890) in Penzance.

GETTING THERE The Old Farm lies on a loop of road off the A394 between Penzance and Helston. Whichever direction you come from, turn off at the sign for Praa Sands and follow the road down the hill. From Penzance the site's on the right near the bottom of the hill. From Helston come round the loop, past the beach, and head back up the hill and you'll see the site on the left.

PUBLIC TRANSPORT Bus no. 2A runs between Helston and Penzance (where there's a handy train station), passing the campsite roughly every hour.

OPEN Late May–early September.

THE DAMAGE Tent, caravan, or campervan plus 2 adults costs £12 per night in low season and £17 after 1st July. Child £3.50, under-3s are free.

henry's

Henry's Campsite, Caerthillian Farm, The Lizard, Helston, Cornwall, TR12 7NX   01326 290596   www.henryscampsite.co.uk

Henry's is different. It's the most southerly campsite in mainland Britain and it's been here for donkey's years. It was just a 'normal' campsite until Ron and Jo Lyne took over from Ron's dad Henry. When asked what he's trying to achieve at Henry's, Ron muttered something like 'I want it to be like a garden'. Well, he's certainly achieved that humble dream, but we think he may be underselling it slightly…

Ron is obviously an artist at heart, constantly creating new marvels for everyone to enjoy. An inquisitive stroll through the site, peering into all the hidden corners, reveals an enchanting arrangement of other-worldly standing stones, Cornish walls, hand-painted murals, and animated sculptures – including a row of cheeky rooftop gulls. Sub-tropical plants are scattered throughout the site and, garden-like or not, the astounding results of Ron's labours speak for themselves.

The surrounding coastal landscape can't have failed to inspire Henry's evolution over the years. The most iconic chunk of coastal scenery hereabouts is Kynance Cove, just a 20-minute walk from the site. Even nearer, but not nearly so beautiful, is Lizard Point.

The unisex ablution arrangements, alien-looking plants hugging an alfresco washing-up sink, and former shipping-container loo block may not be to everyone's taste, but are part and parcel of this unique and personal 'garden'. It's Henry's eccentricity – in equal measure to the stunning surroundings – that entices campers back each year.

COOL FACTOR Quirky landscaping and lovely owners on the glorious Lizard Peninsula.

WHO'S IN? Tents, campervans, caravans, dogs, groups – yes.

ON SITE Campfires allowed in braziers provided. BBQs off the ground. A storyteller in residence for 2 weeks in summer, and plans for theatre groups and acoustic music weekends. Facilities are scattered about and painted in bright hues. Unisex arrangements include toilets, showers, open-air washing-up sink, shop, campers' lounge, and electric hook-ups.

OFF SITE Head to Cornish Camels (01326 231119; www.cornishcamels.com) where there are – you guessed it – camels, as well as a café, organic food, and craft shop. Coo over adorable seals at the National Seal Sanctuary (01326 221874; www.sealsanctuary.co.uk) in the picturesque Helston Estuary.

FOOD AND DRINK Head for one (or more) of Ann's Pasties (01326 290889; www.annspasties.co.uk) in Lizard village. If you fancy fish on the BBQ, go and meet the fishermen who sell their fresh catches at a cooperative shop in Cadgwith Cove. Organic ice cream galore at Roskilly's Farm (01326 280479; www.roskillys.co.uk) near Coverack. Britain's most southerly eatery, the Polpeor Café (01326 290939), has spectacular views and produces a host of home-made fare.

GETTING THERE Take the A30 all the way through Cornwall to Penzance. Then take the A394 to Helston, and then the A3083 to the Lizard. The campsite is accessed from the far side of the car park at the Lizard.

PUBLIC TRANSPORT Take the Lizard Rambler bus no. T3/T34 from Redruth, stopping within 100 metres of the site.

OPEN All year.

THE DAMAGE Adult £7–£9 (depending on season) per night; child (5 years plus) half price.

carnebo barn

Carnebo Barn, Trenoweth, Mabe, Falmouth, Cornwall, TR10 9JJ   07737 778970   roosterswood@yahoo.co.uk

Back then it was known as dropping out. In the 1940s it was a slow boat to Tangier. In the 1960s it was the hippy trail to Kathmandu in a clapped-out combi van. Nowadays it's called going off-grid, and you can do it pretty much anywhere. Just shed the trappings of modern life and live as simply as possible. Some people even manage to do without money altogether; foraging for berries, trapping the odd rabbit, and sleeping wherever they lay the worn-out hat they can't afford to repair or replace.

Now that may be going a bit far when all you want is a weekend away, but Carnebo Barn, in rolling fields just north of Falmouth, gives you a taster of the off-grid life because it doesn't have any electricity.

The place is owned and run by Rufus, a carpenter, and his partner Rebecca, a jazz cellist, and has only recently opened as an official campsite, though friends and family have been enjoying the place for years.

The five-acre smallholding, up a very rough-and-ready track, has a spacious – though slightly sloping – camping field in front of the barn, compost loos and solar showers, and a communal fire pit with wooden seating and some awning to provide shelter from the rain. What power there is comes from a small wind turbine whirring above a gorse bush. (Okay there's a diesel generator as well for calm days, but why spoil a good story?)

A short walk down the hill from the site through thigh-high bracken and you'll find a glorious little swimming hole in a tiny quarry.

Cold, deep, and both discreet and discrete, it's the perfect place for a wake-me-up plunge in the morning or for cooling off after a long hot day of Cornwalling.

The idea at Carnebo Barn is to attract walkers, cyclists, and anyone else with the ingenuity to arrive without the aid of an internal combustion engine; and it's just the spot to give it a go, as there are public footpaths criss-crossing the countryside here, so it is possible to get around just as well on Shanks's pony. Penryn is just a couple of miles away, and Falmouth a bit more of a hike (six miles), though there are plenty of local bus services to take advantage of, as well.

It's worth the trip down to Falmouth as it's really quite a funky little town with an agreeably run-down feel and mix of surfers, students, posh yachters, and tourists. It's a great base for seaborne activities, and there are some cracking beaches nearby if you prefer salt water to fresh. And in the evening there are plenty of hip eateries, bars, and cafés to work your way through.

Elsewhere are all the coastal walks and glorious gardens for which Cornwall is famous. One unmissable spot not far from Carnebo Barn is the National Trust's Glendurgan Garden, where you can lose yourself in the cherry-laurel maze and marvel at the exotic-looking flora that surely shouldn't flourish so far from the Equator.

But the site itself is the main attraction. Rufus and Rebecca are charming and interesting hosts, eager to share stories round the fire of an evening

or maybe break out into an improv jazz session. There are even plans to erect a screen in the field and have film evenings of French New Wave classics and the like. It's all very cool and just sufficiently on-grid not to be too scary to soft city dwellers. After all, you can still get Radio 4 on your wind-up radio, and that's always a sign of civilisation, isn't it?

COOL FACTOR Basic off-grid camping in a field with a log fire and charming hosts.

WHO'S IN? Tents, walkers, cyclists – yes. Well-behaved dogs are fine (there are chickens around). Caravans, campervans, motorbikes – anything with an internal combustion engine – no. That includes cars, preferably. If you do come by car you're encouraged to park in the village and walk to the site.

ON SITE Campfires are allowed if they are off the grass. Tucked away in the bushes in what looks like a small Methodist chapel are the compost loos, and there are solar showers in a corner of the field. There's a cold water tap and some rudimentary tin tubs for doing a bit of washing-up. There's also a communal fire pit with wooden seating and a small canopied area just in case it rains.

OFF SITE Start with the swimming hole a short walk from the campsite or try the nearby sea and boat trips from Falmouth. There are gardens galore, the nearest of which are Glendurgan (01326 252020; see www.nationaltrust.org.uk) and Trebah (01326 252200; www.trebahgarden.co.uk). Down by Falmouth's wharf, the National Maritime Museum (01326 313388; www.nmmc.co.uk) has lots of salty goings-on.

FOOD AND DRINK There are a few basic commodities for sale in the barn – eggs, milk, and bread – otherwise it's bring your own (there's a large Asda a couple of miles back down the road) or go to the Argal Farm's shop (1½ miles away). For a treat, head into Falmouth for award-winning burgers at 5 Degrees West (01326 311288; www.5degreesfalmouth.co.uk) or try Miss Peapod's kitchen café (01326 374424; www.misspeapod.co.uk). In Penryn there's the charming Little Yellow House (01326 377622; www.thelittleyellowhouse.co.uk). Accessible by public footpath in Constantine is the glasshouse café of Potager (01326 341258), though it's only open on weekends in the summer. Otherwise there are plenty of pubs and restaurants along the Falmouth wharfs, including a Latin place called Aguaviva (01326 377943).

GETTING THERE Pen and paper at the ready. On the A30 south from Truro or north from Falmouth, there's a roundabout opposite Asda and B&Q called the Kernick Roundabout (there's a sign bearing its name). Take the Mabe Burnthouse turning and go up the hill to what's known locally as the 'funny junction' with red markings in the road. Turn left past the New Inn and follow the road through Mabe Burnthouse. At the end of the village (by Harmony Cottage, on the left) the road turns sharp left. Almost hidden on the right is the entrance to a small lane. Follow this lane until you reach some houses and the road veers to the right. There's a small postbox just on the left. Take the road that leads straight on and follow it until it becomes a track. Continue along it all the way past some houses and over the brow of the hill. There are telegraph poles on the left, and just where the phone line crosses over the road to the last pole on your right is the entrance to the campsite. Phew.

PUBLIC TRANSPORT The closest bus stop (bus no. 2 runs between Penzance and Falmouth) is at the New Inn in Mabe Burnthouse (about 2 miles from the site) and the closest train station is Penryn (also about 2 miles).

OPEN All year.

THE DAMAGE A simple tariff of £10 per adult, per night. Kids up to age 16 are £5, and the under-5s are free. A pre-erected bell tent is available for £50 per night and sleeps 4.

beacon cottage

Beacon Cottage Farm, Beacon Drive, St Agnes, Cornwall, TR5 0NU   01872 552347   www.beaconcottagefarmholidays.co.uk

Cornwall offers the perfect seaside sojourn for all makes and models of human holidaymaker: surf dudes and dudettes; sand fortress construction engineers (junior or senior); cute-village viewers; ice-cream lickers; and suckers for scenery will all find what they crave when taking a break by the briny in England's south-western corner.

But Cornwall is not simply one place; its north and west fringes are so very different from those on the south and east. The south of the county is sheltered, lush, and very lovely, in a mild-mannered sort of way, with thatched villages sheltering by wooded creeks among the green folds of the rolling countryside – it's many a gentlefolk's dream of the perfect holiday destination.

Beacon Cottage is on the other side of Cornwall, on a hillside directly facing the wrath of the Atlantic, amid some of the wildest, roughest, and most dramatic seaside scenes in Europe. This is not a *nice* place, but an awesome one, where the raw, windswept, surf-washed seaside is, for many, the very essence of Cornwall.

That Beacon Cottage is knocked about by the wind on this rocky, empty, and very beautiful section of Cornish coast just makes it even more awesome. The campsite itself is superb, with a choice of pitches either facing whatever the weather can throw at them in the roomy Ocean View field, or sheltered from the elements in the more intimate orchard around the back of the farm. The facilities (which are top notch) are nearer the latter. So where you end up pitching your tent is a question of priorities: room with a view, or shelter and facilities close by?

For the surf dudes and dudettes, sandcastle builders, and ice-cream lickers there's an eminently suitable beach for every one of their preferred activities, about 150 (very vertical) metres below the site, and less than a mile away along the coast path. The ice cream is provided from a stone hut in the small car park, but nothing else is allowed to spoil Chapel Porth's immaculately wild looks.

The convenience of such a clean and unspoilt beach is the reason Beacon Cottage is such a glam destination for young families in the school holidays, but this campsite's unique selling point has to be its position. And we're not just talking about its geographical location amid all this spectacularly dramatic scenery, but about its historical place within the melancholic setting of Cornwall's industrial past, too.

This part of Cornwall is littered with the haunting ruins of its former metal-mining sites. And the former mining village of St Agnes is about two miles along the coast path from Beacon Cottage. The illuminating walk there passes abandoned engine houses and mine shafts perched precariously on the cliffs along the way, before the path drops down into the rocky cleft of Trevaunance Cove. Here, in addition to the remnants of the county's industrial heritage, you'll find yet more ice-cream licking opportunities, clean surf, and a decent beach on which to while away some time.

Wheal Cotes Mine

St Agnes Head

All the historical roads lead back to Beacon Cottage though, as that classic (and possibly most famous) of Cornwall's picturesque derelict engine houses, at Wheal Coates Mine, is the one nearest to the campsite. For the scenery suckers, and those who have that all-consuming passion to see it while sporting their sturdy hiking boots, this is a walker's Valhalla.

COOL FACTOR Slap bang in the middle of some very intriguing coastal scenery.

WHO'S IN? Tents, campervans, caravans, dogs – yes. Groups – no.

ON SITE The camping fields all have hook-ups, with 43 of the total 70 pitches being thus equipped. The facilities here are modern and very well maintained with toilets, CDP, free showers (4W, 4M), and 2 family bathrooms. There's a laundry, washing-up sinks, and ice packs, and milk, eggs, gas, and newspapers are sold at the farmhouse. No campfires, but BBQs off the ground are okay.

OFF SITE The list of things to see and do in Cornwall is endless, so here are just a few suggestions... Local and lovely (and a 3-mile walk along the cliffs) is Blue Hills Tin Streams (01872 553341; www.bluehillstin.com), where meaning is given to all the ruins emblematic of this area, and especially the coast around Beacon Cottage. Geevor Tin Mine (01736 788662; www.geevor.com) near St Just was a large-scale working mine until 1990; these days the underground tour is the major attraction, while a café provides refreshment and the museum extra info. The Eden Project (01726 811911; www.edenproject.com) near St Austell needs no introduction, but is somewhere everyone needs to see at some point in their brief flight through life, and a really (really) great place to be on a cold, wet day. Paradise Park (01736 753365; www. paradisepark.org.uk) at Hayle is involved in conservation, breeding, and educational programmes (basically a zoo), but has a nice feel to it and makes a fantastic full family day out. Those seeking cuddly cuteness can do no better than the National Seal Sanctuary (www.sealsanctuary.co.uk) at Gweek, where they care for injured and orphaned seals from all over the UK, before releasing them back into the wild.

FOOD AND DRINK Within walking distance (between 2 and 3 miles), both in St Agnes, and both of which can't really be bettered by getting in the car are... the St Agnes Hotel (01872 552307; www.st-agnes-hotel.co.uk), on the main street, offering a decent selection of food and drink and serving bar meals in a traditional-looking dining room at reasonable prices; Sally's Bistro (01872 552194; www. sallysrestaurant.co.uk), with its rather chic decor, is a place for special occasions (like holidays?), serving well-presented meals with a slightly exotic Mediterranean-based theme. Meanwhile, down in Trevaunance Combe (the valley leading to the Cove), the Driftwood Spars Hotel (01872 552428; www.driftwoodspars.com) not only has bar food and a restaurant with a large menu and good children's deals, but also its own brewery. There are 8 beers brewed here, including Blackheads Mild, a traditional, but now rare, dark, malty ale; Blue Hills; and Alfie's Revenge.

GETTING THERE From the A30, just past Blackwater, at the roundabout where the A390 joins, turn right on to the B3277 to St Agnes, and on entering the village at the first mini-roundabout take a sharp left into Goonvrea Road. Follow this for a mile, and then turn right into Beacon Drive (following the caravan site signs). Beacon Cottage is on the right.

PUBLIC TRANSPORT Take a train to Truro, which is the hub of public transport in Cornwall. There you'll find a regular bus service (nos. 85 and 85A) to St Agnes.

OPEN Easter/1 April–end September.

THE DAMAGE Tent plus 2 adults £16–£22 (depending on season); backpacker £7; child £3; dog £2.

golden lion inn

Golden Lion Inn, Stithians Lake, Menherion, Redruth, Cornwall, TR16 6NW   01209 860332   www.golden-lion-inn.co.uk

There are no worries about designated drivers and drink-driving limits when you camp at the Golden Lion. When the landlord calls time and you've drained the last dregs from your pint, you can just roll out the back door and into your tent.

When the current owners took over the inn the land beyond the beer garden was just a field, but they figured they could put it to better use and turned it into a small campsite. There are a couple of hardstandings and some electric hook-ups, so it can be a bit heavy on caravans, but creative uses of the shrubbery can help to camouflage them.

The pub's about midway between Camborne and Falmouth, and abuts the quiet shores of Stithians Lake, a magnet for anglers and water sports enthusiasts. So if the trip to the coast north or south is too much effort, you can buy a fishing permit or hire a windsurfboard at the nearby water sports centre. Whatever you do, it's worth working up a healthy appetite for some good pub nosh and a few fireside pints at the end of the day before it's time to roll out into the garden and try to remember which bush you hid your tent behind.

COOL FACTOR In a lovely garden by an award-winning pub.

WHO'S IN? Tents, campervans, caravans, (well behaved) dogs, groups – yes.

ON SITE Pitches, including 2 hardstandings and 12 with hook-ups, across the land behind the beer garden. There are 2 neat and tidy showers and 2 toilets attached to the side of the inn, accessed by code-locked doors. No campfires.

OFF SITE The site's equidistant from Cornwall's north and south coasts, so take your pick. Otherwise the lake offers plenty of options with all kinds of waterborne craft and conveyance available for hire. See www.swlakestrust.org.uk.

FOOD AND DRINK The pub's bar and restaurant meals have an emphasis on good-quality local produce, particularly beef and game. If you want to DIY there's a farm shop – Cornish Organics – at Four Lanes, along the road.

GETTING THERE From Redruth (off the A30) take the B3297 towards Helston and turn left at Four Lanes on to the B3280 (Stithians Lane). At the T-junction go right, heading for the lake; carry on until you see the Golden Lion on the left.

PUBLIC TRANSPORT Train to Redruth, then bus no. 34 to Four Lanes. It's a 2½-mile walk to the Golden Lion.

OPEN All year.

THE DAMAGE Tent plus 2 adults £12–£14 per night.

porth joke

Porth Joke Campsite, Treago Mill, Crantock, Newquay, Cornwall, TR8 5QS   01637 830213   www.treagomill.co.uk

Lucky campers who've stayed at Porth Joke Campsite know it's an unspoilt, tucked-away, tiny hideout of a site with a warm and genuine atmosphere. Acquiring a pitch here in midsummer will be a challenge because this place is popular and spots are limited, but you'll understand why.

It's seaside camping at its finest. Not only is Surf City Newquay just four miles away, you've also got Porth Joke Beach, which offers privacy and enviable beauty, on your doorstep. You could lose days watching the curling wrath-filled waves of the Atlantic crash against the mighty Cornish dunes.

The site itself is very basic but comes with good facilities, and the jewel in its crown and the single onsite source of entertainment is a giant sandpit, which you are advised to replenish with the sand from Porth Joke Beach.

If, perchance, you do want to venture out of the seductively comfortable Porth Joke confines, then do so on foot. Within a few miles of the site you'll encounter the beauty of Holywell Bay, the endless sands and roaring surf of Perranporth, and the equally sublime Crantock Beach.

COOL FACTOR A beach-tastic site.

WHO'S IN? Tents – yes. Groups – by arrangement. Campervans, caravans, babies under 1 year, dogs – no.

ON SITE Fifty pitches. Shower and toilet block with free hot showers; refurbished washing-up room. Shaving and hairdrying points; free ice pack freezing. Natural sandpit (safe play-space for the kids). BBQs off the ground. No campfires on site – permitted on beach, but bring your own wood.

OFF SITE Take a trip on the quaint Lappa Valley Steam Railway (01872 510317). Or walk through underwater tunnels at Newquay's Blue Reef Aquarium (01637 878134).

FOOD AND DRINK Cornish pies and local fruity ales at the Smugglers' Den Inn (01637 830209). Fine dining at the Crantock Bay Hotel (01637 830229).

GETTING THERE On the A3075 (Newquay to Redruth road), take the first minor road right, signposted Crantock. After 2 miles turn left into a lane, go through Treago Farm on to a track on Cubert Common for ½ mile to the campsite.

PUBLIC TRANSPORT Train to Newquay and then a local bus (no. 585/586) to Crantock and walk to the site.

OPEN April–October.

THE DAMAGE Adult £9.50/£60 per night/week; child £4.50/£35. Weekly bookings only during school holidays.

dennis cove

Dennis Cove Camping, Dennis Lane, Padstow, Cornwall, PL28 8DR   denniscove@freeuk.com – for bookings   www.denniscove.co.uk

Dennis Cove Camping occupies a lovely spot within easy boat-watching proximity of the Camel Estuary, at Cornwall's famous Padstow. Comprising just two simple grass fields – an upper overflow that opens during the busy school holidays, and a sheltered lower field available throughout the season – this well cared-for campsite is all about simple, old-fashioned camping.

The Camel Trail runs adjacent to the site, and any stretch of its incredibly scenic 17 miles makes for a pleasant day of easy walking or cycling. The route follows the estuary and continues inland alongside the River Camel to Poley's Bridge.

But you don't have to stretch your legs much during your relaxing stay at Dennis Cove, for charming Padstow is only a 10-minute walk away. At the heart of this fishing port is its busy harbour, buzzy with activity year-round as fishermen bring in the catch. Fresh off the boat and into the pan, the fish is dished out to hungry tourists at many a fine restaurant here, including those owned by celebrity chef Rick Stein, who's helped transform the tiny town into Cornwall's gastronomic capital.

COOL FACTOR The perfect spot from which to enjoy all that Padstow has to offer.

WHO'S IN? Tents, camper/caravans, dogs – yes. No groups.

ON SITE The lower field is sheltered; busy at peak times. The upper overflow field has unmarked pitches and space. There are 5 electric hook-ups, and a well-maintained shower block (tokens – 40p for 5 minutes), with family shower room; washing-up area; laundry. No campfires, but BBQs allowed.

OFF SITE If you're not whizzing along the Camel Trail in the sun then head to one of north Cornwall's sandy beaches. If it's raining, the waterproof biomes at the Eden Project (01726 811911; www.edenproject.com) are only a 25-minute drive away, in Bodelva.

FOOD AND DRINK Padstow is a Mecca for seafoodies thanks to Rick Stein's empire of quality eateries. Treat yourself to a meal at his Seafood Restaurant (01841 532700).

GETTING THERE Entering Padstow on the A389, turn right at Tesco, drive down the hill, then turn right on to Dennis Lane and continue to the end.

PUBLIC TRANSPORT Train to Bodmin Parkway then bus to Padstow and walk to the site.

OPEN April–September.

THE DAMAGE Tent plus 2 adults and a car £14.50–£19.

botelet farm

Botelet Farm, Herodsfoot, Liskeard, Cornwall, PL14 4RD   01503 220225   www.botelet.com

Fancy this. A farm that's like its own little village, with its own phone box and genuine Victorian red postbox; a couple of yurts and room for a couple of tents. Actually there's room for hundreds of tents in Botelet's 300 acres, but it's a working farm and the owners want to keep the camping small and special. The two tent pitches change with the season, based on where the cows are grazing, how high the grass is, and a number of other random factors like what's in the tea leaves that morning.

It all means that if you come here every year for the rest of your camping days the chances are you'd never pitch in the same place twice. You may be in one of the fields close to the little village of farm buildings with views across the valley, or you may be banished to the wilderness somewhere.

As for the two yurts, one's in the field out front and the other's in a field above the farm. Both have views across the rolling valley, and wood-burning stoves to warm those chilly nights and boil the kettle for your morning cuppa. Just remember to hide the tea leaves afterwards, or the folk in the tents might be asked to move.

COOL FACTOR Remote little farm with freedom to roam.

WHO'S IN? Adults only. Room for 2 tents – maximum of 2 people per tent. Campervans, caravans, dogs, groups – no.

ON SITE There's a single hot shower (with piped Radio 3 so you can sing along in the morning) and 1 loo. Cold taps are dotted around and there's a trough for washing dishes. No campfires, but the yurts have wood-burning stoves.

OFF SITE Try the Polmartin Riding School (01503 220428), just down the road. It offers lessons for all ages and abilities.

FOOD AND DRINK The farm sells eggs when available and serves a veggie breakfast in the farmhouse at £10 per person (book the night before). For a treat, head for Liskeard's Hayloft (01503 240241). Set in a converted barn, it does primarily Italian food, and has a chocolate fountain.

GETTING THERE Come off the A390 between Liskeard and St Austell at East Taphouse and take the B3359 south towards Pelynt. After about 1½ miles turn right at the sign for Botelet and follow the road to the entrance, on the right.

PUBLIC TRANSPORT Train to Liskeard, then bus to East Taphouse, 2 miles away. You can arrange collection from there.

OPEN Easter–mid September (yurts)/end September (tents).

THE DAMAGE £5 per person, per night for tents. The yurts (sleeping 2) are £210 for 3 nights, £310 for a week.

highertown farm

Highertown Farm Campsite, Lansallos, Looe, Cornwall, PL13 2PX   01208 265211   see www.nationaltrust.org.uk

Some people are excited by complexity – calculating the difference between a super-saver off-peak return and two day-rover singles, for example, or explaining the active/passive clause of the offside rule – while for others there's nothing quite so pleasing as simplicity.

You can easily be fooled by the simplicity of Highertown Farm campsite. After all, at first glance it's a fairly square field with a hedge around it and some tents in the middle. There's a church on one side and a sliver of sea to be seen on the other. It might not look like much, but then maybe that's its secret.

There's been a campsite at Highertown Farm since the 1930s, when ruby-cheeked boys with dirty knees and girls in dainty dresses chased wooden hoops or played tic-tac-toe while their parents grumbled about Chamberlain. The site made it through the Second World War and the buttoned-up fifties, let its hair down in the sixties, and went to pieces in the seventies along with the rest of the country. Come the 1980s, though, the National Trust stepped in and took over stewardship of the site. Whether it was the entrepreneurial spirit of the times, or whatever, the NT brought a bit of market discipline to the place – and what a difference it's made.

The site is at the end of a warren of narrow and twisty Cornish country lanes. In summer the grass and hedges at the sides of the road are so high that it's hard to get your bearings, and every now and then you have to act like a meerkat and pop your head out of the sunroof to figure out where you are. With this handy navigational tip you shouldn't have any trouble finding the place, or any other, for that matter.

The site is on a hill at Lansallos looking out towards the coast. A narrow track from beside the church leads down through the trees and opens out into some fields just by a tidy cove with raised cliffs on either side. The South West Coast Path runs along here so don't think you'll have the place all to yourselves, but it makes a great spot to hang-out on sunny days (though the beach is pebbly rather than sandy).

You can also use the path as a starting point to explore some of the coast. Try walking west towards Polruan and taking the ferry across to Fowey, where you can fill up with seafood to fortify you for the return journey. Or go east and you'll eventually reach Shag Rock, where there's nothing to do but, erm, turn around and come back. Unless you have any better ideas.

Once back at the site you can sit yourself down and take in the tranquil atmosphere. The site's limited to 60 people at a time and doesn't accept large groups, so you can be fairly sure of a peaceful stay, though the wardens aren't on site all the time so the system isn't foolproof.

The National Trust owns about 2,000 acres along the Cornish coast here, roughly from Fowey to Shag Rock (the origins of the name are thankfully obscure, but let's hope it refers to the sea bird – a green cormorant, seeing as you ask).

So stewardship of Highertown Farm is just another part of the conservation work the Trust does in the region, and they deserve a hearty slap on the back for preserving this cracking little haven.

The National Trust doesn't own many campsites, but what Highertown Farm proves is that when it does you can be sure that however simple it may look, it'll be pretty darn good.

COOL FACTOR Eco-friendly National Trust site in a sleepy Cornish village.

WHO'S IN? Tents, room for 3 campervans/caravans. Dogs are fine, so long as they are on leads. But no groups allowed and no under-21s without an adult.

ON SITE Pretty good facilities all told. Upstairs in the barn there's a kind of day room (where you'll find plenty of leaflets and info on what to do around the site). Downstairs there are a couple of showers (one of which is a large shower/toilet for the disabled) and a couple of loos. The showers cost 20p for 6 minutes. There are covered washing-up facilities (though hot water is 20p a go) with a washing machine and tumble-dryer. You'll find a further 2 compost toilets off the side of the barn, along with a couple of outdoor sinks, which face the cow field and seem to be fascinating to the cattle as they'll often wander over and watch your plate-rinsing techniques. No campfires, but BBQs are allowed as long as they're raised off the grass.

OFF SITE This is Daphne du Maurier country and in Fowey there's a literary centre (01726 833619) and a festival held in May (www.dumaurierfestival.co.uk) in honour of the author of *Rebecca* and *Jamaica Inn*. For something completely different (and a change from the Eden Project) carry on west from Fowey to the Lost Gardens of Heligan (01726 845100; www.heligan.com), the restored so-called 'Sleeping Beauty' gardens of the seat of the Tremayne family. It's a fabulous story about the rediscovery and restoration of the gardens, which had fallen into ruin after the First World War. Well worth the trip to see its 200 acres.

FOOD AND DRINK If you don't bring your own it's a bit of a hike to the nearest shops. There's a decently stocked Spar in Pelynt for bread, milk, fresh fruit and veg, and a selection of beers and wines. Otherwise head to Fowey for a choice of great seafood options, including the Other Place (01726 833636; www.theotherplacefowey.com), which offers a weekly changing menu and river views. Or nip down to Polperro, a 14th-century port, and try out the Blue Peter Inn (01503 272743; www.thebluepeterinn.co.uk). It's known as 'the last pub before France' and does a wide range of seafood and other more standard pub grub like ham and cheese sandwiches.

GETTING THERE From the A38 between Bodmin and Liskeard get on to the B3359 for Pelynt. In the village turn right past the church and follow the road to a T-junction. Go left and then straight on until a fork in the road by a house (on your right). Take the left fork and follow the road down the hill towards Lansallos and the campsite entrance is on your right, just before the village.

PUBLIC TRANSPORT The closest you can get to the site is to take the Western Greyhound bus no. 573 from Liskeard train station to Polperro Crumplehorn, which is about 2½ miles away.

OPEN Easter–late October.

THE DAMAGE In low season it's £4 per person, per night; £2 for 2- to 12-year-olds and under-2s are free. In high season (21 June–5 September) it's £5 per adult and £2.50 for all kids under the age of 12.

south penquite

South Penquite, Blisland, Bodmin, Cornwall, PL30 4LH   01208 850491   www.southpenquite.co.uk

Just sometimes here at South Penquite Farm on the edge of Bodmin Moor, when it's long gone midnight and there's the sound of rustling in the undergrowth, you might find yourself wondering whatever happened to the Beast of Bodmin Moor?

Supposedly a large wildcat that had either escaped from a sci-fi lab or was a throwback to some kind of sabre-toothed ancestor, it was reputed to prowl the moor scaring the wits out of anyone unlucky enough to cross its path. The story was at its height some years ago and the hoo-ha has died down, but when you're creeping to the loo in the middle of the night and hear a twig snap behind you, you'd better pray the big cat hasn't come back looking for a midnight snack.

Come daylight and you can forget all about it – safety in numbers and all that – and just enjoy the site. It's a fully certified organic farm and takes sustainability very seriously, from using solar energy to recycling everything, even yogurt pots.

Numbers are limited in the camping fields so you shouldn't ever feel penned in. Or if you fancy a bit of luxury you can opt for one of the Three Bears: the Mongolian yurts that occupy a separate field. Daddy Bear's the biggest and sleeps six; then there's Mummy Bear, who sleeps four; and Baby Bear, a snug little place for two.

There's walking galore to be had around the 200-acre farm, and plenty of ducks and hens and horses to entertain the kids, too. Or you can lace up your boots and strike out on to the moor. If you dare...

COOL FACTOR Location, location, location.

WHO'S IN? Tenters and vanners, but no doggies (they don't tend to mix well with the animals).

ON SITE Campfires allowed and wood can be purchased from the farm. New facilities have been installed since the last edition: a shower block with roomy showers, a loo block (watch out for the psychedelic panels made from recycled pencils), with a disabled toilet and shower and covered washing-up areas. There are even bushcraft courses (£20 per person), including the art of fire making. You can also walk the South Penquite trail around the circumference of the farm, taking in standing stones, stone circles, a canyon, and a quarry.

OFF SITE Explore various trails across Bodmin Moor on horseback from Hallagenna Farm (01208 851500; www.hallagenna.co.uk). There are pony treks, which are ideal for kids (over 5), or hacking and trail rides for the more experienced.

FOOD AND DRINK Sausages and burgers are available from the farm to cook over your open fire, but if you fancy something else there's an award-winning pub in the village of Blisland, about a mile away: the Blisland Inn (01208 850739).

GETTING THERE As you head west into Cornwall on the A30 just short of Bodmin the dual carriageway narrows to a single lane. There's a right turn signposted St Breward. Follow this road over the moor for 2½ miles until you see the large South Penquite sign by a rough track on the right.

PUBLIC TRANSPORT The closest you can get really is Bodmin Parkway railway station, but it's nearly 10 miles away.

OPEN May–October.

THE DAMAGE Tent/campervan plus 2 people £14 per night. Additional adult £7; child (5 to 16) £3.50, under-5s free. A week in a yurt £220–£360 (depending on which yurt and season). There's a new wooden pod available for £25 a night.

hole station

Hole Station Campsite, Highampton, Beaworthy, Devon, EX21 5JH   01409 231266   www.freewebs.com/holestationcampsite

Mario loved life at Hole Station. Not only did he make lots of new friends every day; he'd left his previous life of heavy toil in Romania well behind. His English became superb, too, which was no minor feat for a horse.

Mario was the first four-legged fellow to earn his keep by taking Hole Station campers for pony-and-trap rides through the nearby lanes of Highampton Ridge, with its views of Dartmoor on one side and Exmoor (on the other). He learnt to trot, walk, stop, turn, and reverse by voice command, pricking his ears back to hear what owner Liz wanted him to do. When Mario first arrived, Liz had to learn the commands in Romanian before gradually exchanging them for English, so Mario became bilingual – as well as an excellent carthorse.

Since Mario retired, his neighbour, Sanne, has taken up the reigns, and along with Doris, two affable goats, and a couple of dogs and cats, forms part of the scenery at this very special campsite, situated on the land of a former railway station in a sparsely populated part of Devon. Opening its gates to campers as recently as 2009, Hole Station has already become a firm favourite among the camping fraternity, which is hardly surprising given its secluded woodland pitches, campfire encouragement, and natural beauty.

Whether you bring your own tent or opt for a pre-erected Rent-A-Tent here, you're going to love your pitch. There are just 19 of them, each bearing a number and spread about the place in woodland clearings or in the neighbouring Culm meadow. Woodland pitches offer privacy within a magical tree-filled setting, while the meadow pitches are a short stroll from the facilities and enjoy the heaven-scent smells from flowers growing all around them.

Greg and Liz eventually bought Hole Station after keeping their eyes on the property for years. They live in what was the old ticket office while their kids are residents of a renovated old railway carriage (think Annie and Clarabel-style from *Thomas The Tank Engine*) next door. Together they are slowly bringing the wood back to its former forest glory by coppicing and pollarding, which they do in the winter after the last of the season's campers have packed up and gone home.

The cut-down wood is used to create wildlife habitats and fuel for campfires. So feel a little smug, as you sit mesmerised by the licking flames of your fire at night, that you're forming a symbiotic relationship with the trees all around you. In fact, the clearing you're pitched in is helping to shed more life-giving light on the young oaks nearby, enabling them to have a kick-start at growing into huge, majestic trees likely to outlive us for centuries to come.

It's not just the campfire culture, perfect pitches, and woodland restoration that Liz, Greg, and family have got right at Hole Station, though. The loos are of the compost variety and all rubbish (including food waste) is recycled or turned into compost wherever possible in order

to give something back to this lovely corner of England. It's quiet time after 10pm; you can help yourself to free-range eggs, leaving money in an honesty box; and there's a signed Woodland Walk on which you half expect to encounter a fairy or two before reaching (handily labelled) The End –

a top spot for watching the sun go down, especially if you take a bottle along with you.

So Hole Station has earned itself a huge *Cool Camping* endorsement, and if that's not enough for you to book a pitch here, surely the testament of a happy couple of horses is.

COOL FACTOR Camping in magical woodland clearings or a meadow, with campfires and pony-and-trap rides.

WHO'S IN? Tents – yes. Campervans, caravans, dogs, groups, radios, TVs, musical instruments – no.

ON SITE Campfires permitted! Sign up for yours and a kit (consisting of logs chopped by hand on site, kindling, and firelighters) will be ready daily for you to collect from the entrance before evening – if you've remembered to sign your name on the sheet. Hole Station has 19 pitches – 4 of which are pre-erected Rent-A-Tents for hire – most of which are situated within a clearing in the woodland, while the remainder reside in the Culm meadow near the facilities block. Park your vehicle in the car park and transport your gear to your pitch using one of the borrowable barrows. The wooden facilities block has just 2 compost loos – one for men and one for ladies – 2 basins, and 2 hot electric showers. Just outside are 2 washing-up sinks under shelter – hot water available – and a freezer with cool blocks to borrow. It's all kept clean, but can get very busy in the mornings and evenings. There's plenty to do on site: the Woodland Walk, pony courses, pony-and-trap rides. Quiet time from 10pm.

OFF SITE Dartmoor is just a 20-minute drive away, and the beaches of Bude and Widemouth are a 35-/40-minute drive in the opposite direction, so there are plenty of outdoor options. If anyone fancies honing his or her Robin Hood skills there's an archery centre just down the road: Arms of Old (01409 231171; www.armsofold.co.uk). Or Dragon Archery (08000 372466; www.dragonarcherycentre.co.uk), further afield, has exciting courses – come and have a go at the Agincourt course if you and your bow are up to it.

FOOD AND DRINK The Bickford Arms (01409 221318; www.bickfordarms.co.uk) 4 miles away in Brandis Corner uses fresh local ingredients to produce mouth-watering meals. Or you can opt to do all your cooking altento, having stocked up at Farmer Luxtons farm shop (01837 54308) in Stockley (near Okehampton). Its award-winning meat is just waiting to be slapped on the BBQ. The old railway line that once ran through these parts (stopping at the station, of course) is now a cycle track – follow it on foot or by bike towards Highampton and after 20 minutes or so you'll emerge just down the lane from local pub the Golden Inn (01409 231200). This is a cosy place with a wood-burning stove and copper kettles in the large old fireplace, and offers hearty dishes such as Boozey Pie on its menu.

GETTING THERE Take the A30 to Okehampton. In the town centre turn right (signposted Hatherleigh) when you reach the White Hart hotel. Continue along this road towards Hatherleigh then take the first exit (signposted Highampton and Holsworthy) when you reach the roundabout at Hatherleigh. Go through Highampton village, past the Golden Inn and post office, and after 1 mile turn left (signposted footpath and cycle track) opposite the turn off to Black Torrington. Follow the lane down and the white gateway to Hole Station is on the right.

PUBLIC TRANSPORT The nearest train station is Okehampton – take a taxi on to the site.

OPEN April–October.

THE DAMAGE A pitch (bring your own tent) plus 2 adults £12–£14 (depending on season) per night. Rent-A-Tent for 2 adults £21–£27.

lundy island

Lundy Shore Office, The Quay, Bideford, Devon, EX39 2LY   01271 863636   www.lundyisland.co.uk

The bold outcrop of granite that is Lundy Island juts over 120 metres into the air out of the Bristol Channel. It's just 11 miles from the North Devon coast, but feels more remote; the landscape is barren and desolate, with wild, towering cliffs, wind-battered fields, and little in the way of shelter. And like all the best natural campsites, Lundy's is essentially a field with nothing in it. Its peaceful, remote location feels a million miles from modern life, and relies solely on the simple pleasures – clear surrounding waters and dazzling night skies that remain unspoilt by the usual unforgiving streetlights. That said, in case you do start missing certain creature comforts here, such as shelter and the warming fuzz from a gulp of beer, there's a pub on the island that never shuts, so at any time of day or night there's always somewhere to cosy up and swap stories of tents blowing away in Atlantic winds.

Let's be honest, this isn't camping for beginners, but despite its bleak, isolated location, a few nights in a tent here can be invigorating. And when the wind drops and the sun appears, this may well be England's most magical camping experience.

COOL FACTOR Extreme, isolated, miles-away camping.
WHO'S IN? Tents, groups – yes. Campervans, caravans, motorhomes, dogs – no. Maximum of 40 people on site.
ON SITE About 40 pitches; no hook-ups. One shower block with 3 hot showers and 4 toilets. Service washes available and you're only a short walk from the pub and shop. Bring a torch as lights go out after midnight. No campfires or BBQs.
OFF SITE Go on a snorkelling safari with the island warden in the summer months. Or just enjoy the Lundy landscape.
FOOD AND DRINK Lundy lamb is famous and delicious. The Marisco Tavern (01271 431831) is the only pub on the island and serves tasty food including Lundy lamb and locally caught fish; it also has a notice board showing what's on.
GETTING THERE The island ship, MS *Oldenburg*, departs from Bideford and Ilfracombe March–October. A helicopter shuttle service runs during the winter.
PUBLIC TRANSPORT Closest train stations to Bideford are Barnstaple (7½ miles away) and Chapelton (8 miles). From there you can get many frequent local buses to Bideford town centre, then boat straight to Lundy Island.
OPEN Easter–October.
THE DAMAGE £9–£13 (depending on season) per person, per night. Advanced booking essential.

roadford lake

Roadford Lake Campsite, Okehampton, Devon, EX20 4QS   01409 211507   see www.swlakestrust.org.uk

Calling all water babies – Roadford Lake Campsite is, as the name suggests, situated right on the shore of a lake stretching across 730 acres of mid Devon. There are boatloads of opportunities here for campers to immerse themselves in outdoor activities – either on the water in kayaks, canoes, dinghies, and on water skis or around the water's edge on walks, cycle routes, and bridleways. Craft and equipment can be hired or visitors are welcome to bring their own; and private tuition and 'taster' courses are on offer at the friendly onsite centre.

The atmosphere at Roadford is exuberant, as wetsuit-clad campers and visitors stroll around the place with happy smiles on their faces having spent a few hours developing their sea legs on the lake, or sit relaxing by the BBQ after a day moseying around this quiet quarter of Devon.

The site has many pitches, but they're spread across a number of small fields broken up by tall hedges to give them a more intimate feel. The field next to the lake is the one to aim for, right on the shore and offering a fantastic panorama across the water, its boats waiting for you to climb aboard.

COOL FACTOR   Camping on the shore of a sailing lake.

WHO'S IN?   Tents, campervans, caravans, dogs (on leads), groups (discounted rates available) – yes.

ON SITE   Three fields, plus an overflow. Approx. 100 pitches, 10 hook-ups (3 more to come), 9 hardstanding. Five portaloos behind the updated facilities block (with hot showers, loos, sinks, and hairdryer) plus disabled loo/shower room. A new block built in spring 2011 offers more loos and showers (6W, 6M). There are 2 washing-up sinks and 2 covered areas with picnic benches and BBQ. Hire water craft or sign up for sailing lessons and water-skiing at the onsite office. No campfires, but BBQs off the ground allowed.

OFF SITE   Head round to the visitor centre where there's a café, shop, play area, and the starting point for walks, strolls, and off-road cycling. Lots of pretty villages around here too.

FOOD AND DRINK   See South Breazle (p66).

GETTING THERE   Exit the A30 at Stowford Cross. Follow the brown signs for Roadford Lake; continue past the visitor centre and across the dam, until you see a sign for the activity centre. Turn right down the lane to the site.

OPEN   March–October.

THE DAMAGE   Pitch for 2 adults £12–£14 (depending on season) per night. Child £2.50–£3.50. Hook-up £3.50.

south breazle

South Breazle Holidays, Bratton Clovelly, Okehampton, Devon, EX20 4JS   01837 871752   www.southbreazleholidays.co.uk

Come and have an easy Breazle time at this relaxed site surrounded by mid-Devon fields. A great place for first-time campers, South Breazle offers superb facilities and spacious pitches with individual names and separated by pretty flowers. The pitches are looped around the perimeter of a field in a horseshoe shape, within easy reach of the facilities.

Owners Louise and Steve rear cows and a few pigs and sell tasty burgers and sausages in the site shop. They designed the campsite so its nucleus – the field – is open for kids to play cricket and footie, or just run themselves breathless while their parents relax within eyeshot. The track separating the grassy space from the pitches is perfect for cycling around and around before it's time to cool off in the adjacent field's 'fun fountain'.

Camping purists may not love the organised, manicured pitches or the amount of hardstanding and hook-ups here, while the quiet-time at 10pm rule may not appeal to the party crowd. But if you're a new camper or bringing kids it's the perfect site for getting to grips with this sleeping outdoors malarkey, while exploring the heart of Devon.

COOL FACTOR Large pitches and excellent facilities.
WHO'S IN? Tents, campervans, caravans – yes. Dogs, young groups – no.
ON SITE Twenty-nine pitches, most with hook-ups. Large facilities block with power showers, lots of loos, and hairdryer/shaving point. A family room with baby-changing and disabled room. Washing-up sinks, washing machine (£3), and tumble-dryer (£2.50), plus a phone line to the farm. Fantastic onsite shop selling all sorts. Adjacent field with 'fun fountain' and playing space. Free wi-fi, water taps, and CDP. Battery charging. No campfires, but BBQs off the ground okay.
OFF SITE Head horse-riding or over to Roadford Lake (see p65). South Breazle's website is full of ideas.
FOOD AND DRINK The cheery Clovelly Inn (01837 871447) in the village has cosy rooms, real ales, and an excellent menu (fab bacon sarnies). Lifton Farm Shop (01566 784605) sells home-grown produce and cream teas.
GETTING THERE Exit the A30 at Stowford Cross. Follow signs for Roadford Lake then turn right at the top of the hill (signposted Bratton Clovelly), take the second left. Turn right into the lane to South Breazle and follow the right-hand fork.
OPEN 1 March–31 October.
THE DAMAGE Pitch plus 2 adults £12.50–£16.50.

bay view farm

Bay View Farm Caravan and Camping Site, St Martins, Looe, Cornwall, PL13 1NZ   01503 265922   www.looebaycaravans.co.uk

When someone puts love into a campsite, it shows; and Bay View Farm is one loved spot. Welcoming owners Mike and Liz have been smitten with the place since 1972 and, after finally buying the farm and opening it to campers in 1999, they've put a whole lot of love into maintaining it.

The beautifully kept site comprises a modest 25 spaces on a sloping field. Pitch your tent the right way up and the slope only enhances your view, which is about as panoramic and impressive as it gets on the Cornish south coast – stretching to West Looe on the far side of Hanner Fore – a real sight for just-woken eyes. During the summer season, an overflow field ensures there's still plenty of space. But whichever field you pitch on, both are wide open spaces guaranteeing a sea view.

If you like your vistas with a challenge then have a crack at the South West Coast Path – within easy reach of the campsite's cosy confines. On your way back, you can pop into quaint fishing village, Polperro, and take your pick from treats at a host of fudge shops, tea rooms, and fishmongers' with fresh catches – perfect for the evening BBQ.

COOL FACTOR Welcoming owners and incredible views.

WHO'S IN? Every man and his dog in every tent/vehicle.

ON SITE Twenty-five pitches in low season, 40 more in high; hook-ups (£3); wi-fi. Free hot showers, loos, coin-operated laundry. Wooden 'snugs' (3) being built. No campfires.

OFF SITE Say hi to the primates at the Monkey Sanctuary (01503 262532; www.monkeysanctuary.org). Be blown away by the Eden Project (01726 811911; www.edenproject.com) about 10 miles away. For something unusual, try tagging a Cornish shark with the Energy of Looe (01503 265837).

FOOD AND DRINK For a proper Cornish lunch try the Purely Cornish Deli (01503 262696) in Looe and PYO hamper from a range of local produce. The Smugglers Inn (01503 250646) has great local ales and impressive views.

GETTING THERE Take the A38 to Trerulefoot roundabout. From here follow signs for Looe on the B3253/A387 until you reach No Man's Land, where you bear left to follow signs for the Monkey Sanctuary and then Bay View Farm.

PUBLIC TRANSPORT Catch a train to Looe and then hop on bus no. 572 from West Looe to Bay View Farm.

OPEN All year.

THE DAMAGE Pitch, 2 adults, 2 children: £10–20 (depending on season) per night. Snug £35 per night.

karrageen

Karrageen Caravan and Camping Park, Bolberry, Malborough, Kingsbridge, Devon, TQ7 3EN   01548 561230   www.karrageen.co.uk

Karrageen is all about giving its lucky occupants plenty of room to breathe, think, play, and relax. There's no tangle of guy ropes here, and there's even room for those multi-bedroom monstrosities that can take up a good few pitches on their own.

You'll find nothing fancy, nothing flash, and nothing gimmicky: just a simple, very well-maintained and nicely landscaped site in an ever-so-lovely location – with space to spare.

The immediate locality of Karrageen is peaceful and only accessed along a tortuous narrow lane leading down (eventually) to the sea at the lost world of Hope Cove and its little village. After wandering through the sleepy rows of fishermen's cottages you'll think it eminently possible that this is still a place for clandestine meetings of pirates and smugglers – such is the sense of detachment and timelessness in the air.

There are a couple of pubs in the village that serve food, but should lethargy – or the desire not to leave this lovely site – rob the legs of movement, there are decent meals available courtesy of Karrageen's amiable cooking proprietor.

COOL FACTOR Space for families to spread out and relax.
WHO'S IN? Tents, vanners, dogs – yes. Groups – no.
ON SITE A terraced hillside split into small, intimate cul-de-sacs. Excellent facilities: loos and 9 showers (20p; 4W, 4M, 1 family/disabled room equipped for baby-changing). There are 50 hook-ups; freezer access. Downsides: some static caravans lurking about; it's not easily reached by public transport. No campfires, but BBQs off the ground are okay.
OFF SITE Book a boat trip: return sailing from Kingsbridge to Salcombe (01548 853607); River Dart trip from Totnes to Dartmouth (01803 555872; www.dartmouthrailriver.co.uk). Or sea tractor to Burgh Island (www.burghisland.com).
FOOD AND DRINK Posh nosh with a view at the South Sands Hotel (01548 859000) in Salcombe, while in Hope the Sun Bay Hotel (01548 561371) does very good food.
GETTING THERE From the A38 at Wrangaton take the A3121 south; left on to the B3196 to Kingsbridge; and A381 towards Salcombe. After 3 miles take the second turn signposted Hope Cove; the site is a further 2 narrow miles.
OPEN Easter/early April–late September.
THE DAMAGE Tent, car, plus 2 adults and 2 children £13–£27 (depending on season and tent size) per night. Hook-up £3; dog £1.

maelcombe house

Maelcombe House, East Prawle, Kingsbridge, Devon, TQ7 2DE   01548 511521

As camping paradises go, it's hard to beat pitching your tent as close to the beach as you can here at Maelcombe House. Beachside camping coupled with views of some of the most unspoilt, uncrowded stretches of the south coast is enough to enrapture campers here. Many enter into some kind of ecstatic trance as they stare out to sea from this small and almost perfectly rustic campsite.

Maelcombe offers a wild camping experience, comprising a field sloping down to the beach with access via a steep private track. It's unlikely you'll share the site with anything bigger than a campervan, and even that'd be a rarity. Facilities stretch to a water supply, and your sturdiest tent and expedition-grade sleeping gear are de rigueur – it's not unknown for tents to be blown away around these parts. And don't forget your fishing gear; even lobsters and crabs can be caught off the beach.

If this sounds too much like tent-and-trowel camping for you, there are a number of sites up the hill in East Prawle that also offer sea views, but with more in the way of facilities and closer to the village's beating heart, the vibrant Pigs Nose Inn.

COOL FACTOR Wild beachside camping.

WHO'S IN? Wild campers with tents, dogs – yes. Vehicles – not advised.

ON SITE Campfires allowed. Unmarked pitches on a rustic field above the beach with a stunning sea view. No facilities, but you can collect water from the house.

OFF SITE Swim and go rockpooling at the end of the camping field, or head west for more beaches off the coastal path to Start Point Lighthouse (see www.trinityhouse.co.uk). At East Portlemouth you can take a ferry to seaside town Salcombe (www.salcombeinformation.co.uk). If it rains head to Ashby's Easy Stores (www.ashbysonline.co.uk) in East Charleton for hot steak pasties and outdoor-gear shopping.

FOOD AND DRINK For a change from the Pigs Nose Inn (www.pigsnose.co.uk), take a fine cream tea at South Allington House (p70). Or treat yourself at Dartmouth's Michelin-starred New Angel restaurant (01803 839425).

GETTING THERE Take the A379 south, turn left after Frogmore and follow signs for East Prawle. As you enter the village, turn left into School Lane. Continue round to the right, take the first left, and follow signs to Maelcombe House.

OPEN Variable, approx. Easter–October.

THE DAMAGE £7 per tent, per night. Booking advised.

south allington house

South Allington House, Chivelstone, Kingsbridge, Devon, TQ7 2NB   01548 511272   www.southallingtonhouse.co.uk

South Allington House may be slap bang in the middle of a designated Area of Outstanding Natural Beauty between Start and Prawle Points along a sweep of South Devon's coastline, but the fact that you can camp in its grounds is a rather closely guarded secret – the owners don't even mention it on their website. So don't tell them we think their secretive site a bit of a camping oasis, with its facilities offering a cocoon to the least intrepid of campers, while its location in a beautiful valley surrounded by farmland will gently coax the toughest city nuts back to nature.

You can treat yourself to a highly civilised cream tea with dollops of home-made jam at the Georgian manor house while the kids mooch off in search of woodland wildlife. Little ones are kept happy making friends with the grazing sheep, marvelling at frogs in the pond, and trying to keep up with ducklings as they wander around the manicured grounds. And if the weather goes pear-shaped you can always opt for a room in the manor house B&B or other self-catering options. Just be sure to book early during school holidays.

COOL FACTOR A cosy site in the grounds of a Georgian manor house near stunning coastline.

WHO'S IN? Tents, campervans, a couple of small caravans, dogs – yes. Big groups – no.

ON SITE Well maintained facilities in a converted outbuilding near the camping field (35–40 pitches on lawn) include toilets, showers, washing-up sinks, washing machines, tumble-dryers, fridges, and freezers. No electric hook-ups and no campfires unless you take your own brazier.

OFF SITE Besides local beaches and stunning coastal walks, there's the 'hippy haven' of Totnes with its castle and South Devon Steam Railway (www.southdevonrailway.org) to visit.

FOOD AND DRINK Cream teas at the manor house are a must, and in nearby East Prawle there's food and entertainment at the lively Pigs Nose Inn (01548 511209; www.pigsnose.co.uk), or you could try the quieter Piglets Stores and Café (01548 511486) across the road. For local produce, Stokeley Farm Shop (01548 581010) in Stokenham.

GETTING THERE Going south, pass Frogmore on the A379 and follow signs for East Prawle until you reach Chivelstone Cross. Turn left and site is ½ mile further, on the right.

OPEN May–October.

THE DAMAGE Tent plus 2 people £15 per night. Child £1.

beryl's

Beryl's Secret Camping Haven, Beeson, nr Kingsbridge, Devon   01548 580527

The only clue to this campsite's existence is a hand-painted 'camping' sign that looks like it's pointing in the wrong direction. The site doesn't even have a name and is known by locals simply as 'the one run by Beryl'. Beryl herself describes the secretive site, hidden at the end of a tunnel of trees in Beeson village, as her 'unconventional camping haven'. Charming eccentricity is certainly apparent here, not only in the laissez-faire attitude to publicity, but also in the quirky names of the 20 pitches, such as Panoramic and Snug. The 'haven' part of Beryl's description is equally apt for this lush little site, nestled as it is on a hill in the woods with a glorious view of Start Bay.

Venture down the narrow access road – even the odd caravan has been known to brave it – and you're rewarded with a real sanctuary from which to explore the surrounding delights of the Devon coast. You can spy on birds from the hide looking over the local nature reserve's lake. Or take a walk around Slapton Ley lagoon, just over the hill. And the South West Coast Path passes the award-winning beach at Beesands, just below the site.

COOL FACTOR Small, secret, secluded site with a view.

WHO'S IN? Tents, campervans, caravans (narrow access track), dogs – yes. Groups – by arrangement.

ON SITE A small field with 20 named pitches on a hill cradling a pond and embraced by enigmatic woodland. Good facilities with recycling bins, fridges, toilets, showers (coin-operated – 20p), washing-up sinks, electric hook-ups, and power points for charging mobiles. No campfires.

OFF SITE The almost Mediterranean-like Blackpool Sands bay (www.blackpoolsands.co.uk) and its secret gardens are well worth a visit. For a step back in time, take a day trip to Dartmouth (www.discoverdartmouth.com) with its cobbled streets, boutiques, river cruises, and steam railway.

FOOD AND DRINK For seafood fresh off the boat and cream-tea treats, there's the local Britannia (www.britanniashellfish.co.uk) at Beesands. But for the best fish and chips around it's got to be the Start Bay Inn (01548 580553; www.startbayinn.co.uk) in Torcross.

GETTING THERE Take the A379 to Stokenham. Turn right at the roundabout and follow the road for 1½ miles then left to Beeson. In Beeson follow the hand-painted camping signs.

OPEN Easter–October.

THE DAMAGE Adult £6; child (under-16) £3, under-5s free.

old cotmore farm

Old Cotmore Farm, Stokenham, Kingsbridge, Devon, TQ7 2LR   01548 580240   www.oldcotmorefarm.co.uk

When Cornwall is too far, Dorset not far enough, and Somerset too 'inland', then Devon is the perfect West Country destination. To discover the county's true countryside charm and primeval serenity, it's better to journey as far south as possible. Feel all your cares evaporate along the scenic coastal road from Dartmouth all the way to Stokenham, home to Old Cotmore Farm, nuzzled between pretty Torcross and picture-postcard Kingsbridge.

The campsite's run by people who know how to enjoy the finer things in life, and extra touches encourage a comfy stay: spotless facilities, prudent and colourful planting, flat pitches with sweeping views, and an exhaustive choice of walking maps. Tent pitches can be found beyond a field dominated by caravans; three in the Vegetable Patch, and more in the field (above the house) that opens in August.

There's a beach for everyone on the doorstep: Beesands (sandy), Slapton Sands (shingle), Blackpool Sands (award-winning), Mill Bay (dog-friendly), and Pilchards Cove (naturist); and dinky eateries such as the Winking Prawn Beach Café at Salcombe – a must for its popcorn shrimp and creamy ice creams.

COOL FACTOR A glimpse into the 'real' rural Devon.

WHO'S IN? Tents, campervans, caravans, dogs – yes. Groups (even large family groups) – no.

ON SITE Thirty pitches (with hook-ups) in 'the Park' field, where you leave the car; 30 tent-only pitches in the upper field in August, 3 in the Vegetable Patch. A washing block in the Park has power showers (4W, 3M) and loos; 2 loos in the other field. Baby-changing space and a bathroom for the disabled; laundry; small shop; children's play area; games garage. Use of freezers. Quiet curfew 10pm. No campfires.

OFF SITE Salcombe's Island Cruising Club (01548 844300) offers sailing courses, water-skiing, and banana-boat rides.

FOOD AND DRINK Pre-order a luxury Shack Picnic (salmon and crab baguettes, oysters, prawns, strawberries and clotted cream) online from the famous Oyster Shack (www.oystershack.co.uk), a 30-minute drive west.

GETTING THERE Head to Stokenham (at the foot of the A379 between Dartmouth and Kingsbridge) then to Beesands village and after a mile you'll see signs to the farm.

PUBLIC TRANSPORT Bus no. 93 runs between Dartmouth and Kingsbridge every half-hour, stopping at Stokenham.

OPEN Mid March–end October.

THE DAMAGE Tent/motorhome plus 2 adults £11–£19.

prattshayes farm

Prattshayes Farm, Maer Lane, Littleham, Exmouth, Devon, EX8 5DB   01395 276626   see www.nationaltrust.org.uk

The National Trust didn't make a big song and dance about this site until recently when regulars put the word out about their top camping snug in Exmouth's locale, and its sudden popularity nudged the Trust into sprucing up this old favourite.

The long, stone farmhouse and small adjoining field were bequeathed to the Trust in the eighties, but Prattshayes has been operating as a campsite for twice as long. Although you can expect a fair few caravans here, don't be put off; at most there's a 50/50 split between vans and tents.

To maximise privacy, campers aim for the corners of the square-shaped field. The farmhouse borders one side, while the other three are flanked by views of hills, and Exmouth's family-friendly beach – Britain's first ever seaside resort – is a 30-minute stroll along a coastal path. Families are the campsite's target market, too. Young arrivals throw themselves on to the plastic garden toys as their parents hammer in pegs. And after a day of beachcombing, communal games spring into gear. Then, as the moon rises, you might hear a guitar or king whistle serenading your nightcap.

COOL FACTOR A sheltered site by a lovely stretch of coast.

WHO'S IN? Tents, campervans, dogs (breeds are vetted), big groups – yes. Groups of under-18s without adults – no.

ON SITE Thirty pitches; 20 electric hook-ups; 3 well-kept hot (although not very private) showers, loos, a baby-changing stand, and potties. Basic tuck shop. A covered veg prep area, sinks (no plugs), and recycling. Comfy bunkhouse (sleeping 14) for group hire. No campfires. BBQs fine (and free to borrow).

OFF SITE The coast awaits, with rock pools perfect for crabbing. From the docks catch a water ferry with Explorer Water Taxis (07970 918418) across the estuary to Dawlish Warren, a gorgeous nature reserve and beach (no dogs).

FOOD AND DRINK All palates are catered for in Exmouth. The chicest has to be Les Saveurs (01395 269459) tucked down a side street and offering cooking with French twists.

GETTING THERE Head to Exmouth on the A376. At the traffic lights go left, following signs to Littleham. Turn right at the Clinton Arms (Maer Lane), the site is ½ mile on the right.

PUBLIC TRANSPORT Train to Exeter then Exmouth, where bus no. 95 runs the 30-minute journey to Littleham village, alight at the Clinton Arms and walk for 10 minutes.

OPEN 1 April–31 October.

THE DAMAGE Adult £5–£6; child £2–£2.50. Hook-up £2.50.

manor farm

Manor Farm, Daccombe, Newton Abbot, Devon, TQ12 4ST   01803 328294   www.manorfarmcows.com

Manor Farm is a charming, isolated Devonshire idyll located so near the M5 that campers can fall into step with the West Country's calming, unhurried way of life quickly and easily. Signposts to the farm line the main Torquay Road, and just five miles from the motorway and equidistant from the coast a steep detour promptly descends into rural calm. As you pootle along between high hedgerows the campsite jumps into view. Nestled at the foot of a lush green valley is a sprawling farmhouse with a few dozen grazing cows, and not a mobile home on site, or in sight. Better still, far from overflowing with tourists, the nearby dinky (okay, miniscule), thatched-cottage villages of Daccombe and Coffinswell are crowd-free.

The resident owner, Thea, is a chatty lady who raises calves, keeps chickens, and has all manner of friends and family mucking in to keep the farmland in tip-top condition. Simplicity is key to her success and she's never advertised the campsite. The field is spacious and airy, and there's a half-hour walking trail through the neighbouring woods of Orestone Plantation, overlooking fields.

Nearby kiss-me-quick Torquay is typically British; its numerous restaurants and bars ply for custom, and the main beach is heaving in high summer. Prettier, quieter sandy coves in the area include Watcombe and Hollicombe. Reached by either a steep decline or a long walk, they tend to put off new visitors. We say, be a proud tourist – Manor Farm's chilled aura and surroundings can be as relaxing or energetic as you need them to be.

COOL FACTOR Easily accessible, this simple Devonshire idyll is calming and has a cute thatched-roof pub nearby.

WHO'S IN? Tents, campervans (with tents), dogs, groups – yes. Caravans, radios – no.

ON SITE There's room for 75 pitches, plus an overflow field that can fit a further 75. A clean, functional shower block has 15 loos and 4W, 4M electric showers; 3 sinks for washing dishes and clothes, plus a lower-level sink for kids, and washing machine (£1). A mini playground at the bottom has stylish rope swings and a slide. A small shop sells drinks, ice creams, bacon butties, and Pot Noodles. BBQ blocks are free or there are 3 BBQ areas behind the washroom. No campfires.

OFF SITE P-p-pick up a ticket to see a penguin at Living Coasts (www.livingcoasts.org.uk), Torquay's coastal zoo and conservation charity.

FOOD AND DRINK Torquay's inaugural Michelin-starred restaurant the Elephant (01803 200044; www.elephantrestaurant.co.uk) is stylish with pomp, sea views, and posh grub. The Linney (01803 873192; www.thelinny.co.uk) is a local and lovely pub in Coffinswell that serves up more traditional cooking.

GETTING THERE Simples: take the M5 and A38 south then A380 (Torquay Road). Turn left at the traffic lights, following the brown camping signs, then turn right at the top of the hill, and you'll see Manor Farm as you descend.

PUBLIC TRANSPORT Take a train to Newton Abbot, then it's £10 by taxi, or take a bus to Torquay and catch bus no. 31, alight at Barchington Avenue, and walk down Daccombe Hill (10 minutes).

OPEN May–September.

THE DAMAGE £10–£15 (depending on tent size) per pitch, per night; gazebo £1; dog £1.

west middlewick farm

West Middlewick Farm, Nomansland, Tiverton, Devon, EX16 8NP   01884 861235   www.westmiddlewick.co.uk

Ellie and her family were on their third visit to West Middlewick Farm this year. She's given her dad strict instructions to wake her up each morning in time to feed the lambs and help out with anything else in need of an enthusiastic pair of hands here. In fact, Ellie has become such an able farmhand she's even been given her own set of overalls. Because at this working dairy farm, just outside the sleepy hamlet of Nomansland near Tiverton, campers and their kids are encouraged to take an interest in what goes on around here. The farm itself sits between the camping fields and the facilities block, so you'll inevitably wander past and find popping your head into one of the barn doors irresistible, with their welcoming labels and friendly residents. Getting to know the animals and helping with their care comes hoof in hoof with a stay at West Middlewick, and has done since 1933.

As Ellie's parents found out, this refreshing ethos is a huge hit with kids, with some actually begging their parents to leave the beach early so that they're back in time to watch the cows being milked and to help distribute the pig feed. Rabbits in hutches sit on the driveway, chickens roam freely by the barns, and companionable cats prowl around on the hunt for attention. The atmosphere is one of community and conviviality; adults chat cheerfully while their children race around together. And it's not just the kids who get caught up in the West Middlewick way; adults of all ages return year on year to fuss the animals and relax at this no-frills site... By now Ellie and family will be on at least visit number six.

COOL FACTOR Lend a hand on a friendly farm.

WHO'S IN? Tents, campervans, caravans, dogs (on leads and if good with other animals), groups (in lower field) – yes.

ON SITE The site slopes down from the farm. The upper field has a large space in the centre for playing, and track for cycling round, as well as hook-ups and water taps. The more informal lower field has taps and hook-ups at the top. Facilities are a walk away from the site, near the farmhouse. One ladies' block – loos, basins, 2 hot showers (£1 for 10 minutes; 20p for 2 minutes), disabled loo/shower room with baby-changing. Around the corner are 2 washing-up sinks and a washing machine (£4). The gents' has loos and shower (also metered). There are 3 wooden cabins sleeping 6 in another field. No campfires, but BBQs off the ground okay.

OFF SITE Head to Tiverton Castle (01884 253200; www.tivertoncastle.com). With over 9 centuries of history, this compact castle is informative as well as fun. Or find out how honey is made and bees are kept at Quince Honey Farm (01769 572401; www.quincehoney.co.uk).

FOOD AND DRINK The ivy-covered Thelbridge Cross Inn (01884 860316; www.thelbridgecrossinn.co.uk) down the road does cream teas, bar snacks, and has an à la carte menu featuring mouth-watering fish and fowl mains.

GETTING THERE Take the A361 towards Tiverton (off the M5). After 7 miles take the B3137 from the roundabout towards Witheridge, for 9 miles. A mile after Nomansland you'll see the farm on the right.

PUBLIC TRANSPORT Train to Tiverton, then bus no. 155 will drop campers off at the farm.

OPEN All year.

THE DAMAGE Pitch plus 2 people £8–£10 (extra £2 if it's 1 night only); extra adult £2; child £1; dog £1. Hook-up £2–£3.

mitchum's

Mitchum's Campsites, Moor Lane, Croyde, Devon, EX33 1NU   07891 892897 (opening times only)   www.croydebay.co.uk

Acres of sand, pounding surf, and bronzed lifeguards – welcome to the Gold Coast. Not the original Australian Gold Coast, but the North Devon version; slightly cooler and, more importantly, much nearer for us Poms.

There's no disputing the beauty of Croyde Bay, a wide sweep of dune-backed sand flanked by the finest field-green North Devon hills. It's also the closest thing you'll find to a fair dinkum Aussie surf beach in this part of the world, gifting *awesome* waves to pros and beginners alike.

The bay provides a perfect canvas for the Mitchum's Beach campsite masterpiece. It's one of the few sites in the area with direct beach views, meaning you can keep an eye on the surf from your tent and race down with your board when the waves are good. And if you're not here for the surf, it's just as great being able to wake up and see the ocean each morning while cooking your sausages.

The wonderful owner of Mitchum's Beach, Guy, knows how to make you feel welcome, and also appreciates that his site is rather popular. So during the busy summer period he diffuses the camping congestion by opening up a nearby field to campers. This one's called Mitchum's Village campsite, and has the same ambience as its neighbour, just without the ocean outlook.

Regardless of which Mitchum's site you end up in, you're still just a flip-flop away from the beach and guaranteed to fall asleep every night in one incredible location, to the sounds of the crashing Croyde Bay waves.

COOL FACTOR Devon-like chilling with awesome Aussie-like surf.

WHO'S IN? Small tents, small VW campervans without pop-ups or awnings, groups – yes. Motorhomes, large campervans, caravans, dogs, under-17s – no.

ON SITE Approx. 36 pitches; no hook-ups; 2 clean facilities blocks with free hot showers, toilets, and hairdrying, shaving, and phone-charging points. Freezer packs available (£1 deposit, 50p for freezing). Onsite surf hire. No campfires but BBQs off the ground allowed.

OFF SITE Book some lessons with Surfing Croyde Bay (01271 891200; www.surfingcroydebay.co.uk), or take advantage of the stunning heritage coastline path with a walk to Baggy Point. Croyde Bay also hosts the annual Oceanfest (01271 817000; www.goldcoastoceanfest.co.uk) – a free sports and music festival in June.

FOOD AND DRINK Scoff a Devon cream tea at Centery Farm (01271 879603; www.centeryfarm.co.uk). The Thatch (01271 890349; www.thethatchcroyde.com) pub is a lively surfers' hang-out with decent food. And for a quick bite, grab one of the delicious pasties from the village shop.

GETTING THERE Follow the A361 to Braunton, then take the B3231 into Croyde. Turn left in the centre of the village, then left again on to Moor Lane. The Village site is on the left, the Beach site further down on the right.

PUBLIC TRANSPORT From Barnstaple train station, walk the 10 minutes to the bus station and take bus no. 308 to Moor Lane.

OPEN Mitchum's Village: late June–end August. Mitchum's Beach: late July–early September.

THE DAMAGE Book well in advance. Prices vary; contact Mitchum's for details.

little meadow

Little Meadow, Watermouth, Ilfracombe, Devon, EX34 9SJ   01271 866862   www.littlemeadow.co.uk

The ancient South American tribes of Inca and Maya might have invented terracing to help with their crop cultivation, but seldom can they have done it so well as the folk have here at Little Meadow. By levelling off the land in a series of flat lawns, they've ensured that campers benefit from being plumb-line level with the well-tended soft grass for easy tent pegging, while still enjoying views of the stunning North Devon coast. This Area of Outstanding Natural Beauty has everything: dramatic granite cliffs; wide, sandy beaches; and quaint little coves and harbours.

The terracing also helps create privacy – you'd never guess there are 50 pitches on this unassuming, environmentally friendly campsite. Bright splashes of flowers border the pitching areas, providing colourful framing to the views over Watermouth Bay, the Bristol Channel, and the cliffs of Hangman Point. It's a magnificent spot in which to settle comfortably into a deckchair and survey the scenery – you might even spy a seal or a basking shark if you're lucky (and in possession of a good pair of binoculars).

COOL FACTOR Well-tended terraces providing magnificent ocean views.

WHO'S IN? Tents, campervans, caravans, dogs (on leads) – yes. Groups – no.

ON SITE Approx. 50 pitches (draughty in high winds). An octagonal camping pod is being built. The wash-block has toilets, hot showers, and hairdryers. Ice-pack freezing; basic shop selling essentials, fresh organic milk, home-made cakes, and local farm meats. Hook-ups available; small, wooded play area for kids; wi-fi; dog-exercising area. No campfires.

OFF SITE Explore hand-carved tunnels at Tunnels Beaches (01271 879882; www.tunnelsbeaches.co.uk). Watermouth Castle (01271 867474) and its theme park are close by.

FOOD AND DRINK The Quay (01271 868090) in Ilfracombe boasts a wide selection of wines and tasty tapas.

GETTING THERE Take the A361 to Barnstaple. Just past the South Molton exit, turn right to Allercross roundabout (signposted Combe Martin). Go through Combe Martin; the campsite is just past Watermouth Castle on the left.

PUBLIC TRANSPORT Train to Barnstaple then catch a taxi or infrequent bus (no. 301) to Watermouth Castle.

OPEN Easter–late September.

THE DAMAGE Tent, 2 people, and a car £12–£18 per night.

sunny lyn

Sunny Lyn Holiday Park, Lynbridge, Lynton, Devon, EX35 6NS   01598 753384   www.caravandevon.co.uk

There's something slightly 1960s or 1970s about Sunny Lyn… something reminiscent of simpler times. But there's also something mildly exotic about the place too, as though it's not in Britain at all… a hint of France *peut-être*? This heady mix of atmosphere might be a reflection of the pace of life within this deep cleft of North Devon countryside. The loudest sounds in these parts emanate from the West Lyn river, tumbling joyfully through the site, and the hills, shooting skywards on either side, whispering loudly for your attention. The campsite occupies the only patch of level ground in this steep and scenic valley, along with a small clutch of ageing statics and a few houses perched on the precipice on one side of the valley. Nothing else intrudes into this exclusive scene, but the elegant little town of Lynton is only a (stunning) 10-minute stroll away, and the mini holiday resort of Lynmouth is further down the valley's steep hill. Like Sunny Lyn, Lynton and Lynmouth have a slightly exotic appeal and old-fashioned charm. The whole area has a magnetism all its own that doesn't seem to lessen, no matter how often you visit.

COOL FACTOR That lost-world feeling.

WHO'S IN? Tents, vanners, dogs – yes. Groups – no.

ON SITE Thirty pitches on small, level, riverside ground; a section with 8 hook-ups. Decent facilities: toilets, showers (2W, 2M), washing-up sinks, laundry, shop for food, alcohol, and beach combustibles. The small café does traditional breakfasts. No campfires, but BBQs off the ground okay.

OFF SITE Visit the Valley of the Rocks, a 30-minute, almost level, walk from the site. The Lynton Cliff Railway (01598 753486) eases the pain of getting up to Lynton from Lynmouth, where there are a couple of boat trip options from the harbour. Explore the Exmoor Hills on horseback from nearby Outovercott Riding Stables (01598 753341).

FOOD AND DRINK Lynton and Lynmouth have several top-notch eating places. The Vanilla Pod Restaurant (01598 753706) has imaginative, tasty vegetarian and vegan grub, and the Cliff Top Cafaurant (01598 753366) astounding views.

GETTING THERE The site is ¾ mile uphill, next to the B3234 from Lynmouth (off the A39).

PUBLIC TRANSPORT Regular buses from Lynmouth and Lynton to Minehead, Taunton, Ilfracombe, and Barnstaple.

OPEN Mid March–late October.

THE DAMAGE Adult £6.25–£7.50; child £3.25; dog £2.50.

trill farm

Trill Farm, Musbury, Axminster, Devon, EX13 8TU   01297 631113   www.trillfarm.co.uk

Trill Farm is the acquisition of global entrepreneur and founder of Neal's Yard Remedies, Romy Fraser. Her aim is to promote and teach a timetable of sustainable and energy-saving life skills, partly funded by income from the campsite. She created the Trill Trust as a charitable education centre; its ethos greener than the leafy trees that border the land. Campers and day visitors alike can sign up for subsidised courses on nutrition, homeopathy, and vegetable growing (to name but a few) conducted in a striking outbuilding that contains a kitchen and communal working area. Fraser's goal is to build a commune of like-minded businesses committed to creating sustainable lifestyles.

Farmhands will drive camping gear to the top of the hill, and once you've followed them up past herds of cows you're on your own. Two small fields are hedged by surrounding woodland, with hill views in one direction. In keeping with the site's rustic, back-to-basics nature the facilities are simple and cooking is done over fire pits. There are no noise curfews here – you're too far from the farm let alone any neighbours to create a disturbance.

Animal lovers and natural medicine aficionados will appreciate Trill Farm. Join the daily feeding rounds of pigs, chickens, and lambs; explore the woods; and check the website for activities such as food-foraging and bushcraft skills. Otherwise, bring a book, a torch (solar-powered, preferably), and let the world stand still for a few days while you contemplate your own contribution to a sustainable future.

COOL FACTOR Pass lamb pens, chicken runs, and a herd of Ruby Reds to find a rugged hilltop space that accommodates just 20 tents.

WHO'S IN? Tents, groups – yes. Campervans, caravans, dogs – no.

ON SITE Two sloping fields: one wild and one that's kept trim, are largely enclosed and high above the farm, so you don't have to tiptoe around. Two compost loos; a sheltered outdoor eating area; 2 washing-up sinks; benches for gas stoves; and a fire pit where you can grill meat are communal. The upper field has 2 solar-heated showers with warm water. Sustainable living skills courses are held throughout the year – see website for details. A shop sells ice creams and apple juice. There are no hook-ups, and vehicles are not permitted up the hill, it's a short sharp walk. No campfires.

OFF SITE Drop into Ottery St Mary's Escot Park (01404 822188; www.escot-devon.co.uk) for a day of forest games and treasure hunting, and finish off with a cream tea.

FOOD AND DRINK Drive 7 miles south, passing pretty thatched cottages, to the Masons Arms (01297 680300) at Branscombe, where you can feast on steamed West Country mussels and just-caught lobster above a bewitchingly beautiful, sweeping bay.

GETTING THERE At Axminster, take the A358 south and follow signs to Musbury until you see a sign on the left, 'Trill ¾'. The site is the first left turn down a long, potholed track.

PUBLIC TRANSPORT A taxi from Axminster station costs approx. £8, or take bus no. 885 towards Seaton, which stops at the 'Trill ¾' sign, before Musbury.

OPEN Mid July–mid September.

THE DAMAGE Adult £5 per night; under-16s £3, under-5s are free.

the west country

The West Country

Site number		Page number	Cool for campfires	Stunning views	For first-time campers	Middle of nowhere	Beach within reach	Surf's up	Waterside chilling	Walk this way	Great for kids	Dog friendly	High on mountains	For car-less campers	Cool for campervans	Wet 'n' wild	Forest fun	On yer bike	Something different	A friendly welcome	Fish club
35	Westermill Farm	88	●			●			●		●				●						
36	Huntstile Organic	90		●	●	●				●	●	●			●					●	
37	Holly Bush	91			●	●				●					●		●	●		●	
38	Batcombe Vale	92				●			●	●					●				●		●
39	Greenacres	94								●	●				●						
40	Hook Farm	95			●		●				●	●			●					●	
41	Sea Barn Farm	96		●	●		●				●	●			●						
42	Eweleaze Farm	97	●	●			●			●	●				●						
43	Tom's Field	98								●					●						
44	Acton Field	99	T				●			●	●				●					●	
45	Downshay Farm	100	O	●											●						
46	Burnbake	102	O			●				●	●				●		●	●			
47	Wilksworth Farm	103			●					●	●				●			●			
48	Riversidelakes	104	O	●	●				●	●	●				●				●	●	
49	Stowford Manor Farm	108	O						●		●				●	●					
50	The Barge Inn	110							●	●					●				●		
51	Thistledown	112	C	●	●	●				●	●	●			●				●	●	
52	Bracelands	116		●	●	●				●	●	●			●			●		●	
53	Cotswold Farm Park	118		●	●					●	●	●			●					●	
54	Cotswolds Camping	120		●	●					●	●	●		●	●					●	

KEY T – certain times   O – off ground only
     C – communal fire pits

10 km
10 miles

westermill farm

Westermill Farm, Exford, Exmoor, nr Minehead, Somerset, TA24 7NJ   01643 831238   www.westermill.com

In 1938, fed up with army life, Great Grandpa Edwards paid a visit to an unkempt farm hiding in a Somerset valley. Even before his young daughter had scrambled through the farmhouse window to let him in, he'd decided that this was the place for him. On stepping inside, he said simply, 'This'll do'. Within a few years he'd planted thousands of trees, made a home for his cattle and sheep, and transformed the boggy land into something nearing the subtle splendour of today's farm.

The campsite began as a favour to local Girl Guides in need of their camping badges, but swiftly evolved into a green means of diversification. Split into four adjoining fields at the base of the valley, it enjoys the clear, trout-inhabited waters of the River Exe swishing past, and sturdy protection of mottled hills on either side. Furthest from the farmhouse, the fourth field is perfect for those fancying a late night by the campfire. Awaken lost hunter-gatherer instincts by foraging for wood and then building a crackle-tastic fire. By the time you settle down to sleep beneath a star-spattered sky, the neighbouring cattle may have morphed into woolly mammoths.

Exmoor provides a backdrop of varied scenic eye-candy and is eager to please visitors with its plentiful attractions. And for a true taste of locality, pitch up to the monthly skittles tournaments in Westermill's lambing barn. As prevalent in Somerset as cider, this addictive game is open to all, with the added trappings of beer, home-made grub, and the warm feeling that all proceeds go to local charities. In Great Grandpa Edwards' words, 'This'll do'.

COOL FACTOR A secluded, riverside valley in Exmoor.

WHO'S IN? Tents, campervans, caravans, groups, well behaved dogs – yes.

ON SITE Campfires in the fourth field. BBQs off the ground okay. Roughly 60 unmarked pitches altogether. Each field has a spring-water tap. Two separate wash-blocks with toilets, free hot showers, and washing-up sinks. Washing machine (£2) and dryer. Midges are quite bad on warm, damp evenings.

OFF SITE Porlock, Woolacombe, and Puttsburgh beaches aren't far. This part of Devon has some lovely gardens to explore, including Hartland Abbey (01237 441264; www.hartlandabbey.com), where the bluebells in April are gorgeous. Clovelly Court (01237 431781; www.clovelly.co.uk), with the famous village below, is a great place for a walk.

FOOD AND DRINK An onsite shop sells provisions including local bread, free-range eggs, meat reared on the farm, and local Sheppy cider. The best nearby pubs are the Crown Hotel (01643 831554; www.crownhotelexmoor.co.uk) in Exford and the Rest and be Thankful (01643 841222; www.restandbethankful.co.uk) at Wheddon Cross, which does good food in generous portions.

GETTING THERE From Exford take the road to Porlock by the Crown Hotel. After ¼ mile fork left. Continue along this road, past another campsite, and look out for the Westermill sign on a tree. The drive turns left off the road.

PUBLIC TRANSPORT Train to Tiverton, then take bus no. 398 towards Minehead. This stops at Exford – the site is a 20–30-minute walk away. In summer the Exmoor Explorer open-top bus (no. 400) travels from Minehead to Exford.

OPEN Easter–November.

THE DAMAGE Adult £5 per night; child £3; car £2.50; dog £2.50.

huntstile organic

Huntstile Organic Farm, Goathurst, nr Bridgwater, Somerset, TA5 2DQ   01278 662358   www.huntstileorganicfarm.co.uk

Huntstile is foodie heaven. Owners Lizzie and John radiate a passion for good food and the whole place lives and breathes it. The farm covers over 650 acres of organic land nursing vegetables, soft fruit, wheat, oats, and barley, as well as medicinal crops for companies like Neal's Yard Remedies. Beef is produced from the herd of British white cattle, and there are chickens galore, for eggs aplenty. This isn't a dedicated campsite but a farm-cum-B&B-café/restaurant-self-catering-sort-of-a-place – and it's amazing...You can even get married here. There are technically five pitches, but you're more or less welcome to hunker down anywhere. So let your tent snuggle up to an old red-brick wall, the gypsy caravan, or even the pig pen.

You're in Quantock country, so circled by stunning rural Somerset and all its outdoor activities; and onsite walks seek out the ancient woodland or stone circle. It's hard to believe you're near the M5; all you can hear around here is wildlife. And it's lovely to stroll across the farmyard to the café for a cream tea or Full English, happy in the knowledge it's all fair trade with not a GM ingredient in sight.

COOL FACTOR Bijou camping by a 14th-century farmhouse with valley views and organic food.

WHO'S IN? Tents, campervans, caravans, children, dogs – yes. Groups – by arrangement.

ON SITE Five pitches (potentially more soon). No hook-ups or CDP. There's an eco-shower for a quick rinse (eco-friendly soap only), and an electric hot shower next to the main loo and washing-up area. Quiet time 10.30pm–7.30am. Onsite organic café, shop, restaurant, and veg garden. Breakfast available every day; supper by request. Garden games; maps for farm walks. No campfires... at present.

OFF SITE The Quantock Hills (www.quantockonline.co.uk) are close by, offering a range of outdoor activities. The fossils and freshwater ponds of Kilve Beach, on the north Somerset coast, are only a 20-minute drive away.

FOOD AND DRINK All yummy basics can be bought on site. Clavelshay Barn (01278 662629) on a neighbouring farm serves delicious lunches and dinners. The Rising Sun Inn (01823 432575), 5 miles away, serves gastropub food.

GETTING THERE See website for detailed directions.

OPEN March–October.

THE DAMAGE Tent plus 2 people £10 per night. Family tent/campervan/caravan £20.

holly bush

Holly Bush Park, Culmhead, Taunton, Somerset, TA3 7EA   01823 421515   www.hollybushpark.com

This two-acre, get-away-from-it-all site is hidden in the wooded folds of the unknown uplands of Somerset's Blackdown Hills, along a maze of narrow lanes seemingly unreachable by man or machine because so few people seem to stray into this rolling rural idyll. Though surely most have seen these hills from the madness of the M5 and vowed that 'one day' they'll come and explore them. The most famous feature (on the highest point) of the Blackdown Hills is the Wellington Monument, a memorial measuring over 50 metres, and presently awaiting restoration. This elegant obelisk is now enclosed by corrugated iron sheeting painted by local children and is a brilliant example of modern art on the hoof. It would be worth a couple of days' camping at Holly Bush just for the walk (or bike ride) along the shady undulating lanes to view this colossus of remembrance and young artistic endeavour, but that would be doing scant justice to the nature of this glorious glimpse into an unhurried world. The Blackdown Hills are a place for quiet contemplation, lengthy country walks, and long days in the (cycle) saddle.

COOL FACTOR A huge dose of true tranquillity.

WHO'S IN? Tents, campervans, caravans, dogs, quiet families or couples – yes. Groups – no.

ON SITE This little hideaway in the hills has a total of just 30 pitches in an enclosed garden-like setting and tents-only open field with a view. All garden pitches have hook-ups; and this is where you'll find the facilities block, with loos, 6 free showers, disabled facilities, laundry, washing-up sinks, and a fridge. No campfires, but BBQs off ground okay.

OFF SITE This is somewhere to abandon your car once you've arrived; there are some great pub-walks to be had (detailed routes provided by the owners).

FOOD AND DRINK Holman Clavel pub (01823 421432), next door to the site, offers good food and even better local ales (try the Butcombe Gold). The other local pubs to walk to are the Lamb and Flag (01823 421736), the Blagdon Inn (01823 421296), and the Culm Valley Inn (01884 840354).

GETTING THERE From Taunton follow the B3170 for 6½ miles, turn right into a lane with the brown campsite sign. At the T-junction go right. The site is on the left after the pub.

OPEN All year.

THE DAMAGE Pitch for 2 adults £12–£14 per night, plus £3.50 for hook-up and/or hardstanding. Child £2.50–£3.50.

batcombe vale

Batcombe Vale Campsite, Shepton Mallet, Somerset, BA4 6BW 01749 831207 www.batcombevale.co.uk

The first time you enter this secretive place is memorable; as the lane reaches the hill's crest it drops suddenly to reveal a breathtaking view of a veritable Shangri La. This slice of heaven, dropped into the midst of rural Somerset, is Batcombe Vale, where the camping is not so much 'cool', as 'chilled-out-to-the-point-of-being-horizontal'. Around here, rabbits scoot across the grass, buzzards soar on thermals above, and herons pose majestically on the lakesides. Listening to the plops of fish in the water, you half expect the rest of the cast of *The Wind in the Willows* to come marching out of the hedges.

The 30 pitches are on different levels: some with a glorious view, others surrounded by lush, tropical-looking vegetation. There are four small lakes, the largest of which has three colourful rowing boats just for Batcombe's campers to mess about in – Ratty would be proud. Hidden paths snake through the valley's rampant undergrowth and small jetties jut out into the water.

There are numerous genteel activities to undertake near this sheltered camping enclave. Walkers have a choice of paths radiating outwards from Batcombe Vale into the emerald swathes of landscape. Alternatively, within half-an-hour's drive are historic places like Wells (with its amazing cathedral) and Glastonbury (you might have heard of it…). At the other end of the spectrum, there's the Fleet Air Arm Museum at Yeovilton or, in Sparkford, the Haynes Motor Museum. But many visitors just stay put once they've bashed the last peg into the ground of Somerset's answer to paradise.

COOL FACTOR A beautiful and tranquil valley haven.

WHO'S IN? Tents, campervans, caravans, dogs (except certain breeds), small groups (up to 4 units, and only if there's room) – yes. Big group celebrations, noisy types – no.

ON SITE Thirty pitches; electric hook-ups; 4 lakes, 3 of which are stocked. To fish, campers must hold a National Rod Licence. You'll find excellent, eccentric facilities in a log cabin under a huge climbing plant – toilets, free hot showers, basins, laundry, and freezer. Enjoy the lakes aboard one of the free rowing boats; and the 120-acre valley is your playground. Gas or charcoal BBQs only – no campfires.

OFF SITE Petrolheads will love the Haynes Motor Museum (01963 440804; www.haynesmotormuseum.com) in Sparkford. Time flies at the Fleet Air Arm Museum (01935 840565; www.fleetairarm.com) in Yeovilton. Or why not take the train from Bruton to majestic Bath, where you can test Britain's only natural thermal waters at Thermae Bath Spa (www.thermaebathspa.com).

FOOD AND DRINK Gilcombe Organic Farm Shop (01749 813710; www.somersetorganics.co.uk) in Bruton is especially noted for its meat and can supply organic packs for the BBQ. If it's a pub you're after, give the 17th-century Three Horseshoes Inn (01749 850359) a try. It's in Batcombe – a mile's stroll from the campsite.

GETTING THERE The easiest approach is via Bruton or Evercreech on the B3081, then follow the brown campsite signs to Batcombe Vale.

PUBLIC TRANSPORT The campsite is 3 miles from Bruton train station.

OPEN Easter–end September.

THE DAMAGE Pitch plus 2 adults £16.50 per night; child (3 to 15 years) £3, under-3s free.

greenacres

Greenacres Camping, Barrow Lane, North Wootton, nr Shepton Mallet, Somerset, BA4 4HL   01749 890497   www.greenacres-camping.co.u

Once upon a time, an enchanting couple created a peaceful outdoor living area that was both safe and comfortable for young families and lots of fun for children. They called this place Greenacres – a gigantic 4½-acre field with just 40 pitches spread around three sides of the perimeter, while the entire central swathe is reserved for various dragon-slaying and spell-casting playtime activities. There's no visual electronic entertainment here; but a host of classic old-fashioned toys and activities, such as Wendy houses, see-saws, swings, and plenty of bikes for hire. There are even a couple of valiant battery-powered quad buggies.

If all this has left you imagining a site full of spellbound kids chaotically running through the site among all the cars and tents, then relax. All the magic takes place in car- and tent-free zones.

There's plenty of fun to be had in the environs of this fairy-tale campsite, too. The moody Somerset Levels provide excellent walking, or if you fancy something that doesn't require wearing boots then hippy-central Glastonbury is only three miles away – just the spot for picking up a magic wand…

COOL FACTOR Spellbinding family campsite.

WHO'S IN? Tents, small campervans, groups – yes. Caravans, motorhomes, dogs – no.

ON SITE Forty jumbo pitches; electric hook-ups. Retro wash-block with WCs, clean showers, washbasins, fridge/freezers, washing-up sinks, iron, ironing board; hairdryers on request. Nearby bike hire. No campfires. BBQs off ground.

OFF SITE Head witch-spotting and explore the famous caves at Wookey Hole (01749 672243; www.wookey.co.uk), 5 miles away. Check out the myths and legends at the Glastonbury Tor (www.glastonburytor.org.uk).

FOOD AND DRINK Two fantastic local producers sell their fare on site in high season. The Pilton Pig (01749 890252), a 5-minute drive, has a tea room and produces exquisite home-cured bacon and sausages. For a special dining treat try the 6-course tasting menu at Goodfellows Seafood Restaurant (01749 673866) in Wells.

GETTING THERE Take the A361 towards Glastonbury. After Pilton, turn right at the brown campsite sign. Pass North Wootton and the site's 2 miles further, on the left.

PUBLIC TRANSPORT Train to Castle Cary, then taxi.

OPEN March–October.

THE DAMAGE Adult £8 per night; child £2.50.

hook farm

Hook Farm Caravan Park, Gore Lane, Uplyme, Lyme Regis, Dorset, DT7 3UU   01297 442801   www.hookfarm-uplyme.co.uk

Island-hopping dinosaurs were part of the scenery in these parts some 190 million years ago. Many lost their footing and fell into the sea, leaving their mark on what became known as the Jurassic Coast. Hunting down their fossils is a popular sport in the quaint harbour resort of Lyme Regis. A couple of miles inland is Hook Farm, where a few steps is all it takes to be warmly welcomed at reception, whisked past a section for caravans, and ushered into a beautiful, terraced garden valley.

Spacious pitches allow room to spread out with gazebos and blankets. A dozen are tucked beside various bushy nooks and crannies, offering a little more privacy. You could select your patch according to your sleeping habits: early risers should head west to enjoy the morning sun, and night owls looking for a lie in can camp east, where the last of the day's rays fall. Sunsets look best from the top of the hill, while the lower area is better shielded from the elements. To lift the spirits of any young fossil-hunters who return empty-handed from a day's beachcombing, plastic dinosaur eggs are sold in the campsite shop.

COOL FACTOR Terraced site in a prime fossil-hunting spot.
WHO'S IN? Tents, campervans, caravans, dogs (certain breeds only) – yes. Groups – no.
ON SITE A total of 100 pitches including 17 for caravans; 56 hook-ups (£3). Two clean modern blocks of 5W, 5M loos and showers (20p for 4 minutes; 3 are solar-powered). Washing machine and tumble-dryer. Freezers are free; an onsite shop; a small play area. Arrive before 8pm and leave by 11am. No campfires; off-ground BBQs allowed (blocks available).
OFF SITE Guided 3-hour fossil walks along the coast, Sat–Tues (www.lymeregisfossilwalks.com). Visit the Dinosaurland Fossil Museum (01297 443541) in town, open daily.
FOOD AND DRINK Visit Hugh Fearnley-Whittingstall's own deli, cookery school, and canteen at River Cottage (www.rivercottage.net; booking advised) near Axminster.
GETTING THERE Head south on the A35 then right on to the B3165 (Lyme Road). In Uplyme, turn right opposite the Talbot Arms pub into Gore Lane; the campsite's on the right.
PUBLIC TRANSPORT Train to Axminster, Dorchester, or Weymouth, then bus no. 31 (www.firstgroup.com) to the Talbot Arms stop, then walk up the steep hill to the site.
OPEN March–October.
THE DAMAGE Tent plus 2 adults £15–£26; child £2.50.

sea barn farm

Sea Barn Farm Camping Park, Fleet, Weymouth, Dorset, DT3 4ED   01305 782218   www.seabarnfarm.co.uk

As you turn off the main road and head for Sea Barn Farm through narrow, mostly single-track country roads, shaded with tall trees on either side, it feels like a pioneering journey of discovery in forgotten Dorset. And then you find this gorgeous little tenters' campsite, neatly contained by a low stone wall, with the most fantastic panorama as a backdrop. The view of Fleet Lagoon, Lyme Bay, and the Jurassic Coast can be seen from many of the pitches; others have countryside views and some have no view at all, as pitches are arranged across a sequence of small fieldlets with differing outlooks.

In truth, the low-key, undiscovered ambience at Sea Barn Farm is something of an illusion. The site's actually part of a larger operation that includes the adjacent campsite and a touring caravan park. Although they're separate from Sea Barn Farm, guests can use their facilities, which include an outdoor heated swimming pool and a bar and clubhouse. So, it's the best of both worlds at Sea Barn Farm – quiet and peaceful camping, with extra entertainment just next door.

COOL FACTOR Sea views and farm landscapes.

WHO'S IN? Tents, campervans, motorhomes, dogs (on leads) – yes. Groups – by arrangement. Caravans – no.

ON SITE Approx. 250 pitches; 50 hook-ups (£3). No hardstanding. Two blocks with free hot showers and toilets; 2 family shower rooms and disabled facilities. Laundry (£3; £3–4 for drying). A bar/clubhouse and swimming pool at adjacent West Fleet Farm during peak season. No campfires.

OFF SITE There are 2 great attractions nearby: the Bovington Tank Museum (01929 405096) and Monkey World (01929 462537). The site also runs right down into the Fleet Lagoon – a protected nature reserve.

FOOD AND DRINK Incredible views at Café Oasis (01305 833054) in Weymouth. Some of Dorset's best seafood is at the Hive (01308 897070; www.hivebeachcafe.co.uk).

GETTING THERE Take the A354, follow signs for Bridport and the B3157. After Chickerell, left at the mini roundabout to Fleet. At the top of the hill, after the church, turn left at the crossroads to site. (Satnav may lead you to the rear entrance.)

PUBLIC TRANSPORT Bus no. 8 from Weymouth to Chickerell, then a short walk.

OPEN March–October.

THE DAMAGE Pitch plus 2 adults £11–£21; child £1–£2.50.

eweleaze farm

Eweleaze Farm, Osmington Hill, Osmington, Dorset, DT3 6ED   01305 833690   www.eweleaze.co.uk

Dorset's protected Jurassic coastline is a gloriously undeveloped stretch of hidden bays, beaches, and pristine countryside. Blissfully roadless, the stretch of coast between Durdle Door and Weymouth is best explored along the South West Coast Path. Part-way along this route lies Eweleaze Farm, which, through a combination of fortuitous geography and formidable effort, is one of the most agreeable places to camp in England. The views are one of the many things that make Eweleaze a cut above the average campsite. They are quite staggering from most pitches: a curve of coast meandering round to Weymouth Harbour, and finishing at the raised lump of land at Portland. And while plenty of sites can boast views, not many can offer a private beach with direct access. This small but adequate shingle bay with shallow waters is what makes Eweleaze the first choice for carefree family camping. The campsite has eco credentials, too, including campfire wood donated by a local tree surgeon. But the downside is that the campsite is open only in August. So bag a pitch asap and don't let Eweleaze Farm be the one that got away this summer.

COOL FACTOR Spacious campsite with a private beach.

WHO'S IN? Every man and his dog.

ON SITE Campfires allowed. Around 250 pitches over several fields; 23 showers – 4 outdoor solar-powered; toilets in each field; firewood available; access to private beach.

OFF SITE In Dorchester you'll find museums devoted to terracotta warriors, dinosaurs, teddy bears and even Tutankhamun. Try a sailing course or hire a sailing boat through SailLaser (www.sail-laser.com) in Weymouth.

FOOD AND DRINK Organic onsite farm shop (8am–9pm); various stalls (12–9pm) sell wood-fired pizzas, organic pies and chips, kebabs and salads, as well as organic breakfasts (8–11am). The Smuggler's Inn (01305 833125) in Osmington is a view-tastic 40-minute walk away.

GETTING THERE Take the A353 to Osmington. From the east, after passing the village, look out for a speed limit sign, and turn left here on to a dirt track to the farm. From the west, the sign's just before the village, dirt track on the right.

PUBLIC TRANSPORT Take bus no. 503 from Weymouth to Waterside Holiday Park then walk the final 300 metres.

OPEN August only.

THE DAMAGE Adult £6/£12 (per weeknight/weekend); child £3/£6. Vehicle £10 flat fee.

tom's field

Tom's Field, Tom's Field Road, Langton Matravers, Swanage, Dorset, BH19 3HN   01929 427110   www.tomsfieldcamping.co.uk

Located in the rustic Purbeck Hills is a pastoral marvel of a campsite, once owned by Tom. Alas, you won't find Tom here anymore, but he leaves the ruggedly beautiful stretches of Tom's Field and its surroundings as his camping legacy, deep in the heart of Dorset. The site is idyllic both in size and appearance, comprising just over four acres of gently rolling soft grass bounded by old stone walling. It's divided into a flat lower field and a slightly more undulating higher field, which is compensated for by the view. Look the right way and you'll get long seaward panoramas across the sweeping Swanage Bay. Look even harder, on a cloudless day, and you might just catch a glimpse of the Isle of Wight.

You won't have a shortage of things to do here. Not only do you have the nearby pubs – which have become attractions in their own right – you've also got the Jurassic Coast and the coastal path on your doorstep. These massive stretches of lithic coastline and rustic views juxtaposed with the cosy, grassy comfort that comes with field camping, really complete this beautifully Arcadian campsite.

COOL FACTOR A pastoral haven, complete with panoptic vistas and rugged landscapes.

WHO'S IN? Tents, motorhomes, dogs (on leads) – yes. Groups – by arrangement. Tents over 8 metres, caravans – no.

ON SITE Approx. 100 pitches; shower block with solar hot water system, token-operated showers, 2 family shower rooms, disabled facilities, laundry room, baby-changing area, washing-up areas, CDP, and hook-ups. Recycling. Onsite shop for daily essentials. No campfires. BBQs off the ground okay.

OFF SITE The National Trust's Corfe Castle (01929 481294; see www.nationaltrust.org.uk) shouldn't be missed.

FOOD AND DRINK Grab a great cream tea from the Corfe Castle National Trust tea room (01929 481332). Order an unbelievably tasty BBQ hamper from the Purbeck Products (01929 439121). For pubs see opposite page.

GETTING THERE Take the A351 to Harman's Cross and turn right on to Haycrafts Lane; after a mile turn left on to the B3069 and then it's right, on to Tom's Field Road.

PUBLIC TRANSPORT Train to Wareham and one of the numerous local buses towards Swanage that stop at the site.

OPEN March–October.

THE DAMAGE Tent plus 2 people and a car £10–£12 per night. Advance bookings only during school holidays.

acton field

Acton Field, Langton Matravers, Swanage, Dorset, BH19 3HS   01929 439424   www.actonfieldcampsite.co.uk

Hidden behind a discreet residential slip road in Langton Matravers, random tufts of wild flowers adorn the natural bumps and curves of Acton Field on the Purbeck Hills. The unspoilt – verging on wild – terrain comprises a wide, sloping, grassy campsite, with a view of Swanage Bay glistening in the distance. Arrive early in peak season to claim the best-sheltered and flattest spot you can find, as exposed parts can get very windy. Advance booking is essential from late July to the end of August, and outside those dates campers need to be members of DEFRA-approved clubs such as the Camping and Caravanning Club. It's worth the joining fee for this beautifully rugged camping experience that not every man and his dog can overpopulate.

Essential day trips include the scenic cliff-top walk from the village to swim at the Dancing Ledge tidal rock pool and caves. In 40 minutes you can walk down to Swanage Bay for a fish-and-chip beach supper, or to the famous Square and Compass in Worth Matravers. Buy a pint of cider and a pasty through a hole in the wall before relaxing on the pub's little slope… it could be a long stagger back.

COOL FACTOR Expansive, no-frills camping with sea views on the horizon.

WHO'S IN? Everyone.

ON SITE Campfires allowed at certain times – inquire with the owners. An unlimited number of pitches on the (sometimes steeply) sloping field. No hook-ups. Basic but spotless hut with showers (2W, 2M; 20p for 3 minutes). Two washing-up sinks; freezer for ice packs only. A mobile grocer visits every morning selling essentials and fresh bread.

OFF SITE Steam trains at Corfe Castle (01929 425800; www.swanagerailway.co.uk), big pasties at the Square and Compass (01929 439229), or cliff-top walks to Dancing Ledge, Seacombe Cliff, and Winspit – what will it be?

FOOD AND DRINK Delicious Jamaican food with a side of reggae and calypso tunes: weekends only at the Jerk Shack in the garden of the Scott Arms (01929 480270).

GETTING THERE Take the A351 to Corfe Castle then the B3069 through Kingston towards Langton Matravers. The campsite is on the right as you enter the village.

PUBLIC TRANSPORT As opposite. Alight at Capstan Field.

OPEN Spring Bank Holiday week, then late July–late August. Members of DEFRA-approved clubs Easter–late October.

THE DAMAGE £6–£12 per adult, per night.

downshay farm

Downshay Farm, Haycrafts Lane, Swanage, Dorset, BH19 3EB 01929 480316   www.downshayfarm.co.uk

It was William the Conqueror who commissioned the building of Corfe Castle on its lofty Purbeck perch, thinking it the prime location – with its views over vast expanses of Dorset countryside – from which to ward off any impending attacks. But had his castle scouts taken the trouble to visit a superior spot in the neighbourhood, where Downshay Farm resides today, the landscape in these parts might have looked very different – perhaps even with a castle that's still intact.

The views from the sloping campsite at Downshay stretch out across this scenic part of Britain like a Turner painting. A palette of greens and browns forms a patchwork of fields that fold neatly behind one another where the shallow hills meet, and at the centre of this canvas sit the ruins of Corfe Castle, forming a stunning silhouette against the glowing embers of an evening sky.

The farm's large tent field lies beyond a rusty, rickety gate and is no modern, manicured camping ground. In fact, it's best to pitch your tent in a particular direction to ensure a good night's sleep, as the gradients are challenging – but just remember the views you'll be treated to in the morning. Pitch around the perimeter of the field as its middle is normally kept empty for games of footie or frisbee, and there's a flatter field below for caravans and campervans.

To reach Downshay Farm in a manner in keeping with the stylish views offered here, take an ancient steam locomotive from Swanage through the countryside, past Corfe Castle's iconic ruins.

COOL FACTOR Splendiferous views out across Dorset and its iconic Corfe Castle.

WHO'S IN? Tents, campervans, caravans, well-behaved groups, dogs (on leads) – yes. Transit vans, motorbikes – no.

ON SITE Room for about 90 tents. Caravan field has 12 pitches (all with hook-ups) and separate facilities block. Each block contains hot showers (5W, 4M, 2 unisex), and toilets. Hairdrying point; freezers for ice packs; washing-up areas. BBQs off the ground are okay; barrels available for fires.

OFF SITE On sunny days head to Swanage, Studland, or Shell Bay beaches – or take the ferry over to Sandbanks. When the weather isn't so good head to the Tank Museum (01929 462359; www.tankmuseum.org) in Bovington – a real winner with the kids with its vast array of tanks and interactive experiences – or the Teddy Bear Museum (01305 266040; www.teddybearmuseum.co.uk) in Dorchester. Then, of course, there's Corfe Castle (01929 481294).

FOOD AND DRINK Corfe Castle village has a good selection of pubs and a fantastic ice cream shop – Box of Delights (01929 481060).

GETTING THERE Take the A351 past Corfe Castle to the crossroads at Harman's Cross. Turn right into Haycrafts Lane and continue for ½ mile. Campsite signs are on the right.

PUBLIC TRANSPORT Train to Wareham/Swanage then bus (no. 29/92/142/X43) to Harman's Cross, then a short walk up the hill. Or take a romantic steam-train ride from Swanage to Harman's Cross.

OPEN For 10 days around Whitsun weekend, then mid July–early September. Caravan field April–October.

THE DAMAGE Adult £5 per night; child (over-10) £2, (under-11) £1. Plus £2/£3/£4 for small/medium/large tent; car £1. Minimum fee per night £10.

burnbake

Burnbake Campsite, Rempstone, Corfe Castle, Wareham, Dorset, BH20 5JH   01929 480570   www.burnbake.com

There are those rare occasions when you arrive at a site and within minutes know you'd like to stay all season. Burnbake is one of these instantaneous hits. Its many plus points quickly add up to create a vibe so agreeable that before you know it, you're down at the office negotiating a second week's stay. There are no designated pitches among Burnbake's ancient woodland site – 12 acres of secluded, level ground, complete with burbling stream – it's all about having a proper nose around to discover your perfect nomadic nook or camping cranny.

This location couldn't be better for exploring the Isle of Purbeck. Studland Bay's beaches are a short drive away and provide miles of sandy fun. Cyclists – take the private road to the beach; walkers – try the more scenic hour-and-a-half heathland route. Helpful maps are available on site. Back at base, why not give the bright blue yurt-café a whirl? Run by Liz Moody throughout the school holidays, this funky little joint is just the ticket if you don't want to cook. Liz has obviously decided there are worse things than spending long, idyllic summers among the trees at Burnbake. She's not wrong.

COOL FACTOR Woodland campsite with a relaxed vibe.

WHO'S IN? Tents, campervans, groups, dogs – yes. Caravans – no.

ON SITE Campfires allowed in containers off the ground; 130 pitches. Two large wooden huts house 7 showers each (shower cards cost 30p or 4 for £1), plus a family room, 2 washing machines (£2), and outside washing-up sinks. A shop opens for 2 hours each morning and evening, selling camping food and equipment. Safe play area with slide and swinging tyres. The site can get a bit muddy after rain.

OFF SITE If you tire of beaches, head to Monkey World (01929 462537; www.monkeyworld.org) near Wareham.

FOOD AND DRINK The onsite yurt-café is open 9–11am and 6–9pm. The Square and Compass and Scott Arms (see Acton Field, p99 for contact) are both only a short drive.

GETTING THERE From Wareham take the A351 to Corfe Castle, turn left under the castle on to Studland Road, taking the third left turn, signposted Rempstone. Then follow the campsite signs for a mile; Burnbake is on the right.

PUBLIC TRANSPORT Train to Wareham, then a taxi.

OPEN March–September.

THE DAMAGE Pitch plus 2 adults £8–£10 per night. Extra adult £2–£4. Child (3 to 16 years) £1–£3.

wilksworth farm

Wilksworth Farm, Cranborne Road, Wimborne, Dorset, BH21 4HW   01202 885467   www.wilksworthfarmcaravanpark.co.uk

Wilksworth Farm is more compact than most campsites, with excellent facilities and a safe environment that appeals to anyone looking to grant their kids some freedom during their holidays. Arrivals check in at reception, which doubles as a shop selling essentials, then cart their tent across the road to the tent field.

Aim for the opposite end of the field to the wash-block and communal games room to escape the clamour of guests using both. Tents are shoehorned around the perimeter, so it's useful to pack a windbreak for privacy. Better still, invite a couple of friends and huddle up close together.

The site's selling points include the Olde Cart Shed café, where reasonably priced, generously portioned meals are served up in a sheltered, friendly ambience. Up the hill and past a sea of caravans is a heated outdoor pool surrounded by sun loungers. Add tennis courts, a BMX track, sandpit, and a dog-walking path, and you won't have to plan any entertainment for the kids...You might even be able to escape unnoticed to nearby Bournemouth for a little retail therapy.

COOL FACTOR Safe, smart, sociable, and family-centric.
WHO'S IN? Tents, campervans, caravans, dogs – yes. Big groups, nature- and space-lovers – no.
ON SITE The tent field has 25 pitches and there are 60 in the caravan/campervan field. All have hook-ups. Excellent, award-winning wash-rooms have underfloor heating, showers, and hairdryers. Amenities galore include an info booth, heated swimming pool, and shop selling all sorts, from breakfast groceries to postcards. The Olde Cart Shed serves takeaways as well as eat-in meals. The laundry (£3), washing-up, and BBQ areas are communal. No campfires.
OFF SITE Bournemouth's beaches and shops are nearby, as are the unspoilt country walks of Cranborne Chase.
FOOD AND DRINK The Stocks Inn (01202 882481; www.thestocksinn.com) in Furzehill, with original village stocks outside, offers Dorset-farmed steaks, local coastal catches, and a pretty country beer garden.
GETTING THERE From the A31, take the B3078 through Wimborne Minster towards Cranborne; the site is signposted.
PUBLIC TRANSPORT Train to Poole then one of the regular buses to Wimborne Minster, then a short walk.
OPEN April–October (swimming pool May–September).
THE DAMAGE Tent plus 2 people and a car £18–£28.

Riversidelakes is, in a word, magical.

Checking out campsites has got to be one of the best jobs in the world. Never more so than when we find one that surpasses all expectations. And Riversidelakes is an utter gem. A jewel. A gold mine…You get the picture.

Owners Maggie and Chris are instinctive hosts. Born and bred in Dorset, Chris lured Maggie, a former nurse, out of the Home Counties; they married, bought a farm, built a golf course, then fell into the business of property development and renovation.

Maggie's dream to run a campsite was next on the checklist. Riversidelakes was already a much-loved secret among locals when the couple first arrived for a recce. But it was winter and the site looked barren. Two years later the property was still on the market, and on a second visit in the spring they fell hook, line, and sinker in love. On the eve of summer 2010, the couple and their two sons took possession of 26 acres, five Chinese geese, one duck, one swan, a cat, 20 chickens, and the season's entire campsite bookings.

The West Country's Horton is so near the M27 that you could be driving through Kent or Hampshire, not among the old, stone towns you find in deeper, rural Dorset. Despite the easy access, Riversidelakes has hitherto retained an aura

riversidelakes

Riversidelakes, Slough Lane, Horton, Wimborne, Dorset, BH21 7JL 01202 821212 www.riverside-lakes.co.uk

of secrecy, whether intentional or not. Low-key signposting (if you hit Drusilla's Inn you've gone too far) does little to hint at the magic that lies ahead. But once you're in, park up and head for reception, where you'll probably meet the very affable Maggie.

Pile your gear on to a quad-bike trailer that will be driven to your pitch. Or, if you've booked one of the lofty tree-edged spots, there's a path you can drive along to your grassy door, where you can unload all your gear. It couldn't be any smoother.

The camping area comprises 12 acres of dreamy natural meadow and woodland, with three lakes enclosed by circumferential paths and thick shrubbery. Mown pathways lead to clusters of pitches separated by long, wild grasses that offer great privacy; all that sedentary campers can see of their neighbours are the wafts of smoke rising from their braziers. At dusk the overall vista resembles the basecamp of an intrepid expedition into the wild unknown. There's a stillness in the air... Total enchantment.

Groups really do love it here, and often book out entire pitch clusters. Each cluster bears its own helpful name. So you can choose your spot according to your requirements – great lake views, proximity to the facilities, sheltered woodland, treelined or ridgeway pitches, and isolated

individual hideaways that provide additional privacy – you choose.

The middle lake and its old, battered boat are popular with swimmers. The pond-brown water, muddy floor, or the thought of brushing against carp may put some off, but a lot of visitors just embrace their inner wild-swimmers and hop in.

Many campers bring bicycles along to Riversidelakes so that their charges can tear along the grassy paths. If they're not doing that the kids are climbing trees, playing on rope swings, or watching their dads fish in the lakes. As for everyone else, they're just kicking back and enjoying the magic.

COOL FACTOR Spacious, relaxing, comfortable, and easily accessible. Regulars already know they have to book in advance, so newbies will need to be quick off the mark.

WHO'S IN? Tents, campervans, caravans, dogs, groups – yes.

ON SITE Campfires in borrowed braziers only, which come with BBQ grills. Logs are £4 a bundle. There are 55 tent spots in the variously named pitches, and room for 5 campervans or caravans with hook-ups (£4 per night) in the 'Main' area, near the entrance at the bottom of the site. Tent pitches: Viewpoint allows parents to keep an eye on toddlers as they run up and down the meadow. Isolation spots suit single bookings and are nearest to the showers. Chill Out is furthest from the owners' bungalow, which might appeal to chatterboxes. Centre Point attracts the fewest passers-by. Three Woodland pitches offer protection from the elements among the trees; while Overview looks out across the middle lake and suits small tents, and the top Treeline and Ridgeway clusters have views of the site and also share an eco-loo. A new shower block will have 8 solar-powered showers, loos, a family bath, disabled toilet, and baby-changing facilities. New Soul Pad bell tents – 7 – come with camp kitchens, beds, and a table. A communal area with a fridge, 2 washing-up sinks, and an electric power point faces a huge fire pit that groups can use. Recycling bins include a swap shop, where you leave/pick up anything that campers might use. Experienced anglers only can acquire an Environment Agency rod licence to fish in the lakes (from the post office, £8 per day). Two tyre swings; ice packs are available.

OFF SITE Of course, you might want to do more than just kick back by the lakes. The historic market town of Wimborne Minster has a farmers' market on Fridays and flea market on Saturdays. Moors Valley Country Park (01425 470721; www.moors-valley.co.uk) is down the road. Pay to park (2 hours: £4.50) to make use of its picnic areas and cycling tracks for free; pay extra for golf, croquet, and high-wire tree-climbing (£20–£30). Bournemouth beach is a 20-minute drive away, as is the town's bustling shopping centre.

FOOD AND DRINK Pretty Drusilla's Inn (01258 840297; www.drusillasinn.co.uk) is right out of the campsite and sells a whole range of pub grub including Sunday roasts, cider-roasted hams, and kids' meals. Friday morning is farmers' market day (7am–2pm) at Wimborne Minster, with organic and locally produced cheeses and meats.

GETTING THERE Take the M27 west and then the A31. At the A338 at Ringwood turn towards Bournemouth then follow signs to the Moors Valley Park/Three Legged Cross, and the site is 3 miles after the park on the right, after 2 mini roundabouts.

PUBLIC TRANSPORT Bournemouth train station is a 20-minute taxi ride away (£28). National Express run coaches to Ringwood, and a taxi from here is about £16.

OPEN May–September.

THE DAMAGE Adult £10 high season/£7 in low season per night; child £7/£5, under-5s free. Soul Pad bell tent £38–£90 per night.

stowford manor farm

Stowford Manor Farm, Wingfield, Trowbridge, Wiltshire, BA14 9LH   01225 752253   www.stowfordmanorfarm.co.uk

We can't all be to the manor born, but camping in the grounds of Stowford Manor allows you to channel your inner Margot despite sleeping in a field. The stunning 13th-century farmhouse and accompanying mill provide the backdrop to two small camping fields. The site was mentioned in the Domesday Book, although camping started more recently (about 40 years ago). Since then the Bryant family have mastered the art of running a working farm and a delightfully relaxed campsite on the verdant Wiltshire/Somerset border.

Afternoons at Stowford Manor can be whiled away in the garden, where cream teas are served using dairy from the farmer's two Jersey cows. From here you can watch hens peck around the millpond as the gurgling River Frome flows by. Bliss... Unless it's late July, when the site is taken over by the folky Trowbridge Village Pump Festival.

Camping at Stowford Manor isn't about being completely indolent, though – Farleigh and District River Swimming Club is half a mile downstream. Many wild swimmers stay here, and campers are allowed access to the club for £1 a day. An alternative (drier) activity is to cycle all the way along the canal to Bath – in less than an hour – and enjoy a day spent ogling the sweeping Georgian crescents and noble golden-stone houses.

Knowing what makes their campers tick, the Bryants have printed a map of three pubs within walking distance, all of which have rewarding views and serve good food. What more could you want? Another cream tea? Go on then...

COOL FACTOR Rural England at her finest: an historic setting offering river swimming and yummy cream teas.

WHO'S IN? Tents, campervans, caravans, dogs, groups – yes.

ON SITE Campfires allowed off the ground. Thirty pitches with hook-ups are spread across 2 fields; the best pitches are by the river – not by the A366. The bathroom is inside a converted barn with rustic antique furniture and a retro jukebox. Three showers (50p tokens available at the café) – the water's hot, but they aren't very powerful; 3 loos. Tea and scones £4.50, served 3–6pm. Shiatsu masseur Nik Greenheart (07870 944742) practises in the mill building, £35 per hour.

OFF SITE Go on safari in the grounds of a stately home at nearby Longleat (01985 844400; www.longleat.co.uk). Special Plants (01225 891686; www.specialplants.net) in nearby Chippenham is a nursery with beautiful gardens that runs practical gardening courses.

FOOD AND DRINK The New Inn (01225 863123; www.labourinvain.com) at Westwood is less than a steep mile's walk away. Cross the A366 and follow signs to Westwood, across the fields in a north-westerly direction. Sample local Cheddar cheese (and Brie, Stilton, and ham) in their ploughman's lunch, or hand-made sausages from Bath with mash and onion gravy. A couple of miles along the A366 is the well-stocked Woody's Farm Shop (01225 720006; www.woodysfarmshop.co.uk), with a cracking café open daily.

GETTING THERE From Bath take the A36 south before turning east on to the A366 (or west if you've come down the A363). The site is east of Farleigh Hungerford, 3 miles before you reach Trowbridge (or 3 miles west of Trowbridge).

OPEN Easter–late September.

THE DAMAGE Tent plus 2 people £12 per night; family tent £14; motorhome £14; hook-up £2.

the barge inn

The Barge Inn, Honeystreet, Pewsey, Wiltshire, SN9 5PS   01672 851705   www.the-barge-inn.com

Like a wayward child tired of rebelling, the Barge Inn and its sibling campsite are growing up and moving on. For years the campsite has attracted travellers, locals, and crop-circle enthusiasts, who – unable to make advanced bookings – would turn up, pay a fiver to a chap in a caravan, sink a few pints, then strum their guitars until the early hours. The facilities were unkempt, children weren't welcomed and getting a good night's sleep was implausible. But because the location is so utterly fantastic and full of character, the sense of camaraderie among campers felt unique.

Now the pub has been scrubbed clean to every inch of its 200-year-old life and is undergoing a facelift. A Lottery grant has funded a new shower block, reception, exhibition space, and a communal day-yurt for hire outside, all masterminded by the new owners, a local community group. And there's now a noise ban after 11pm.

The Kennet and Avon Canal runs alongside the pub with moorings for barges. From the towpath you can see one of Wiltshire's numerous white chalk horses etched into Milk Hill. But the county is really famous for the crop circles that appear mysteriously overnight (Pewsey's most famous one was used by Led Zeppelin as album artwork). Whether the work of aliens or creative locals, they make eccentric Britain proud. And don't be alarmed if, in the twilight hours, you wake up to what sounds like a spaceship vibrating slowly above your tent – it's just a cargo train crawling by on its way to London.

COOL FACTOR Quirky and characterful, with crop circles and a pub at your feet.

WHO'S IN? Tents, campervans, caravans, dogs (on leads), groups – yes.

ON SITE One long, narrow field contains 35 pitches, but no hook-ups. Regular campers will breathe a sigh of relief to see a new washing block with 2W, 2M showers. A reception room replaces the old caravan, and a new shop will sell camping essentials. No campfires, but BBQs are permitted.

OFF SITE For information on the crop circles (most tend to appear in spring) direct enquiries to the Wiltshire Crop Circle Study Group (01380 739966; www.wccsg.com). Hire a canal boat (from £250 for 2 days) from Devizes Wharf (01380 728504; www.whitehorseboats.co.uk); the Barge Inn is just 3 moorings along.

FOOD AND DRINK The owner-chefs of the Red Lion (01980 671124; www.redlionfreehouse.com), 15 minutes away in East Chisenbury, have more credentials than the number of items on their daily changing menu. Accumulating skills from Leiths Cookery School, world-famous chefs, and a Michelin-starred restaurant in Spain, this couple is food-obsessed. And it shows – Valrhona chocolate *crémeux* with cocoa crumbs, anyone?

GETTING THERE Head to Marlborough then carry on west along the A4 before turning left to Lockeridge. Follow the road south for 8 miles and turn right when you see signs for the pub. The drive leads to the car park.

PUBLIC TRANSPORT Take a train to Pewsey and pre-book a taxi (01980 630094) to the site.

OPEN Easter–October.

THE DAMAGE No advance bookings. Tent £6 per person, per night; motorhome £10–£12.

thistledown

Thistledown Farm, Tinkley Lane, Nympsfield, Gloucestershire, GL10 3UH   01453 860420/07868 713180   www.thistledown.org.uk

Thistledown is, quite simply, enchanting. More than just a beautiful campsite nestled among 70 acres of organic meadow and woodland, it is inspirational, too. It was a dream realised by Richard Kelly, who has years of experience in environmental design and construction, as well as farming. He has nurtured Thistledown since 1993, when he began creating habitats for the wide range of local plants and wildlife. Richard now runs it as an environmental learning centre with his son Ryan, and neither could be more helpful or enthusiastic about this camping environment.

It's easy to find Thistledown; just head towards a majestic wind turbine located 300 metres from the entrance. The turbine was one of the first to be erected by the increasingly popular Ecotricity, the UK's first provider of mainstream electricity produced from renewable sources. It's a part of the genuine green vibe in this neck of the Gloucestershire woods, so if you've ever fancied living the sustainable *Good Life*, then this is probably the place in which to settle.

But, in the meantime, you can camp in three main areas at Thistledown, where up to 40 pitches are available in each. But don't for a minute think that you will be crowded out. Richard and Ryan ensure that no one camps on top of one another, and the 70 acres take in trees, undulating pasture, glades of wild flowers, and space – everywhere. Even if there's a wedding in one of the pastures (think hay bales for pews and canvas bell tents decorated with hand-made bunting), with all the

tree cover at Thistledown Farm it's unlikely that you'll even be aware of it.

The top site allows cars and offers camping in pitches individually mown into a pretty elderflower orchard, while the bottom two pastures are car free. Perfection. You can stretch out knowing nothing (save the odd startled deer) will drive into you. And for those with children, real freedom is a reality here. The pastures are flanked by woodland offering numerous opportunities for lengthy walks, nature watching, or just some good old-fashioned hooning around.

Thistledown is a wildlife receptor site, which means species disturbed by developments in the area are rehoused here. Richard and Ryan often run talks, walks, and events that are free for campers – from BBQs to bird walks and bat evenings. At dusk you can actually wander down to a spot where badgers come out to feed and, as long as the wind is in the right direction (so they can't smell or hear you), you'll be able to stay transfixed for ages.

All three camping areas have fire pits (most pitches have their own) and there are a few braziers for hire. In the evening, Richard will whizz by on his little off-road vehicle selling wood by the heaped barrowful. You can take your own, but are asked not to collect it from the woods as it provides shelter for creatures such as snakes and slow worms.

Picnic tables and sawn logs are dotted around for campers as well as the day trippers who come

to enjoy this tranquil environment, its stunning views, and the nature trails on offer. Streams spouting from Roman drainage systems into small ponds gurgle in the background, and the rope swings near them offer great excitement.

And the really magical thing about Thistledown is its colour. The trees, grassland, and space are all green. Green in colour, and green in ethos.

COOL FACTOR Camping under the stars in an ancient valley surrounded by nothing but wildlife, or (if you want your car next to you) in an elderflower orchard.

WHO'S IN? Tents, groups, dogs (on leads) – yes. Campervans – yes (in elderflower orchard). Caravans – no.

ON SITE Campfires allowed in pre-dug fire pits. There are 3 main camping areas (40 pitches in each) on this 70-acre site: the elderflower orchard, where cars are allowed, and the car-free second and third pastures. The second pasture only tends to be used as an overflow. Pitches are unmarked, but there's plenty of room (and we mean metres, not centimetres) to stretch out and play ball games. The elderflower orchard is upgrading (from portaloos) to compost loos and showers. The pastures have compost loos, solar-powered hot showers, and basins, plus an outdoor washing-up sink. The site has numerous walks, lakes, a birdwatching hide, and a simple observatory for stargazing. You can borrow a wheelbarrow to transport your gear into the no-car zones, or pay £2.50 to be whizzed down in the off-road buggy, as long as the guys are available. Wood is available to buy by the barrowload (£10), or bring your own (just no scavenging).

OFF SITE A walk through the woods from Thistledown will take you to the fascinating Woodchester Mansion and Park (01453 861541; see www.nationaltrust.org.uk). The house is an unfinished Gothic manor, so you can open doors that go nowhere and get an idea of the building process. Don't visit after dark though; it's haunted... The area surrounding Thistledown is also known for its burial mounds. The Neolithic Nympsfield Long Barrow (see www.english-heritage.org.uk) has spectacular views over the Severn Valley, as well as internal burial chambers for viewing. Just along the ridge is the Uley Long Barrow (aka Hetty Pegler's Tump) – take a torch if you want to see inside. On the other side of Stroud is the beautiful Slad Valley.

FOOD AND DRINK There are plans to offer locally produced organic food boxes on site, so watch this space... Foodie heaven Nailsworth is only 3 miles away. Bread will never be the same again once you've tasted the stuff at Hobbs House Bakery (www.hobbshousebakery.co.uk), and for an upmarket deli visit William's Foodhall (01453 832240; www.williamsfoodhall.co.uk). The award-winning Stroud farmers' market (6 miles away) is open every Saturday from 9am–2pm; you can buy everything from locally produced meat, bread, and cheese to Thai takeaways. Good local pubs offering food include: the Old Spot (01453 542870) at Uley, with its own microbrewery; and the Black Horse (01453 872556) at Amberley. Or for a pub within walking distance, try Nympsfield's Rose & Crown (01453 860240).

GETTING THERE From the M5 take the A419 towards Stonehouse. After a mile take the third exit to Eastington at the roundabout and head on to Frocester. At the crossroads at the top of Frocester Hill go straight over and turn left after about 300 metres, towards Nympsfield. At the staggered junction go straight across to Tinkley Lane, signposted Nailsworth. After 1 mile Thistledown is on your left. (If you reach the wind turbine you've gone too far.)

PUBLIC TRANSPORT Train to Stroud, then (twice-daily) bus no. 35 to Nympsfield. Then it's about a 15-minute walk.

OPEN April–December.

THE DAMAGE Tent £5 per night; adult £5; child (over 3 years) £2, under-3s free. Dogs free.

bracelands

Bracelands, Bracelands Drive, Christchurch, nr Coleford, Gloucestershire, GL16 7NN   01594 837165   see www.forestholidays.co.uk

Some may wonder why we'd feature such a big, 'corporately run' site, but as soon as you drive under the barrier at Bracelands you'll get it. Location, location, location: huge, immaculately manicured grass pitches with the most stunning forest backdrop, amid the freshest, pine-scented air that Gloucestershire has to offer.

Bracelands covers 38 acres and is divided into three main areas: top, middle, and far field. Each has its own regularly cleaned facilities block, and there are well-organised refuse stations dotted about. Tarmacked 'roads' – great for those who want to bomb around on bikes – join up the fields. The site is run by Forest Holidays, owned by the Caravan and Camping Club and the Forestry Commission. So yes, there are lots of gleaming white caravans and motorhomes about, but everyone seems to rub along nicely together. The bottom of the far field is where the tenters tend to congregate, as there aren't any hook-ups, so there seems to be a more traditional canvas approach.

There is a rather quaint 1950s holiday-camp feel about this place, especially when you check in. You half expect to see loud speakers announcing the day's activities, but don't worry, there aren't any redcoats around. There are really helpful rangers, though, who are happy to take you on guided walks or point you in the right direction of the numerous trails into the surrounding Forest of Dean. There are rules – hardly surprising on a site of such scale – but they really are only there to ensure everyone has a great stay.

COOL FACTOR Camping on the edge of the pine forest that is 27,000 acres of the Forest of Dean.

WHO'S IN? Tents, campervans, caravans, dogs (on leads), groups – yes.

ON SITE There are 520 pitches here, including some pre-pitched tents, but there's plenty of space for ball games, and faultless facilities. All the washrooms have free hot showers with rows of basins to match. Disabled and baby-changing facilities are available in the first field. Water taps are dotted throughout the site and all fields have clothes- and dish-washing sinks. No campfires, but BBQs allowed.

OFF SITE The Forest of Dean has an abundance of outdoor activities to offer. Head to nearby Beechenhurst Lodge for the Sculpture Trail set among the pines. Hire bikes from Pedalabikeaway (01594 860065; www.pedalabikeaway.co.uk) and take advantage of the award-winning and car-free trails.

FOOD AND DRINK The *pains au chocolat* at the grocery store in nearby Christchurch Campsite are worth getting up early for. The Saracens Head Inn (01600 890435; www.saracensheadinn.co.uk) at Symonds Yat serves excellent food that you can enjoy while watching canoeists on the River Wye.

GETTING THERE From the A40, take the A4136 towards Coleford. Turn left on to the B4432 (Park Road) at the Pike House Inn. Continue, towards Symonds Yat, then turn left, following campsite signs. Bracelands' reception is at Christchurch Campsite.

PUBLIC TRANSPORT Take the train to Lydney, then a bus to Christchurch crossroads, then a 5-minute walk to reception.

OPEN April–September.

THE DAMAGE Tent plus 2 people £8–£22 (depending on size of pitch, servicing, and season), plus £10 refundable deposit for the barrier key.

cotswold farm park

Cotswold Farm Park, Bemborough Farm, Guiting Power, Gloucestershire, GL54 5UG   01451 850307   www.cotswoldfarmpark.co.uk

Being able to pitch a tent in the Cotswolds is an extremely rare occurrence, so somewhat apt that it is possible here – at a rare breeds farm. This place is a huge hit with families, as you're next to the popular Cotswold Farm Park, also known as Adam's Farm on the BBC's *Countryfile* programme. You're surrounded by the sights, snorts, and smells of all creatures great and small; from Highland cattle and Gloucester Old Spot pigs to chickens and donkeys. Most campers take advantage of the one-off entrance fee for unlimited visits to the farm park. Kids love the adventure playground and the Touch Barn, where you can cuddle such cuties as newborn chicks, rabbits, and ducklings.

And then there are the views. You're camping in a flat field on top of a Cotswold ridge, with stunning vistas in every direction. And, because all the land surrounding you is farmed by the park, you have access to the most amazing footpaths. The Wildlife Walk is a two-mile wander from the campsite gate into a beautiful valley and back up again. Even the locals can't believe how lovely it is. Many campers use the site as a basecamp for exploring the Cotswolds and its variety of attractions. From the chocolate-box stone cottages of villages like Stanway and Guiting Power, to the 'bright lights' of the spa town of Cheltenham, now more famed for its shops and eateries than its water.

The bonus here is that when all the tour buses and day trippers have left, you and the animals are still there. You're at one with nature – albeit you're tucked up in a tent and they're in a stable.

COOL FACTOR Animal-tastic site nestled on top of the Cotswolds... gold dust in this neck of the woods.

WHO'S IN? Tents, campervans, caravans, groups, dogs (on leads, and not allowed into the farm park) – yes.

ON SITE There are 40 pitches, 16 with hook-ups. The facilities are fairly basic, but very clean. They offer men's and ladies' toilet blocks, with free showers and 2 washing-up sinks in a separate shelter. Baby-changing and disabled facilities are just across the yard. An onsite shop offers BBQ packs including home-grown/reared and local produce; ice-block freezing; camping gas; and so on. There's plenty of room in the field to play outdoor games. Huge adventure playground next door at Farm Park. BBQs allowed, but no campfires.

OFF SITE The main attractions are right on your 'farm-step'. You're surrounded by 1,600 acres of farmland, with access to wonderful walks. A one-off entry fee gives you unlimited access to Farm Park. You're also in the heart of the Cotswolds, so the famous Cotswold Way footpath is never far from you.

FOOD AND DRINK The Cotswold Kitchen at Farm Park offers a hearty cooked breakfast and food throughout the day. Local pubs serving food are the Plough Inn (01386 584215) at Ford and the Half Way House (01451 850344) at Kineton. Bourton-on-the-Water (4 miles) has facilities including a small supermarket and bakery. For home-grown veg visit Pauline's honesty box stall on the side of the road in Taddington (2 miles away). Winchcombe (6 miles) boasts the Michelin-starred Restaurant 5 North Street (01242 604566).

GETTING THERE From Stow-on-the-Wold or Bourton-on-the-Water (both on the A429), follow the camping signs.

OPEN March–October.

THE DAMAGE From £11 per night for a pitch with hook-up in low season, to £19 in high season.

cotswolds camping

Cotswolds Camping, Spelsbury Road, Charlbury, Oxfordshire, OX7 3LL   01608 810810   www.cotswoldscamping.co.uk

Cotswolds Camping is run by two hard-working friends (with some help from their husbands). No one lives on site, but a lot of work goes on in the background to ensure that it's a well organised but relaxed experience for everyone who stays.

The campsite is on the edge of the beautiful market town of Charlbury, with stunning views across the Evenlode Valley. It offers a couple of grass fields flanked by pine trees, with walks across open countryside accessible through a gate at the back. There's a compact and bijou summerhouse for those seeking indoor space in inclement weather; the washing facilities are all housed in the yard next to the field; and there's even a small modern kitchen. So all in all it's a very civilised affair. And everything's so clean that you could eat your free-range eggs (from the resident hens) off it. Caravans aren't banned, but the simplicity of this site appeals far more to dedicated tenters. It's a perfect place to kick back, treat your lungs to fresh air, read the paper, and listen to the surrounding cows, sheep, and chickens. Oh, and waking up to the sounds of resident wood pigeons is priceless.

As well as being a great springboard for visiting the lovely local villages of honey-coloured stone buildings, Cotswolds Camping is surrounded by yumminess of the food variety. Wander into Charlbury for its many pubs, or to the little village of Chadlington for a community-managed shop at its best, complemented by a café that sprawls out on to the pavement a few doors down. You're not in the middle of nowhere here, but it feels like it.

COOL FACTOR Simple Cotswolds site.

WHO'S IN? Tents, campervans, caravans, groups, well-behaved dogs – yes.

ON SITE Ten pitches, 3 with hook-ups. The facilities are new and immaculate, including separate toilet blocks with free showers and shaver points. Kitchen with free use of a fridge, toaster, kettle, and washing-up sink. Field for outdoor games, and basketball hoop. A couple of old ponies in the adjoining field enjoy company. There's a little wood for hide-and-seek, as well as access to miles of footpaths through the campsite gate. No campfires, but BBQs allowed.

OFF SITE Chadlington village (2 miles away) has an excellent wooden adventure playground. The stately home of Blenheim Palace (www.blenheimpalace.com) in Woodstock is only 6 miles away. The picture-postcard town of Burford is 9 miles away, and boasts the Cotswold Wildlife Park (01993 823006; www.cotswoldwildlifepark.co.uk), home to rhinos, wolves, and leopards.

FOOD AND DRINK You can buy (even collect) fresh eggs on site. Nearby Charlbury offers many food shops, the CAMRA-award-winning Rose & Crown pub (01608 810103), and the Bull Inn (01608 810689) for excellent food. If you really want to live the high life, cruise on over to Daylesford Organic (01608 731700) near Kingham for upmarket cream teas and the most beautifully packaged pint of milk in the UK.

GETTING THERE From Charlbury (off the A44) go north on the B4026 towards Spelsbury. After about a mile, the site entrance is on a bend on the right.

PUBLIC TRANSPORT Train to Charlbury then bus no. X9, towards Chipping Norton, will drop you off at the gate.

OPEN April–October.

THE DAMAGE Tent plus 2 adults £12.

south east

South East

Site number		Page number	Cool for campfires	Stunning views	For first-time campers	Middle of nowhere	Beach within reach	Surf's up	Waterside chilling	Walk this way	Great for kids	Dog friendly	High on mountains	For car-less campers	Cool for campervans	Wet 'n' wild	Forest fun	On yer bike	Something different	A friendly welcome	Fish club
55	Stoats Farm	126		●	●	●	●			●		●		●	●		●			●	
56	Grange Farm	128		●			●	●				●			●						
57	Roundhill	129								●		●					●				
58	Ashurst	130								●	●				●		●	●			
59	Basingstoke Canal	131							●	●											●
60	Stubcroft Farm	132	O	●	●		●	●		●	●	●			●		●				
61	Spring Barn Farm	134	O	●			●			●	●	●									
62	The Sustainability Centre	136	C							●	●	●					●		●	●	
63	Blackberry Wood	137	●							●		●					●				
64	Wapsbourne Manor Farm	138	F							●	●	●							●	●	
65	Kitts Cottage	140	F							●	●	●								●	
66	Woodland Camping	144	●			●						●					●	●	●	●	
67	Heaven Farm	146	●						●		●				●						
68	St Ives Farm	147	●			●			●	●	●	●			●						
69	ForgeWood	148	●							●	●	●		●			●			●	
70	Dernwood Farm	152	F		●	●				●	●	●					●			●	
71	Hidden Spring	154	F	●	●					●	●	●								●	
72	Brakes Coppice	156	F							●	●	●			●						●
73	Bedgebury	157	●		●					●	●	●							●		
74	Welsummer	158	●		●					●	●	●		●			●				
75	Folkestone	160		●	●		●			●					●						
76	Palace Farm	161	F									●								●	
77	Bouncers Farm	162	F	●						●	●	●		●			●		●	●	
78	Debden House	164	F							●		●		●	●		●				
79	Town Farm	165	F	●						●	●	●									

KEY C – communal fire pits
O – off grass only
F – in fire pits only

stoats farm

Stoats Farm Camping, Weston Lane, Totland, Isle of Wight, PO39 0HE   01983 755258   www.stoats-farm.co.uk

Small, shy, retiring kinds of campsites are as rare as hen's teeth on the Isle of Wight, so while Stoats Farm may not entice the bat of a cockerel's eyelid anywhere else in Britain, here on Holiday Park Isle this is a campsite to treasure. Stoats Farm has a great location, nestling in a shallow valley at the far-western tip of the island. Rural is the effect – very rural – but it's all a cunning deception, for this is really a coastal site of some distinction.

Sitting outside your tent gazing quietly over the rolling fields; listening to the horses chatting to one another; absently tracking the hens pecking about; and casting your eye over the ancient farmhouse and its lovely ramshackle collection of outbuildings is a deeply calming, countryside experience. But if you wander up the hill across the lane, this charade of countryside rurality is completely unmasked at the top. For this isn't a hill at all, but the top of a ghostly white precipice falling away into the azure ocean below.

The quiet bucolic bliss, which had wrapped such a warm, safe blanket of gentleness right around you, has been ripped asunder by one of the most dramatic and vertiginous views in the land, and Stoats Farm now seems to belong to a different world. The cliff-top path soon leads to that icon of coastal views at The Needles, and then, on the way back to the warm embrace of the campsite, The Needles Park (a theme park firmly rooted in nostalgic soil) vies for your attention.

Shy, retiring, and a little ordinary this campsite may be, but its surroundings are anything but.

COOL FACTOR A countryside campsite on the coast.

WHO'S IN? Tents, campervans, caravans, dogs – yes. Groups – by prior arrangement.

ON SITE About 100 pitches; the simple but well-maintained facilities (toilets, 9 free showers, laundry, washing-up sinks, disabled loo) may be stretched if they are all occupied. Electric hook-ups available; ice packs can be frozen; and the onsite shop sells basics and home-produced veg and dairy. No campfires, but BBQs off the ground are okay.

OFF SITE The cliff walk from the site to either Freshwater Bay or The Needles is stunning, and a great day can be made of all of it by walking the rural route to Freshwater, then along the cliffs to The Needles, before heading back up the valley.

FOOD AND DRINK The High Down Inn (01983 752450; www.highdowninn.com), right next to the campsite, is excellent, offering imaginative pub grub, decent wine, and delicious vegetarian meals. In nearby Yarmouth, the Kings Head (01983 760351) is rated highly by the friendly folk at Stoats Farm for its traditional food and good cider.

GETTING THERE From Yarmouth's ferry terminal, follow the A3054 to Totland, then the B3322 towards The Needles. After 1½ miles turn sharp left into a minor road signposted Freshwater. The site is ½ mile ahead, just where the road turns sharply right.

PUBLIC TRANSPORT The regular Needles Coastal Cruiser bus travels between the site and Yarmouth in the summer.

OPEN 1 March–31 October. (Though a very well-behaved motorcycling group occupies almost the whole site on the August Bank Holiday weekend.)

THE DAMAGE Tent plus 2 people £12–£14 (depending on season) per night; additional person (over 4 years) £3.50, under-5s free; hook-up £3.75.

grange farm

Grange Farm, Brighstone Bay, Isle of Wight, PO30 4DA   01983 740296   www.grangefarmholidays.com

The ultra-green, festival-hosting Isle of Wight has reinvented itself into a hip little island offering something for everyone today, with exceptional waves for surfers, as well as kite-surfing, paragliding, and summer events that attract new crowds every year. The isle is shaped a bit like a front-on cow's head. At its temple is, fittingly, a town, called Cowes. At its respective ears sit the towns of Yarmouth and Ryde, both of which have regular ferry services to the mainland. And perched atop tall cliffs, behind the beach at Brighstone (about midway down the left of the cow's jawline), sits Grange Farm campsite. Two flat, grassy fields go right to the edge of the cliff, and there's an overflow field across the road, aptly christened the Cool Camping Field. You'll need a sturdy tent for the winds blowing across the top of these fields, but the reward is a panoramic view across the sea and an easy scramble down to the beach below. This is a family-run, family-friendly site – kids will love getting close to a Noah's Ark of farm animals, including llamas, kune-kune pigs, goats, water buffalo, and a variety of poultry. A varied site on a varied isle.

COOL FACTOR Cliff-top, adventurous camping with panoramic sea views.

WHO'S IN? Tents, campervans, caravans, dogs – yes. Groups – sometimes, by arrangement.

ON SITE Campfires allowed on the beach below. Two fields with 60 pitches, most with hook-ups; extra Cool Camping Field only open for 28 days in July/August. A heated block has 15 showers, a coin-operated bath, toilets, and washing-up sinks. Laundry, hairdryers, phone, and drinks machine.

OFF SITE Head out surfing/paragliding/kite-surfing, or take it easy exploring the main town of Newport.

FOOD AND DRINK The Blacksmiths Arms (01983 529263) has a pleasant beer garden. See how far English wine has come at Adgestone Vineyard (01983 402503) in Sandown.

GETTING THERE From Yarmouth, follow signs to Freshwater Bay, then take the A3055 for 5 miles, Grange Farm is on the right. Contact Wightlink (www.wightlink.co.uk) or Red Funnel (www.redfunnel.co.uk) for ferry info.

PUBLIC TRANSPORT From Yarmouth/Newport, take bus no. 7 to Brighstone. Alight at the Three Bishops pub and walk ¾ mile to the site.

OPEN March–November.

THE DAMAGE Standard tent, 2 people, plus car £12–£17.

roundhill

Roundhill, Beaulieu Road, Brockenhurst, Hampshire, SO42 7QL   01590 624344   see www.forestholidays.co.uk

Get ready for a change of pace in the New Forest, where horses and all manner of other woodland wildlife rule, but if you're very good, they might just agree to put you up for a few nights. Why not practice living harmoniously alongside these creatures at Roundhill, one of Forest Holidays' most outstanding campsites? Once an airfield, this expanse of heathland is at the forest's centre, and the sheltered pockets of land created by its numerous trees and shrubs provide the perfect pitching space. The rules are simple – find yourself a spot six metres from your nearest neighbours and it's yours. The lakeside area near reception and the adjacent pine woods are popular with regulars. Animals have grazing rights here, so expect to see horses, donkeys, cows, and even pigs wandering freely around the campsite. For the most part, they keep their distance, but keep your food locked away. The donkeys are highly skilled at unzipping tents, and rumour has it they can even open ring-pulls on cans. So, make like a woodland elf in this heathered heaven and be at one with the free-roaming animals… Wait, has that donkey got one of your beers?

COOL FACTOR Forest camping with added animal antics.

WHO'S IN? Tents, campervans, caravans, groups, dogs (maximum of 3 per pitch) – yes.

ON SITE Total of 550 pitches; 3 facilities blocks with hot showers (4W, 4M), 11 basins, 14 toilets, and hairdryers (20p). Disabled, baby-changing, and dog-washing facilities. Reception sells batteries, tent pegs, maps, bread, and milk. Charcoal BBQs only, off the ground. No campfires.

OFF SITE The National Motor Museum (01590 614650; www.nationalmotormuseum.org.uk) at Beaulieu is open every day. Home to the record-breaking Bluebird and Golden Arrow, or try the James Bond Experience.

FOOD AND DRINK Check out Simply Poussin (01590 623063; www.simplypoussin.com) brasserie in Brockenhurst. The old-style Filly Inn (01590 623449; www.fillyinn.co.uk) at Setley is a 10-minute drive. Beaulieu hosts a farmers' market full of local produce on the middle Sunday of each month.

GETTING THERE From the B3055 at Brockenhurst, turn on to Beaulieu Road and head east for 2 miles.

PUBLIC TRANSPORT Brockenhurst station is just over 1½ miles from the site.

OPEN March–October.

THE DAMAGE Standard pitch plus 2 adults £9.50–£18.50.

ashurst

Ashurst Caravan Park and Campsite, Lyndhurst Road, Ashurst, Hampshire, SO40 7AR   02380 292097   see www.forestholidays.co.uk

New Forest Ponies can be traced back as far as 1016. Renowned for their friendliness, they don't restrict themselves to their own company. So when you're settling down to drink your hot cocoa under the myriad stars at Ashurst, you'll probably hear something munching close by; it's not a warthog or slavering beast watching you from the treeline, it's one of those gregarious gee-gees come to say hello.

Founded by William the Conqueror as a hunting ground, the New Forest offers some of the most picturesque woodland scenery in the UK – be it on a frosty morning when the vermilion heather is flecked with ice; autumn, when the leaves are a riot of coppery golds; or the full bloom of spring and summer, when the trees burst with foliage.

Ashurst's 55 acres lie at the heart of this wilderness, a vast 280-pitch site of centuries-old oaks and beech providing shade and atmosphere. Don't expect many mod cons beyond a shower and loo block; it's a site that's aiming for a small carbon footprint. Nature is your playground here – explore endless dark woods, play hide-and-seek, and, of course, mingle with the friendly equine neighbours.

COOL FACTOR The god of the forest *must* live here.

WHO'S IN? Tents, campervans, caravans, groups (minimal noise from 10pm, though) – yes. Dogs – no.

ON SITE Loads of space, with around 280 pitches. Central shower and loo block (hot showers, sinks, space for baby-changing) and helpful staff at reception. There are some caravans, but not many. No campfires.

OFF SITE Ashurst is close to a range of things to do from wolf-watching at the New Forest Wildlife Park (02380 292408; www.newforestwildlifepark.co.uk) to teddy bears' picnics, deer-watching, and rambles with rangers – see www.forestry.gov.uk for info. Great biking around here, too.

FOOD AND DRINK The Happy Cheese (02380 293929) is an easy walk away: a nice place with decent pub grub, ales, and snooker table. Or head to Lyndhurst's Herb Pot Bistro (02380 293996) for a more comprehensive menu.

GETTING THERE Take the A31 heading west, then the A337 to Lyndhurst, turning left at the roundabout on to the A35 that becomes Lyndhurst Road. Ashurst is on your right.

PUBLIC TRANSPORT Ashurst station is just round the corner from the campsite.

OPEN Easter–late September.

THE DAMAGE Tent & 2 adults £10–£21; child £2.25–£4.25.

basingstoke canal

Basingstoke Canal Visitor Centre, Mytchett Place Road, Mytchett, Surrey, GU16 6DD   01252 370073   www.basingstoke-canal.co.uk

With a functional name like Basingstoke Canal Visitor Centre campsite, you might guess that this is an efficiently run, no-nonsense sort of operation that tells it how it is. You might also deduce that there's a canal nearby – the Basingstoke Canal runs along one edge of the site, mostly hidden behind trees but appearing at one corner along with a cute black-and-white swing bridge and narrowboats moored up for photo opportunities. This is the gateway to 32 miles of towpath on a beautiful British waterway offering cycling, walking, fishing, and boating. The canal isn't the only means of transport in evidence around here: a railway runs along the far side of the canal; the occasional small aircraft buzzes overhead en route to nearby Farnborough Airport; and there's the faint swoosh of traffic noise, but not enough to drown out the warbling jays or the laughing ducks. This might not be 'proper' countryside camping, attached as it is to Farnborough's outskirts, but it is a lovely canalside location and thanks to its transport connections you could board a train in London and be camping here less than an hour later. Commuter camping, no less.

COOL FACTOR Camping à la canal, barely half an hour from London.

WHO'S IN? Tents, caravans, motorhomes, dogs (on leads), groups (up to 3 tents) – yes.

ON SITE Unmarked pitches across a grassy 6 acres. A small kids' playground, hot showers, disabled/baby-changing room, (both a bit of a distance from the campsite), and a Tea Room (open daily). Fishing permits and boat trips are available at the visitor centre. No hook-ups. No campfires.

OFF SITE The main attraction is the canal, with 32 miles of towpath to explore; maps at reception. For a change of pace, scream the day away at Thorpe Park (www.thorpepark.com).

FOOD AND DRINK The Swan (01252 325212) at Ash Vale has all you need from a pub: good food, local ales, old oak beams, exposed brickwork, log fires, and a warm welcome.

GETTING THERE Follow the A331 towards Farnham. Take the Mytchett turning and follow the Canal Visitor Centre signs.

PUBLIC TRANSPORT Train to either Farnborough or Ash Vale, then a 5-minute taxi ride (£6).

OPEN All year (booking essential in summer).

THE DAMAGE Tent plus 2 people £8 per night; caravans/motorhomes/trailer tents £9.50; extra person £1.50. A deposit is required when booking.

stubcroft farm

Stubcroft Farm, Stubcroft Lane, East Wittering, Chichester, West Sussex, PO20 8PJ   01243 671469   www.stubcroft.com

Run by a gregarious environmentalist and professional photographer, Stubcroft Farm is a sustainable lambing farm set in 50 acres close to the beautiful coastline of West Wittering. The campsite sits next to a handsome red-brick farmhouse, which, with its old pumps and nearby beehives, gives the place a real whiff of 'olde' England.

Stubcroft is proudly green in approach, with its use of fair trade and organic products, as well as environmentally friendly loos. The 90 pitches are pretty compact, having been bordered with specially planted hedges and a wealth of trees to provide privacy and shelter from those landlubbing sea winds. However, on a busy summer weekend you'll be close quartered with your fellow campers, as the place is extremely popular. You'll soon see why; the sky is huge here, and there's an immediately calming effect when you look out across the wild paddock and beyond to the distant smudge of Chichester on one side and the sparkling sea on the other.

Kids will be able to run free (thanks to the site's secluded lane and surrounding fields) while you busy yourself buying home-made burgers from the shop and setting up your barbie. You may even find yourself helping owner Simon with the extraction of honey, or staying during one of the farm's organised vintage-tractor rallies. April is a great time to visit, as there are newborn lambs to bottle-feed; and bring your binoculars – you might just spot some of the deer or 72 species of birds drawn to the area's secluded tranquillity.

COOL FACTOR Basic camping on the doorstep of stunning scenery.

WHO'S IN? Everyone – from dogs on leads to exuberant teenagers and groups.

ON SITE Campfires in containers off the ground. Some can be rented out (£5 per night); logs also sold. Ninety pitches, 6 eco-loos, 6 conventional flush loos, and 5 modern showers. Drinking taps, a CDP, 8 electric hook-ups. Bike hire available so you can head off exploring the miles of cycle paths.

OFF SITE Easy access to some of the UK's best beaches: Bracklesham Bay for surfing; the East Head spit for walking – 50 acres of *Lawrence of Arabia* sand dunes to live out those 'take Aqaba' fantasies; West Wittering beach has some of the cleanest, clearest water in the country. For kids, there's the South Downs Planetarium in Chichester, the Old Windmill in Halnaker, or Portsmouth's impressive Blue Reef Aquarium.

FOOD AND DRINK That smell of bacon winding its way to your tent is emanating from the farmhouse and Stubcroft's famous breakfasts. For lunch head for fish and chips at Bracklesham Bay, then take dinner at East Wittering's 16th-century Thatched Tavern (01243 673087), which offers mouth-watering, locally produced dishes.

GETTING THERE Take the A286 towards the Witterings and Bracklesham. Go through Birdham village then left on to the B2198 (Bell Lane) at the mini roundabout by a Total garage. After the Bell pub take the second right into Tile Barn Lane, then turn left and follow signs to the farm.

PUBLIC TRANSPORT A regular Stagecoach bus (Chichester–Bracklesham Corner), stops just past the Bell pub.

OPEN All year.

THE DAMAGE Tent plus adult £7–£8 per night; child £3.50; dog £1; campervan/caravan and 2 adults £20–£25.

spring barn farm

Spring Barn Farm Park, Kingston Road, Lewes, East Sussex, BN7 3ND   01273 488450   www.springbarnfarmpark.co.uk

Surely one of the prettiest towns in Sussex, with its mixture of medieval and 18th-century houses, Lewes is bursting at its timbered seams with history. Whether Sir Arthur Conan Doyle or Virginia Woolf lost themselves in its cobbled alleys and antique bookshops, or visited Normanesque Lewes Castle while they lived here is anyone's guess, but the town continues to draw celebrities, from pop stars to actors. Beer lovers will be delighted to know that Sussex's premier ale, Harveys, is brewed in town, and there are plenty of cosy pubs in which to sample it. Lewes is also famous for its Bonfire Night, which sees a cast of thousands parading through the streets in fancy dress with burning crosses before the pièce de résistance: effigies are burned in the nearby fields.

Located on the undulating South Downs, in a vista of buttery hills and widescreen skies, Spring Barn Farm is manna from heaven for kids, and perfect for campers who like a good walk. Let's start with the secluded campsite: it's basic – little more than a field with a nearby loo block – but the views are fantastic. Look out over the downs, peer into the adjacent *Children of the Corn* maize field, and hear the myriad calls of animals from the adjoining farm. Kids love the petting zoo in the farm's central building and the menagerie outside. If goats, rabbits, and chickens are passé, then show them the cheeky Shetland ponies and South American alpacas with their *Thunderbird*-puppet lips. The maze is great fun too; three acres of twisting turns in which to lose yourself.

COOL FACTOR History and great walks just beyond your tent flaps.

WHO'S IN? Tents, small groups – yes. Campervans, caravans, dogs, big groups – no.

ON SITE Campfires allowed off the ground, as are BBQs. A total of 32 pitches; a water pipe; no electricity; solitary loo block. For the kids: zip wire, pedal go-kart track, trampoline, swings, sandpit, pirate play ship, adventure playground, and the maze and menagerie of animals. Come in Easter to bottle-feed newborn lambs, and meet chicks and rabbits. Campers get a 50 per cent discount on entry into the farm.

OFF SITE Lewes has its photogenic castle (01273 486290) – built during the days of William the Conqueror – and just south of the town centre, historic Anne of Cleves House (01273 474610) makes for an interesting visit. Divorced, beheaded, divorced... hmm? Time for a history lesson.

FOOD AND DRINK Spring Barn's farmhouse kitchen is a cosy place to hole up for breakfast before setting out for a long walk on the South Downs. Not far away, in neighbouring File, is a treat for gastronomes – the Ram Inn (01273 858222; www.raminn.co.uk) does wonderful traditional Sunday lunches and has a range of local draught beers, and a pretty garden.

GETTING THERE Follow the A27 towards Lewes and, at the Kingston roundabout, take the exit for Kingston village. Drive through the village to the T-junction opposite Wyevale Garden Centre and turn left. Spring Barn Farm is on the left.

PUBLIC TRANSPORT Take a train to Lewes, and you'll need to catch a local cab to the site.

OPEN Late March–late September.

THE DAMAGE Pitch plus adult £7 per night; child (2 to 16 years) £3.50.

the sustainability centre

The Sustainability Centre, Droxford Road, East Meon, Petersfield, Hampshire, GU32 1HR   01730 823166   www.sustainability-centre.org

In 1998 the Sustainability Centre sprang to life in the South Downs to teach people about economical and environmental reform. Among its 55 acres of woodland and natural chalk downs, visitors can learn how to draw on conservation craft and natural remedies for healthy and sustainable living. The Earthworks Trust, which owns and runs the centre, is funded in part through the income generated by its campsite, yurt, and two tipis. Various onsite courses (in the likes of herbal first aid, willow basket making, and permaculture) are run throughout the year and conducted in a rather grand outdoor eco-classroom. The tipis and yurt are nestled in individual camping bays: Forget-Me-Not, Hazel, and Olive. The interiors have a wonderfully earthy smell, enhancing the site's natural concept. A rug and cushion or two adorn the tipis, while the large yurt features two single beds and a log-burning stove. A clearing in the woods has space for up to 40 tents, too; surrounded by nothing but trees it's a magical setting. Whichever canvas space you choose to spend the night in, you'll find the cost of your stay eco-nomical, which is always a bonus.

COOL FACTOR With eco-credentials this high, what's not to like?

WHO'S IN? Tents, glampers, dogs, groups – yes. Campervans, caravans – no.

ON SITE Campfires allowed in 2 fire pits, and there's a communal covered BBQ (wood/charcoal £5). Space for 40 tents; 2 tipis (sleeping 6/10 – bit of a squeeze; no standing room); yurt (sleeping 10) has 2 single beds (bring the rest of the bedding). Comfy eco-lodge for hire. Three solar showers, 2 basins, and 3 compost loos. Onsite Beech Café serves organic, fair-trade vegetarian meals (open Thur–Sun).

OFF SITE Plenty of walks; the nearest starts in Petersfield and winds up in Exton (see www.southdownsway.co.uk).

FOOD AND DRINK Treat yourself to Michelin-starred modern British fare at JSW (01730 262030) in Petersfield.

GETTING THERE Take the Clanfield exit off the A3 and follow the brown campsite signs. The centre is on the left.

PUBLIC TRANSPORT Train to Petersfield, 8 miles away, then take a taxi. The centre has a minibus that runs on vegetable oil for groups needing lifts (for a fee).

OPEN All year (yurt and tipis April–October).

THE DAMAGE Adult £8 per night; child (5 to 13 years) £4, under-5s free. Yurt £40 for 2 people. Tipi £30 for 2.

blackberry wood

Blackberry Wood, Streat Lane, Streat, nr Ditchling, East Sussex, BN6 8RS   01273 890035   www.blackberrywood.com

Experience the magic of falling asleep by a crackling fire in your own woodland clearing at Blackberry Wood, nestled in the foothills of the South Downs. Situated beyond the eclectic aesthetics of the permanent-caravan, double-decker bus, gypsy wagon, and campervan field at the site's entrance, the dense woodland forms a rambling straggle of trees and thicket, with a few footpaths criss-crossing through the undergrowth. The footpaths lead to 20 individual clearings dotted among the nature-filled woods, each with its own unique personality and name. There's Fruity (in the shade of a crab apple tree), Minty (with its gloriously fresh-smelling herbs), Avalon (large and beautifully shaded), Ahora (meaning 'love' in Maori, this one's even had its own authentic blessing)... Which will you choose?

Spend easy days in your very own woodland suite, listening to the birds sing their hymns and the breezes sough their songs through the trees. It's all part and parcel of the reconnecting-with-the-earth experience that Blackberry Wood unjealously doles out to its campers.

COOL FACTOR Back-to-nature woodland camping.

WHO'S IN? Tents (large ones too big for some clearings), dogs on leads, groups – yes. Campervans, caravans, radios – no.

ON SITE Campfires allowed. Twenty clearings for tents, or stay in the double-decker bus, retro caravan, or gypsy caravan in the field (prices online). Hot showers (20p), flush toilets, washing-up facilities, and campfire grills. Bike hire and logs for sale in the onsite shop (which also stocks essentials).

OFF SITE The site provides route maps for lovely local walks. Chilled-out Lewes (see Spring Barn Farm, p134) is just 5 miles away; or it's 8 miles to the dazzling lights of Brighton.

FOOD AND DRINK The Jolly Sportsman (01273 890400), just a 40-minute walk away, has a cosy atmosphere and serves up gourmet dishes from its regularly changing menu.

GETTING THERE Take the A23 then left on to the A273 for about a mile and bear right on to B2112 (New Road) for 2 miles before going right, on to Lewes Road, and left on to Streat Lane after 2 miles. You'll see the site on the right.

PUBLIC TRANSPORT Plumpton is the closest station (30-minute bridleway walk to site).

OPEN April–September.

THE DAMAGE £5 per tent, per night, plus £8–£9 per adult; child (3 to 12 years) £4–£4.50. Book (online) well in advance.

wapsbourne manor farm

Wapsbourne Manor Farm, Sheffield Park, East Sussex, TN22 3QT   01825 723414   www.wowo.co.uk

Wapsbourne Manor Farm, or 'Wowo', as it's affectionately known by a growing band of regulars, is a rare and beautiful thing – a great campsite within two hours' drive of London. It's small on unnecessary rules and regulations, and big on fun and freedom. Campfires are allowed, facilitated by a firewood delivery-man who appears at dusk on his little tractor; camping's equivalent to room service and evening turn-down all in one. Saturday night is music night: free camping for musicians in return for an 'open campfire' policy allowing all-comers to join in a sing-song around the fire. It's a hippified rule alright, but fitting for mildly bohemian Wowo. Kids' entertainment is strictly old-school: climbing trees, swinging on tyres, and making camps in the undergrowth. In fact, the entire 150-acre site is a huge, natural adventure playground extending well beyond the four main camping areas.

This magical spot always seems to have something new to reveal: another field hidden behind the thicket, a secret pathway, a yurt nestled among the trees. And there's a whole separate site that you might not see unless you go looking: the premium woodland camping pitches, otherwise known as Tipi Trail. These eight pitches are secreted away from the riff-raff in their own exclusive woodland setting, ideal for celebrities, politicians, and newlywed royal couples looking for seclusion. With the evening air scented with campfire smoke, the soft murmur of sociability and perhaps a sing-song soundtrack, this wonderful place just oozes rustic, back-to-basics appeal.

COOL FACTOR A cracking, chilled-out atmosphere and to-your-tent firewood delivery.

WHO'S IN? Tents, campervans, dogs – yes. Caravans, motorhomes, groups of unsupervised under-18s – no.

ON SITE Campfires (in designated fire pits) and BBQs off ground are allowed. Forty standard pitches and 8 Tipi Trail secluded woodland pitches (each with benches, chairs, and a trivet for your fire); 4 yurts too. There are 4 compost toilets plus 2 basic, clean shower blocks with free hot showers. (No shaving/hairdryer points). A communal barn has a ping-pong table; free communal fridges and freezers; wi-fi; an honesty bookshelf; coin-operated laundry. An onsite shop stocks a small range of organic food. Ask about weekend bushcraft activities, plus the earth ovens – great for making pizza.

OFF SITE Sheffield Park is a mile up the road, while the Bluebell Railway is practically next door (see p143 for info).

FOOD AND DRINK A few miles up the A275, Trading Boundaries (01825 790200) is a delightful café and eclectic furniture/antiques shop. For foodies, there are 2 excellent gastropubs; the Coach and Horses at Danehill (01825 740369) and the Griffin Inn (01825 722890) in Fletching, both less than 10 minutes' drive.

GETTING THERE Follow the Bluebell Railway signs along the A22. Pass the railway on the right and Wowo is the second entrance on the right.

PUBLIC TRANSPORT The nearest station is Haywards Heath from where a taxi costs about £15.

OPEN All year; Tipi Trail and yurts November–February.

THE DAMAGE Adult £10 per night; child £5, under-3s free. Firewood £5; one-off charge for dogs (£5) and cars (£10). Tipi Trail pitches an extra £10 per night except during winter. Yurts £112–£250 per 2-night stay. Book early. Min. 2 nights.

kitts cottage

Kitts Cottage Camp, Freshfield Place Farm, Sloop Lane, Scaynes Hill, West Sussex, RH17 7NP   07733 103309   www.kittscamp.co.uk

James, the manager of both the local affiliated gastropub, the Sloop, and Kitts Cottage campsite, is a wry chap; he looks as if he might have been a highwayman or pirate in a former life, so we're not sure whether or not to believe him when he points to the campsite's eastern treeline and says there's a ghost of a lady who sometimes walks through there from the woods. Certainly it's an atmospheric spot, and on those creepy *Sleepy Hollow* nights, as the north wind wraps its teeth around your guy pegs and whistles at your door, you might wish that we'd never mentioned it. To be honest, but for your imagination, there's nothing faintly spectral about Kitts Cottage.

The story (coupled with James) just adds to the site's charm, for Kitts is bordered by forest, rolling meadow, and fields. Sandwiched between Lewes and Haywards Heath, the 18-acre site takes its name from a house that used to stand here hundreds of years ago… that's as much as we know, though – perhaps our researcher got lost in the local ales at the Sloop.

There are no style awards or glamping brownie points being won here, Kitts is all about bowling up with your tent and doing all the hard stuff like pitching up and cracking open your cool box, as well as stoking the flames on one of the many designated fire pits. Essentially it's a huge meadow bookended on two sides by alluringly ancient woods and bordered by sheep-grazing fields; there's an area for families shaded by mature oaks, a section for groups further away, and the remainder

is left for couples and singles. The eastern treeline is always kept free and uninterrupted for aesthetic purposes – an arboreal canvas that might have come from the brush of John Constable. It makes a pleasant change for taste and nature to triumph over wanton greed.

James runs it this way to keep things in balance, just like the unspoken eco-agreement with the forest critters that watch you sleep. Your side of the bargain is not to gather logs, or any kindling whatsoever – it's provided to you on arrival. And, in return, the creatures leave you alone, just like in that film *The Village*. Fires are positively encouraged, though, as part of the site's back-to-basics ethos – returning to camping the way it used to be.

The site sits on a slight elevation, giving great views from the top of the hill. Gazing across the woolly backs of sheep and rusted ploughs, you have to pinch yourself when you remember you're less than an hour from London.

The surrounding woodlands are criss-crossed with public footpaths, one of which leads directly to the much-celebrated Bluebell Railway, a journey into yesteryear with a fully working steam railway system. With its old-fashioned stations peppered with nostalgic signs, octogenarian conductors, and steam billowing from *Thomas the Tank Engine* funnels, it's a delight for even the weariest of cynics. The footpaths from the site are perfect for getting back to nature, and if you don't fancy walking then bring your bike to explore the

woody glades, sunburnt fields, and pretty hamlets. The local Cuckoo Trail is a cyclist's paradise – 11 miles of disused railway track, choking on wildlife and woodland as it meanders gently through quiet hamlets, monuments, and the best of Sussex countryside. It starts in Polegate and zigzags through Hailsham, Horam, and Heathfield. There are plenty of places en route to stop for a cheeky cool pint or a snack, as well as various sculptures in wood and steel to look out for. In May, keep an eye out for the Orange-tip butterfly, and orchids growing near the path.

COOL FACTOR Back to basics, camping au naturel. Ditch the iPod speakers and lace up your walking boots.

WHO'S IN Tents, well-behaved dogs (on leads), groups, all folk – yes. Caravans are not welcome, however this is prime ground for campervans.

ON SITE Campfires positively encouraged in the fire pits. Pick up all your wood and kindling on arrival and James will direct you to the appropriate area that will best suit you. As Kitts aims to have the minimum human footprint on the area's eco-system, there are barely any facilities for your convenience beyond a few loos and a central alfresco washing-up area. There's no hot water and just a single exposed cold-water shower.

OFF SITE There's plenty to do if you're looking for organised activities: Sheffield Park and Garden (01825 790231; see www.nationaltrust.org.uk) features 18th-century ornamental gardens (laid out by Capability Brown) bursting with azaleas, rhododendrons, monkey trees, and views to set the soul alight – plus soothing lakes and a nice little tea room to quieten the groaning belly. Twenty minutes' walk from Kitts, the Bluebell Railway (01825 720800; www.bluebell-railway.com) is a heritage steam railway running between Sheffield Park and Kingscote, and a real journey back through time. The old boys that operate it are charming and take you back to another era as they doff their caps, wrinkle their leathery faces, and guide you on to the glorious old carriages, with smoke billowing from the funnels as if you were off to Hogwarts School. Bring on the lemonade and slammy doors, the cucumber sandwiches, and

the *Famous Five* – this is a rare and evocative slice of olde England.

FOOD AND DRINK Apart from food cooked by yourself you'll have to seek warming fare at your local tavern – the Sloop Inn (01444 831219; www.thesloopinn.com), a welcoming gastropub with organic meats from local butchers, seasonal produce, and prices to match the affable atmosphere. Nearby too, at the end of Ketches Lane on the A275, is the Trading Boundaries (01825 790200; www. tradingboundaries.com) – a group of wonderful shops containing treasures from around the world, grouped around an old house, courtyard, and gardens. The café there sells light lunches all day. Both places can be reached by public footpaths, and the campsite actually has 3 separate footpaths that meet in Long Kitts and can take you to the south, west, and east.

GETTING THERE Take the A22 through East Grinstead and Forest Row, 100 metres after the Wych Cross crossroads turn right on to the A275 towards Lewes. When you reach the church at Danehill, turn right following signs to Freshfield (2 miles). Stay on that road past Brickworks and a mile after that you'll see the Sloop Inn on your left. The campsite entrance is approx. 300 metres further on the left-hand side.

OPEN 1 April–late October.

THE DAMAGE Tent plus adult £12 per night, weekend £20 for 1 or 2 nights; child (under-15) £5, weekend £10 for 1 or 2 nights.

woodland camping

Woodland Camping Eco, Ashwood Farm, West Hoathly Road, East Grinstead, West Sussex, RH19 4ND   01342 316129
www.woodlandcampingeco.wordpress.com

This woodland escape in the very heart of the Ashdown Forest is nothing short of magical. Its owners, Wendy and Patrick, are fiercely eco-minded and their sense of respect for the land resonates throughout the site.

On arrival, plant your bags in a wheelbarrow and make your way past the fairy knoll and maze to the enchanted woodland area – your very own Rivendell – a sanctuary of oak and silver birch at the source of a river. Speaking of *The Lord of the Rings*, there's something a little 'Galadrielesque' about Wendy, with her gentle demeanour, wise eyes, and belief in a person's right to privacy. There's every encouragement for you to get reacquainted with nature here – build a fire, recline, relax, and listen to the breeze. There aren't any mod cons, just one of the best locations in wild Sussex to get in touch with your inner bushman. In the centre of the wood there's a maypole for pagan festivities, and the trees are strung in brightly hued ribbons and trinkets – fortunately no wicker effigies with burning policemen inside.

On a warm night, sit around the fire or shoot the breeze with your fellow eco-people. Nearby is a tipi, erected by a chap who wanted to live like his ancestors did thousands of years ago. By day he's a fireman, by night he eats raw meat and berries. Is he a werewolf? 'No,' replies Wendy, 'he's remarkably healthy – and very handsome.' There's a compost loo in the wood, but for showers you'll have to pop back to the block by reception. In order to keep things natural there are no electric hook-ups.

COOL FACTOR Hidden-away pitches in an ancient forest.

WHO'S IN? Tents, campervans – yes. Dogs, groups – no.

ON SITE Campfires allowed – collect your own wood from the forest, £5 per fire pit, per night. There are 10 pitches; a compost loo in the wood; and a canvas shelter for communal dinners. Water vats are brought to the clearing every morning. If you've got loads of stuff, owner Patrick can take you on his tractor (£5 each way) or else use the site's wheelbarrows. There's a shower block by reception; pigs and ducks for the kids to watch, plus a kids-only fairy knoll. And just to continue that elfin trend, archery lessons can be requested (£40 per hour).

OFF SITE Sheffield Park (see www.nationaltrust.org.uk) is a few minutes' drive away and makes for a wonderful excursion if you like ornamental gardens. Wander past monkey puzzle trees and lily-studded lakes to the centrepiece cascade. Deers Leap Bikes (01342 325858) are round the corner from the site; hire a bike (£20 per day) and head for pretty Weir Wood Reservoir (www.weirwoodreservoir.co.uk) or further explore Ashdown Forest.

FOOD AND DRINK You can buy organic eggs, milk, and bread at reception. Nearby, the Old Mill (01342 326341) is a homely gastropub in a 15th-century building.

GETTING THERE From East Grinstead, take the A22. Turn right on to the B2110 (Turners Hill Road), then right again on to Saint Hill Road. Finally, go left to West Hoathly Road and Ashwood Farm is about 1/3 mile up, on your right.

PUBLIC TRANSPORT Take the train to East Grinstead, and a cab from there.

OPEN 1 April–late October.

THE DAMAGE Tent plus adult £12 (£8 if you come by carless means) per night; child (up to 13 years) £6 (£4).

heaven farm

Heaven Farm, Furners Green, Uckfield, East Sussex, TN22 3RG   01825 790226   www.heavenfarm.co.uk

Discover your own slice of camping heaven in deepest, darkest Sussex. If you wander down to the tucked away, forgotten corner of Heaven Farm you'll find a spacious, quiet field, cuddled by trees and hidden from the world. Less than two hours from London, this unassuming, unpretentious, undersubscribed campsite is a quintessentially beautiful and easy weekend getaway.

Due to the large number of accessible activities and surrounding beauty, this campsite seems more like an ingenious afterthought, perhaps to complement the award-winning neighbouring Nature Trail. Comprising a large circuit through wooded parkland and alongside streams, the trail offers different natural surprises depending on the time of year you visit. Foxgloves in the summer, visual explosions of reds, browns, and golds in autumn; Bambi deer and robins in winter; and a magical carpet of bluebells in the spring.

And if all your badgering about in the woods leaves you a little parched, you can always end your nature-filled afternoon with an impressive cream tea at the Heaven Farm Stables Tea Rooms.

COOL FACTOR Peaceful spot in heavenly scenery.

WHO'S IN? Everyone welcome (groups by arrangement).

ON SITE Campfires allowed. Thirty pitches (some not quite level); a separate section of 5 Caravan Club pitches with electric hook-ups. Additional hook-ups available. Three well-maintained showers (not available 10am–5pm). Bring a torch – there's no lighting here after dark. The Stables Tea Rooms are open 10am–5pm. There's an onsite organic shop selling home-made marmalades, chutneys, and nut-butters, and a craft shop, open 11am–5pm.

OFF SITE Besides the Nature Trail, the Bluebell Railway (01825 720800; www.bluebell-railway.com), Ashdown Forest, and Sheffield Park are all within reach.

FOOD AND DRINK Tuck into Ashdown venison with black pudding at the Coach and Horses (01825 740369) in Danehill. Or dine on the terrace at the Griffin Inn (01825 722810) – humble by nature, appetising in taste.

GETTING THERE The site is well signposted off the A275, 3 miles south of Chelwood Gate; 5 miles north of Chailey.

OPEN Tents: 1 May–31 October. Touring caravans: all year.

THE DAMAGE Adult £9–£10 (depending on season) per night; child £4–£5, under-5s free. Hook-up £2–£2.50. Book in advance to avoid disappointment.

st ives farm

St Ives Farm, Butcherfield Lane, Hartfield, East Sussex, TN7 4JX   01892 770213

'Three cheers for Pooh! (For who?) For Pooh! (Why, what did he do?) I thought you knew…' Of the many things that the great Winnie the Pooh did, the most significant, as far as we're concerned, is choosing to spend his entire fictional life in this little corner of East Sussex. What's not known is if he ever came across St Ives Farm, a countryside campsite just outside Hartfield, the village where AA Milne penned his famous stories. Using the rural idyll of St Ives Farm as a base, you can follow in the footsteps of Christopher Robin and all the gang. Just pick up a special map to discover all their beloved haunts – 100 Acre Wood, Galleon's Lap, and Poohsticks Bridge. St Ives Farm sits beside a pretty fishing lake surrounded by arable farmland, and the Weald Way runs alongside. The farm has a peaceful ambience, enhanced by the softly crackling fires scenting the air with sizzling sausages and melting marshmallows. The site often gets booked out at weekends, so, as Pooh would say, 'you can't stay in your corner of the Forest waiting for others to come to you. You have to go to them sometimes.' What are you waiting for? Book your spot, too.

COOL FACTOR Secluded lakeside setting with added Pooh-phernalia.

WHO'S IN? Every man and his dog.

ON SITE Campfires allowed. Twenty pitches; updated facilities include a new shower block with 6 showers, toilets, and 4 separate portaloos. Fishing in the lake (carp and perch) £8/£4 per day for adult/child.

OFF SITE Go walking with llamas (no, really) at the Ashdown Forest Llama Park (www.llamapark.co.uk) in Forest Row. A llama each costs £30; a llama between 2 costs £50.

FOOD AND DRINK For top-notch food with an emphasis on locally sourced, seasonal produce, head for the Hatch Inn (01342 822363) at Colemans Hatch. It's a quaint little country pub on the edge of Ashdown Forest, a 10-minute drive from St Ives Farm and handy for Poohsticks Bridge. The St Ives Tea Room at the farm next door does cream teas.

GETTING THERE Take the B2026 north from Hartfield. Take the first turning left on to Butcherfield Lane and continue for 1½ miles. Take the next left and follow signs.

PUBLIC TRANSPORT Bus no. 291 calls at various local train stations and stops at Hartfield, 2 miles from the site.

OPEN April–October.

THE DAMAGE Adult £7 per night; child £4.

One of a bright young generation of new campsites, ForgeWood has taken *Cool Camping* principles and applied them beautifully. The site opened fully in 2010 after a low-key try-out the previous season, and it has proved to be an instant hit with that killer combination of campfires, woodland pitches, a tents-only rule (with the exception of the odd vintage campervan), and a laid-back approach.

ForgeWood – like Bedgebury (p157) about 15 miles away, and Wowo (p138) in East Sussex – is a solid example of the new breed of simple yet contemporary campsites, a movement that's been gathering momentum for a few years now. These sites totally 'get' that people want to let their kids roam around woods making camps and dens and getting dirty. They totally get the importance of the campfire, of providing a generous hoard of chopped wood and plentiful marshmallows. They get that people don't want rules and regulations and just want to go with the flow. They get that a camping trip is about being out amid nature, immersed in the experience of the wild. And they totally get that today's tent campers don't want to share these magical pockets of nature with shiny white caravans sporting satellite dishes on their roofs. Banning caravans is always a popular move among the tent fraternity.

forgewood

ForgeWood Barn, Sham Farm Road, Danegate, nr Tunbridge Wells, Kent, TN3 9JD   07720 290229   www.forgewoodcamping.co.uk

What Forge Wood and others are doing so well is putting the unassuming tent camper back at the centre of things. With an attractive mix of ancient woodland and open fields, this site gives tenters space and freedom. But the pitches within the woodland are the ones that stand out – surrounded by a sprawling, undulating thicket, unkempt and scattered with fallen branches, and left to the influences of weather, nature, and time. It's a beautiful place to camp. If truth be told, it's not entirely untouched – a regular visit from the tree surgeon ensures that all potentially dangerous overhanging branches are removed before they fall on an unsuspecting camper's head. But don't let small details get in the way of the romantic ideas – it looks untouched, and you do feel like you're camping out in the wilds. A bit.

Such splendorous surroundings are a result of the fact that Forge Wood is situated in a quiet corner of the vast Eridge Park Estate, a 3,000-acre expanse of countryside and farmland incorporating Britain's oldest deer park. The countryside site has been preserved since the 11th century, when William the Conqueror gave the estate to his half-brother Odo, a man of vast wealth and questionable morals who ended up in prison for embezzlement. Today the estate belongs to the Marquess of Abergavenny, and although it's not open to the

public, there are rights of way along parts. Venison from the estate is available at Forge Wood in the form of sausages, burgers, and steaks – ideal for the campfire. Firewood and marshmallows are also sold at reception, as are handy little cooking thingamajigs, which allow you to use your pots and pans on the fire instead of the gas burner, so there's no doubt this place supports a strong campfire culture. In case this site needed anything else to recommend it, then the fact that there's a pub and a station nearby would seem to top it all off nicely. So for London-based campers, it's possible to get here in just over an hour, including a stop for a pint of Badger at the Huntsman.

COOL FACTOR Expansive ancient woodlands and a campfire culture.

WHO'S IN? Tents, occasional vintage campervan, dogs – yes. Caravans, motorhomes, groups of under-21s – no.

ON SITE Campfires encouraged. Pitches available in the woods or the fields. Many pitches are inaccessible by car; campers are encouraged to leave them in the car park. Rope swings and random kids' shelters can be found in the woods, which are used as a giant playground for young campers. Portakabins are used for the facilities and reception – part of the plan, the managers say, to provide a truly low-impact environment. Without permanent buildings, this entire site can disappear out of season and be returned to nature with no sign that a summer campsite exists. The facilities include free hot showers, washing-up sinks, disabled facilities, and ice-pack freezing. There is no shop as such, but fire grills (from £5 per night) and cooking equipment are available to rent or buy; firewood, marshmallows, and other bits and bobs are also available at reception. At the other side of the car park is a tea room, open daily in summer, which serves snacks, afternoon teas, and light meals.

OFF SITE Walks through the Eridge Park Estate start from the campsite; maps are available at reception, which will take you variously to historic ice caves, a Victorian folly, and a Saxon fort. A trip to nearby Groombridge Place (01892 861444; www.groombridge.co.uk) is a very worthwhile excursion, with its renowned formal gardens and the excellent Enchanted Forest attraction for kids, which includes treetop walkways, birds of prey, and huge swings. Further afield, but equally worthwhile, is Bewl Water (www.bewlwater.co.uk), a huge, picturesque reservoir with an activity centre, kayaking, sailing, a zip wire, and a big playground for children. Kids can also go 'Hydroballing' – walking across water in a giant, transparent bubble. The Waterside Bistro (01892 893923) has views out across the water. The historic spa town of Tunbridge Wells is only 4 miles away, and has castles, gardens, and aged houses to explore.

FOOD AND DRINK The Huntsman pub (01892 864258), next to Eridge station, has a pleasant beer garden, ales from the Badger Brewery, and a changing menu with an emphasis on locally sourced, seasonal produce. Head into Tunbridge Wells for a host of options including, for something a bit special, Thackeray's (01892 511921; www.thackerays-restaurant.co.uk) on London Road – a modern French restaurant in a beautiful 17th-century weather-boarded villa.

GETTING THERE Eridge Park is just off the A26, between Tunbridge Wells and Crowborough. Take the turning on the south side of the A26, towards Rotherfield and Mayfield. This is Sham Farm Road; follow for a mile and the site's on the left.

PUBLIC TRANSPORT Direct trains run from London Bridge to Eridge station in as little as 50 minutes; other connections are available via East Croydon. From Eridge station, it's about half an hour on foot (about 2 miles), or 5 minutes in a taxi. Tunbridge Wells station is 4 miles from the campsite and has better taxi connections.

OPEN April–October.

THE DAMAGE Adult (over 16 years old) £12.50 per night; for families, the rates are £10 adult/£5 child over 3 years old.

dernwood farm

Little Dernwood Farm, Dern Lane, Waldron, Heathfield, East Sussex, TN21 0PN   01435 812726   www.dernwoodfarm.co.uk

Dernwood Farm is hidden away down a rolling country lane in the patchwork fields of Sussex. Like a Russian doll-within-a-doll, the campsite itself is further secreted inside an eight-acre clearing in the middle of a coppice wood originally grown for charcoal burning. Isn't it fitting, then, that fires are a welcome addition to the earthy, authentic camping experience on offer here?

On arrival you make yourself known at reception, pick up your organic eggs and choose from a rich selection of fresh flavoursome beef (produced here) to roast on your BBQ. Then, armed with some logs, pop it all into one of the trolleys or wheelbarrows provided and make your hobbit-like journey through the woods to the fairy-tale field that truly earns its moniker of 'wild'.

'It's a kind of filter,' says Amanda, your welcoming host, of the 10-minute walk through the woods, 'a real discovery as you shed your city skin and unwind. It also keeps away noisy campers looking for a quick fix.' There's no electricity here; this is a low impact, eco-friendly campsite, so it's just you, your canvas, and delicious food cooked by your own fair hands over the fire pits provided.

Come spring the three adjoining semi-natural ancient woods are aglow with thousands of bluebells. When you take a walk through them keep an eye out for the small pits once dug for the mining of ore in centuries past.

This is a place to really lose yourself for a few days, zone out from the urban noise you left behind, and tune in to the wildlife around you.

COOL FACTOR? As hidden and earthy as it gets.

WHO'S IN? Tents, dogs (on leads) – yes. Campervans, caravans, groups – no. It's a family campsite: no electronic noise or raucous explosions after the North Star appears.

ON SITE Campfires allowed in designated pits. Shop sells meat and eggs. There are 2 toilets, a cold washing-up area, a standpipe, and a log store (£5 per load), as well as solar-shower sacks. Wheelbarrows to transport your kit. Kids love to explore the fallen trunks and play hide-and-seek in the endless expanses, and Amanda can show them the animals. The yellow trail is a 40-minute rough walk through the woods. The nearest road is 2 miles away – and that's a mere country lane.

OFF SITE The Cuckoo Trail, a spit from the site, is a great option for cycling or walks – weaving through woods, fields, and the best of Sussex countryside. Normans Bay, named after the conquerors who landed here a thousand years ago, is just 20 minutes away. Pop into The Observatory Science Centre (01323 832731; www.the-observatory.org) – on selected evenings you can look through their telescopes at events in the night sky.

FOOD AND DRINK Stock up on steaks before heading to camp – they're hung for 21 days so are bursting with flavour. Beyond the wood in Chiddingly, the Six Bells (01825 872227) comes highly recommended (voted Best Bargain Pub in Britain) for its tasty fare and shabby-chic decor.

GETTING THERE Head to Horam on the A267 and, just before the garage on your left, head right down Furnace Lane. A mile on take the first left turn to Chiddingly and Little Dernwood Farm is on your left, opposite Copfold Farm.

OPEN 1 April–late September.

THE DAMAGE Tent plus adult £8 per night; child (over-5) £5, under-5s free. Family (2 adults and 2 children) £20.

hidden spring

Hidden Spring Vineyard, Vines Cross Road, Horam, Heathfield, East Sussex, TN21 0HG   01435 812640   www.hiddenspring.co.uk

Hidden Spring does what it says on the tin: family camping *à la ferme*, squirrelled away in fields corduroyed by vineyards and apple orchards. It's situated near the sleepy village of Horam – which has all you might need from a bakery, off licence, and fish and chippy – and there's a palpable sense of calm that slips over you as soon as you drive up the rutted road and catch your first view of the campsite. It's basic, but *good* basic, and for a reason too – owners Tamzin and David want their visitors to experience a back-to-nature treat, a place where kids can make dens in the copse, run wild through the orchard, and play hide-and-seek in the woods.

There are two fields to choose from – a tents-only option, and one for campervans and caravans. But don't worry, given the site's pursuit of aesthetics over rampant profit, there are only a select number of caravans allowed at any one time, so the views of the undulating fields, grass-munching horses, and sweeping vineyards are unbroken. There are fire pits like witches' cauldrons in the campervan field. You can buy wood and firelighters from Hidden Spring's little shop (which operates an honesty tab) and do the Neanderthal thing. Of an evening you can listen to the owls begin their calling while your flames turn a rich Halloween orange and carbonise your burgers; it's a beautiful spot to sit back and chill. The endless vistas of hay fields, soft chalky backdrop of the South Downs, and first-class pubs of East Sussex make a trip here well worth it, and there are more local attractions than you could hope to cover in a weekend, from castles to stately homes.

COOL FACTOR Eco-camping on a gloriously pretty farm.

WHO'S IN? Glampers, tents, campervans, caravans, dogs (on leads) – yes. Young noisy groups – no.

ON SITE Campfires allowed in fire pits. There are 10 pitches in the caravan field with electric hook-ups; 10 pitches in the camping meadow; and a couple of fully furnished 'luxury' tents. Kids' swings; dens in the woods; and the farm shop sells locally sourced meat (BBQs for hire), eggs, milk, and logs. The shower and loo block is spotlessly clean. The farm produces red and white wine and its own apple juice. Wood sculpture classes can be organised on request.

OFF SITE Wilderness Wood (01825 830509) is a family-run working woodland park in the Sussex Weald. There are woodland walks, a café, and play area. Drusillas Park (01323 874100) is a great place to entertain the kids, with its menagerie of animals – from monkeys to tarantulas, lizards to otters. Finally, the nearby Cuckoo Trail is a cyclist's paradise; built upon 11 miles of disused railway track, it weaves through woods, fields, and the best of the Sussex countryside.

FOOD AND DRINK BBQing that locally produced meat under the stars makes for a perfect dinner. Otherwise, try the Brewer's Arms (01435 812288) in nearby Vines Cross. It offers shabby-chic decor, a great atmosphere, and an earthy menu.

GETTING THERE From East Grinstead head to Uckfield on the A22. Then take the B2102 to Cross In Hand. From here take the A267, turning left for Horam and heading through the little high street shortly before turning into Vines Cross Road.

PUBLIC TRANSPORT Train to Eastbourne then Stagecoach bus no. 52 to Horam.

OPEN 1 March–31 October.

THE DAMAGE Tent plus adult £12 per night; child (3 to 14 years) £3. Bell tent £25 per night; dome £40; yurt £50.

brakes coppice

Brakes Coppice Park, Forewood Lane, Crowhurst, Battle, East Sussex, TN33 9AB   01424 830322   www.brakescoppicepark.co.uk

Back in the days of knights and armour the little village of Battle was but a blip on the map. Then came that fateful day in 1066, when a bunch of French fellas dragged their boats on to English shores to wage war on the Saxons. After one king's-eye of an arrow shot, the Norman Conquest was complete and Battle became one of the most historically significant towns in England.

The modern-day town exudes a deep sense of history, probably because its main draw, the 11th-century abbey, is built on the very ground upon which the conflict took place. It's flanked by pretty wood-timbered tea houses, a central street awash with bric-a-brac shops, and surrounded by countryside Americans in sneakers would die for.

A short drive away is Brakes Coppice, an immaculate campsite with plenty of room to pitch in the skirts of its deep coppice woods. The facilities are basic, but the spot is lovely. There's a shaded adults-only area in a little glade and two other areas for families. Admittedly there are a few caravans lurking like sheep in an allocated area, but generally this is a camper's campsite.

COOL FACTOR Close to historic Battle, not far from the sea, and set in spacious, shielded woodland and pasture.

WHO'S IN? Tents, campervans, caravans, dogs, young groups (only if adult-supervised) – yes.

ON SITE Thirty pitches over 4 acres; kids' play area; toilets and showers with laundry facilities. Reception sells milk and bread, but you're better off going to Battle to stock up. There's a fishing lake at the bottom. No campfires.

OFF SITE Battle Abbey has a great exhibition and film all about the Battle of Hastings. Bexhill's De La Warr Pavilion (01424 229111) is a stunning 1930s modernist building with an impressively large art gallery and a café roof terrace.

FOOD AND DRINK De La Warr Pavilion's restaurant serves up fresh, tasty, food with a sea view to match. Try the period-charm-oozing Pilgrims Rest (01424 772314) in Battle.

GETTING THERE Head to Battle on the A21 then A2100. Continue along the High Street and on towards Hastings for 2 miles, then turn right on to Telham Lane (towards Crowhurst). Continue on to Forewood Lane and the site is on the left.

PUBLIC TRANSPORT Train to Crowhurst, then walk: along the path by the southbound platform to Forewood Lane.

OPEN 1 April–early September.

THE DAMAGE Tent plus 2 adults £14–£18; child £2.

bedgebury

Bedgebury Camping, Pattenden Farm, Goudhurst, Kent, TN17 2QX   01580 213487   bedgeburycamping.co.uk

You can instantly tell that more than the average amounts of thought and love have gone into Bedgebury Camping. It's the little extras: a communal tipi for campfire gatherings and general hanging-out; the cute little wooden compost toilet blocks, hand-built by owner Jim; the campfire starter packs, which include straw bales to sit on in addition to the more predictable logs, kindling, and marshmallows. Small things – big difference. And it's a big site, too. Although camping is restricted to four acres, there are another 20 acres to explore, including woodland and a small stream. It's a tranquil, picturesque spot, set away from the main road in a green, wooded vale. You might catch the occasional glimpse of an oast house amid the trees – these distinctive buildings serve as a reminder of the hop-farming heritage of the area. Bedgebury itself was a hop farm in times gone by, but now the rows of old hop-drying huts have found another use as perfectly proportioned cycle storage sheds. Bring your bike to explore the exhilarating single-track trails at Bedgebury Forest, or the more sedate, family ambles around nearby Bewl Water.

COOL FACTOR Spacious, chilled-out camping loveliness.

WHO'S IN? Tents, dogs – yes. Campervans, caravans – no. Well-behaved groups – yes (separate field for large groups).

ON SITE The main, L-shaped camping field is largely flat. Atmospheric communal tipi open 24/7; tea and cakes served in the afternoon. Eight compost toilets; clean showers and WCs in a portaloo cabin; and washing-up sinks next to the bike-storage huts. Maps detailing local footpaths at reception. Campfires allowed; starter pack including 2 hay bales, logs, matches, kindling, and marshmallows £20.

OFF SITE Fantastic area for walking and cycling, including Bewl Water (see p151) and Bedgebury Forest. Sissinghurst Castle (01580 710701) with its remarkable gardens isn't far.

FOOD AND DRINK The stylish Globe & Rainbow (01892 890803) at Kilndown serves excellent seasonal food sourced largely from Kentish farms – a 45-minute walk.

GETTING THERE Take the A21 towards Hastings. After Blue Boys services turn left at the next roundabout on to the A262. Turn right at Goudhurst village pond, follow the road down into the valley, then look for Bedgebury on the right.

OPEN For 28 days during August only.

THE DAMAGE Adult/child (3 to 14 years) £8–£10/£4–£5 per night (depending on day). Pets £2.

welsummer

Welsummer Camping, Chalk House, Lenham Road, Kent, ME17 1NQ   01622 844048   welsummercamping.com

Named after an old (and sadly long-since departed) rescue hen called Welsummer, Med and Laura Benagounne's campsite is the epitome of laid-back cool – not something, admittedly, that you immediately associate with Kent. A multicoloured windsock hangs from a tree, chickens roam free, and acoustic instruments and fireside singalongs are the order of the day – or rather, the night.

The range of camping experiences on offer at what is quite a bijou site – just three-fifths of an acre, plus a small wood – is pretty impressive. Traditionalists can pitch in one of the two small fields, backwoods types can set up their tent (as long as it's small) in the copse, and those with no canvas home to call their own have the choice of a bell tent or an old-school ridge tent to sleep in.

The owners' organic garden produces veg for sale in the small onsite shop, where campers can also pick up basic supplies – at weekends this may even include a loaf of home-made bread or some scrumptious dish fresh from the oven. Meanwhile, the site's eco-credentials are bolstered in the wash-rooms, where water for the showers is heated by a wood-burning stove fed with fuel from the locality.

But it's the woodland life here that sets this campsite apart from most others. Laura used to camp among these same trees as a child, and it was her desire to let others share this formative experience that led her to opening this smallholding as a campsite. And should you wish to explore the area, the path out of the woods leads straight on to Kent's Greensand Ridge.

COOL FACTOR Something for every sort of cool camper.

WHO'S IN? Tents, dogs (maximum of 3 on site at any one time) – yes. Campervans, caravans, groups – no.

ON SITE Most of the 20 pitches have their own fire pit (firewood £3.50, starter kit £5). There are 2 loos and 2 showers. Kids are free to climb the trees. The tiny shop sells the smallholding's free-range eggs and serves hot drinks and hot snacks all day. The distant murmur of the M20 can be heard – but that's the only downside.

OFF SITE Leeds Castle (www.leeds-castle.com), less than 4 miles away, is every child's dream of an ancient stronghold and has a fantastic play area for kids, too. Grown-ups may reward themselves afterwards with a wine-tasting and wander through Biddenden Vineyards (01580 291726; www.biddendenvineyards.com).

FOOD AND DRINK The food at the nearby Pepperbox Inn (01622 842558; www.thepepperboxinn.co.uk) comes highly recommended (no under-14s inside the pub, but there is a beer garden). The small and rather appealing market town of Lenham boasts the tempting Lurcocks Delicatessen (01622 858345) with its good stock of local produce.

GETTING THERE It can be tricky, so follow the excellent instructions and photos on welsummercamping.com, which will guide you in from the M20.

PUBLIC TRANSPORT Take a train to Lenham, 2 miles away, then cycle, walk, or taxi to the site (costs about £7 with Streamline or Express Cabs, 01622 750000 and 01622 690000 respectively).

OPEN April–October.

THE DAMAGE Small tent £12 per night; large tent £20; bell tent £45; ridge tent £45. Plus adult £3 per night; child (3 to 13 years) £1. Booking strongly advised.

folkestone

Folkestone Camping, The Warren, Folkestone, Kent, CT19 6NQ   01303 255093   see www.campingandcaravanningclub.co.uk

The soaring white cliffs of Folkestone and nearby Dover are infamous. Welcoming yet overwhelming, the cliffs are nothing short of spectacular. And because cliffs like these need an equally spectacular viewing spot, the Camping and Caravanning Club created Folkestone campsite. It's set in a particularly attractive curve of the Kentish coast and has an outlook of Channel waters and crumbly crags, and (as one of the closest spots to continental Europe) is handy for a ferry or Channel Tunnel excursion. The main camping field is an immaculate grassland strip with flat unmarked pitches. Those nearest reception are the most unsheltered, but your views across the Channel are uninhibited, and there are some stealthy little spots among the trees – including the surreptitiously placed Honeymoon pitch. Wake up each morning to cliffs, coastline, and beaches – the site's position means you're only a path away from the shingle and sand beach below. Trek a bit further and you'll find the man-made Samphire Hoe nature reserve – one of the newest parts of England (thanks to the leftovers from the Channel Tunnel excavation) juxtaposed with the old and wise cliffs.

COOL FACTOR Cliff-top camping with Channel views.
WHO'S IN? Every man and his dog welcome.
ON SITE Eighty pitches – 42 standard tent; 15 hardstanding and 15 grass with hook-ups; 2 jumbo pitches; 15 tiny pitches. Two blocks each with 2 hot showers and 2 toilets; 2 washing-up sinks, washing machine, dryer. Freezer pack £1 deposit; hairdryer 20p. CDP; mini-shop. BBQs off ground. No campfires.
OFF SITE Samphire Hoe nature reserve (01304 225649) is a must-see. And the impenetrable fortress of Dover Castle (01304 211067) is well worth a visit.
FOOD AND DRINK The Valiant Sailor (01303 252401) offers hearty pub grub. Enjoy a pint of Ramsgate No 5 and cracking sea views at the Lighthouse (01303 223300). Pick up fresh seafood from Folkestone Harbour.
GETTING THERE Follow the A260 towards Folkestone; turn left on to Hill Road, following signs for the Country Park. At the junction of Dover Road, turn left then immediately right, on to Wear Bay Road. Take the second turning on the left and follow the track for ½ mile to the campsite.
PUBLIC TRANSPORT Train to Folkestone, then taxi (£5).
OPEN April–October.
THE DAMAGE Adult £7.70–£11.10 per night; child £2.80–£6.40, under-6s free. A £7 non-member pitch fee per group.

palace farm

Palace Farm, Down Court Road, Doddington, nr Faversham, Kent, ME9 0AU   01795 886200   www.palacefarm.com

The cockerel may crow or the goats may mutter as you enter Palace Farm, but that's as noisy as it gets here. It's a quiet old place, off the beaten track (but not far from some very worthwhile places to visit) and with a 10pm quiet rule that's largely respected. It's a simple set-up: a flat, grassy field holds up to 25 tents around its hedgerow edges, with an adjoining field left free for games or general haring around. Two pre-erected bell tents provide the slightest hint of camping glamour, but this is good, honest Kentish camping with no pretensions to be anything else. Don't confuse quietness with strictness, though. Campfires are allowed, campers can help themselves to plums from the orchard or blackberries from the old hedgerows around the farm, and edible mushrooms are permitted to grow prolifically across the site in the autumn. (We're told they're not hallucinogenic which, apparently, is a good thing.) While you're hunting and gathering, have a forage at the honesty shop, where zero-food-mile courgettes, pumpkins, and other seasonal veg are available fresh from the farm. Busy days, quiet nights. Life's good at Palace Farm.

COOL FACTOR Unpretentious camping in underrated spot.

WHO'S IN? Tents, dogs (on leads; must be pre-booked), well-behaved groups – yes. Motorhomes, caravans – no.

ON SITE Campfires allowed (in fire pits); 25 pitches plus 2 bell tents on a field of about an acre with a wooden shower block (3 showers, 3 toilets including family/disabled room). Tourist info and walking maps available at the reception hut, where you can also freeze ice packs and charge phones. Reduced noise after 10pm and no noise after 11pm.

OFF SITE Lots to explore in the wider area including Leeds Castle (10 miles), Challock Forest (10 miles), Canterbury (14 miles), and Whitstable (16 miles); owners happy to help.

FOOD AND DRINK The George Inn (01795 890237) in Newnham is a dependable old pub with a popular restaurant.

GETTING THERE From the A2 between Sittingbourne and Faversham turn south at Teynham, signposted Lynsted. Go through Lynsted, over the M2 bridge, then take the second right into Down Court Road. Palace Farm is on the left.

PUBLIC TRANSPORT Train to Sittingbourne, then a bus to Doddington (up to 4.30pm), or hop in a taxi for about £12.

OPEN April–October.

THE DAMAGE Adult £8 per night; child (3 to 15) £4. Fire pit £2, logs £3.50/bag. Bell-tent hire £50/night, £250/week.

bouncers farm

Bouncers Farm, Wickham Hall Lane, Wickham Bishops, Essex, CM8 3JJ   01621 894112   www.operaintheorchard.co.uk

If you've been searching in vain for years for a campsite that offers its own pony-and-trap taxi service, then search no more. Get within a few miles of Bouncers Farm – to Witham station, say – and, for a small fee, Ann will collect you and your fellow campers and take you clip-clopping down narrow country lanes to her lovely woody site in the surprisingly bucolic Essex countryside. Greenies will also be happy to note that there are discounts for those who get most of the way to Bouncers by some form of sustainable transport.

The campsite is spread out across Ann's smallholding, and with just 10 pitches there's plenty of room to sprawl. The eight acres of woods are a magnet for children, who can play on a tyre swing, climb up into the tree house Ann herself played in as a girl, make dens, or explore a little hollow of bulrushes just made for hiding from grown-ups and all their outmoded ways of being. Said grown-ups, meanwhile, might like to relax by slinging up a hammock between the 300-year-old trees.

If ever out of the woods, younger children can take part in organised mini-beast hunts, or be led for a ride on a pony (after doing all the fun grooming and tacking up, of course). Unlike most campsites in Britain, there's a professional opera held here for two nights every July, and an art exhibition in the last week of September.

And if you want to try something a little different you can book the two gypsy caravans and bender tent and cook your supper in a proper steaming cauldron over an open fire.

COOL FACTOR The almost magical quality of the woods.

WHO'S IN? Tents, dogs (1 per family and on leads) – yes. Campervans, caravans, groups – no.

ON SITE Numerous fire pits for campfires. There are 10 pitches; a wet room with double shower and loo; Portakabin with 2 loos and a solar-heated shower; and a fridge/freezer. For children there's a tyre swing, sandpit, and tree house. Pony ride £12; mini-beast hunt £12.

OFF SITE Learn how to sail at West Mersea with ex-Olympian Jane Richardson, or have a session at a riding school (Ann can arrange booking for both). At Paper Mill Lock (01245 225520; www.papermilllock.co.uk) you can hire a rowing boat or canoe, or go for a canal cruise along the Chelmer and Blackwater Navigation.

FOOD AND DRINK The Du Cane Arms (01621 891697) in Great Braxted is very highly regarded for its food. Olivers Nurseries (01376 513239), south of Witham, is a PYO fruit farm, café, and farm shop. Or give Ann a shopping list before you arrive and a local independent shop will deliver.

GETTING THERE From the A12 take the B1389 into Witham and then the B1018 (Maldon Road) south towards Wickham Bishops, and turn left up Wickham Hall Lane. Bouncers Farm is on the left, after ½ mile.

PUBLIC TRANSPORT Train to Witham then cycle or walk along the Blackwater Rail Trail, or take bus no. 90 (Stephensons; 01702 541511) to Snows Corner, and wander up from there. Or arrive in style in the pony-and-trap.

OPEN Easter–Oct and 4 weeks over Christmas and New Year.

THE DAMAGE Small tent and 1 person £12 per night; medium tent £15; large tent £24; extra adult £4; child £3; dog £1. Pre-erected 3-man tent £20 per night; family-of-5 tent £30; gypsy caravan (sleeping up to 5) £80.

debden house

Debden House, Debden Green, Loughton, Essex, IG10 2NZ   020 8508 3008   www.debdenhouse.com

If campsites had their own Zodiac signs, then Debden House's would be Libra. It manages to pull off a unique balancing act between size (this place is huge, taking up 60 acres of prime Essex countryside) and privacy. Backing directly on to vast Epping Forest, with its magnificent ancient trees, flower-carpeted meadows, mirrored ponds, and abundance of wildlife, the campsite is divided into seven fields. Two of these are given over to large groups so that campers after a quieter stay can enjoy peace elsewhere. Our favourite is Field 2, for its back-of-beyond feel within a narrow strip of green enclosed by the forest; but then there's the Fire Field, where you can have a campfire in any of the designated spots.

It's a joy to be so close to London, and yet be surrounded by all this woodland. Footpaths lead off from the camp's edges, taking you deep into the heart of the forest – many linking up with other walking paths. You can enjoy a weekend communing with nature and then hop on the tube to be in the heart of the capital within the hour. The best of both worlds indeed.

COOL FACTOR Fireside camping in a forest setting.

WHO'S IN? Tents, campervans, caravans, large groups, dogs (on leads) – yes. Caravans over 5.5 metres – no.

ON SITE Campfires in designated pits in the Fire Field (pre-book; photo ID required on arrival). Pitches over 7 fields. Bit of a walk to the toilet and shower (6, hot water) block at the site's entrance, but there's another loo block in the middle, with a washing-up area. Two children's play areas; electric hook-ups on Fields 1 and 4; laundry with token-operated machines; shop and café in the house. Busy at peak times; motorway traffic and planes audible. Book weekends.

OFF SITE Queen Elizabeth's Hunting Lodge (020 8529 6681) in Chingford is worth a visit. And you're only an hour from all the sights and sounds of the capital.

FOOD AND DRINK It's well worth stocking up at the local farmers' market on the first Sunday of the month.

GETTING THERE Take the A1168 towards Loughton. Turn right on to Pyrles Lane, right into Englands Road, and follow the brown campsite signs, turning left into Debden Road.

PUBLIC TRANSPORT From Theydon Bois tube station catch bus no. 167/20 onwards.

OPEN May–September.

THE DAMAGE Adult £7; child £3.50. Hook-up £3.50.

town farm

Town Farm, Ivinghoe, Leighton Buzzard, Bedfordshire, LU7 9EL   07906 265435   www.townfarmcamping.co.uk

Whipsnade Zoo; hot air ballooning above the Chilterns; the Grand Union Canal; parks aplenty; and endless cycling, walking, and riding trails – with the area offering all this, surely the BBC's *Room 101* was wrong to consign Leighton Buzzard to the bin?

The sheep-rearing Town Farm family-owners have enjoyed living here for generations regardless, and have opened their land to campers looking to extol this part of Bedfordshire, too. Their vast camping field is behind a barn. Tents can be pitched at the foot of Ivinghoe Beacon, where the famous Ridgeway Walk starts its journey to Wiltshire, or overlooking the Vale of Aylesbury. Ignore the pylon wire running along the right of the site, and head left towards the Chilterns, past a hip, new, chalet-style wash-block, to pitch at the far end.

Frazzled parents looking for activities to wear out their brood have so much choice both off and on site (there are swings, goalposts, and a trampoline on the grounds, plus a pick-your-own farm open in summer) that everyone will sleep soundly at night. *Room 101* obviously wasn't thinking about parents; we think Leighton Buzzard is a keeper.

COOL FACTOR An ideal trial location for first-time campers and Londoners not wanting to stay far from home.

WHO'S IN? Tents, campervans, caravans, obedient dogs (that won't bother sheep), groups – yes. Noisy groups – no.

ON SITE Campfires allowed in the onsite fire pits (rented for £5; wood bundle £5) and BBQs on blocks. A total of 50 pitches, with 12 hook-ups for caravans/motorhomes. The facilities block has 2 showers, a washing machine (£3.50), tumble-dryer (50p/8 mins), freezer, wi-fi, and electricity points. There is a distant hum of local traffic.

OFF SITE Whipsnade Zoo (01582 872171) is 10 miles away, and the elephants and tigers at Woburn Safari Park (01525 290407) half an hour. The Chiltern Cycleway (www.chilternsociety.org.uk) details 170 miles of routes in the area.

FOOD AND DRINK Eat local goods fresh from the Pecks Farm Shop (01525 211859); lovely pies and pickles. Leighton Buzzard farmers' market takes place every third Saturday.

GETTING THERE Town Farm is just off the B489 between Ivinghoe and Dunstable (on your right if travelling west).

PUBLIC TRANSPORT Train to Tring, then a taxi (£10).

OPEN All year.

THE DAMAGE Adult £8–£10 (depending on length of stay); child (6 to 18 years) £5, under-5s and dogs free.

east

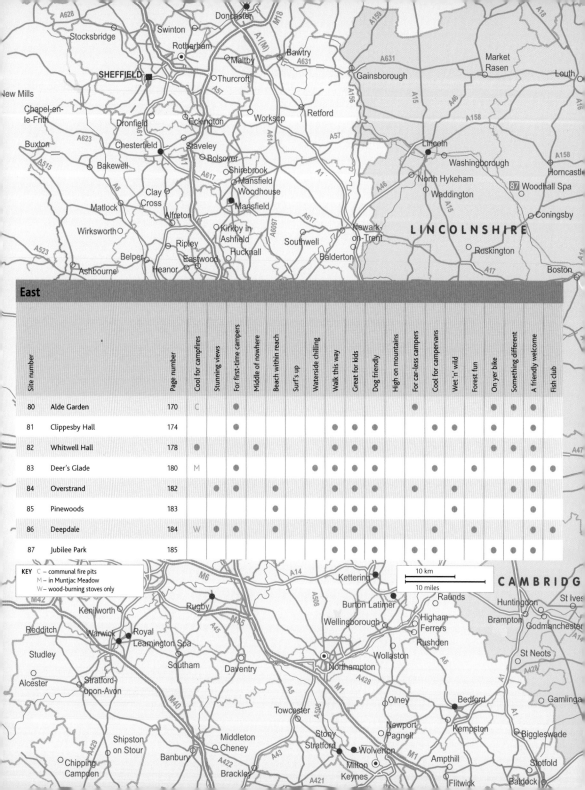

East

Site number		Page number	Cool for campfires	Stunning views	For first-time campers	Middle of nowhere	Beach within reach	Surf's up	Waterside chilling	Walk this way	Great for kids	Dog friendly	High on mountains	For car-less campers	Cool for campervans	Wet 'n' wild	Forest fun	On yer bike	Something different	A friendly welcome	Fish club
80	Alde Garden	170	C		●									●				●	●	●	
81	Clippesby Hall	174			●					●	●	●		●	●			●		●	
82	Whitwell Hall	178	●			●				●	●	●						●		●	
83	Deer's Glade	180	M		●				●	●	●	●					●			●	●
84	Overstrand	182		●	●		●							●				●		●	
85	Pinewoods	183					●				●	●						●			
86	Deepdale	184	W	●	●		●		●			●		●		●		●		●	●
87	Jubilee Park	185								●	●	●						●	●	●	

KEY C – communal fire pits
M – in Muntjac Meadow
W – wood-burning stoves only

10 km
10 miles

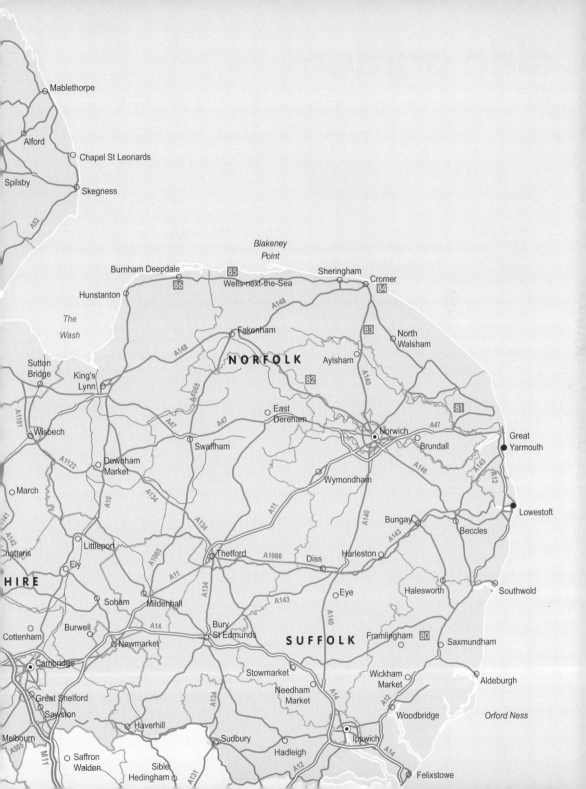

alde garden

Alde Garden, The White Horse Inn, Low Road, Sweffling, Suffolk, IP17 2BB   01728 664178   www.aldegarden.co.uk

If there were an annual award for 'English campsite with the greatest diversity of accommodation', the owners of Alde Garden would be permanently practising their acceptance speeches and making mental notes not to blub on discovering that they've triumphed over Angelina Jolie again.

Guests to this former pub garden, on the edge of the little village of Sweffling, can choose between a stay in a bell tent, a yurt, a tipi, a gypsy caravan, and a 'wooden tent on stilts' (inspired by a trip to New Zealand). Alternatively, they can bring along their own tent and camp in the time-honoured fashion. Indeed, youthful owners Marie and Mark encourage non-campers who have booked into the more glampy accommodation to bring along a tent to give traditional camping a try. Battle-hardened tentophiles, meanwhile, can spend their final night in the yurt or the gypsy caravan, say, as a bit of a naughty treat (there's even a cute self-catering cottage for those who need to bait the hook for less enthusiastic campers).

However you decide to stay here, the vibe remains the same. A garden kept deliberately wild (and with its own friendly hedgehog) combined with facilities artfully constructed from reclaimed and recycled materials engender a laid-back atmosphere, where the sixties and the tenties collide to rather pleasing effect.

Take the brilliant jungle shower, for example, made from wood Marie and Mark have picked up. Showerers can hitch up one of the site's bags of solar-heated water to enjoy an (entirely modest)

outdoor shower. It's definitely worth a go; not only is it pleasantly surprising how warm the sun can make the water, but there's the added bonus of a view of next door's free-range pigs. (There are also two spotless conventional showers for those for whom cleanliness is next to indoorsiness.)

The pathways around the 0.89-acre (they've measured it) site; the Donkey Shed shelter that trebles as a kitchen and dining room (the straw-bale seats are a particular hit with kids); the bookcase in the yurt... they've all been lovingly crafted by hand with materials that would otherwise have gone to waste. Even the wood-burning stoves have been created from discarded gas bottles by a friend of the couple. And if you're more into cycling than recycling, you can borrow a bike from the cluster, which even includes a tandem, kept on site.

After dark, myriad colourful solar-powered lights and sun jars give the place a magical dingly dell feel, an impression enhanced by the soft glow from the brick pizza oven (bring your own ingredients and become *italiano* for the night), and the rosy blush of the communal fire.

There are big plans afoot for the coming years. Aside from building the wooden tent on stilts, Marie and Mark are reopening the pub – The White Horse – whose garden forms the campsite. They also plan to build a compost loo and open a little shop selling hand-made recycled crafts.

Visitors should note that there's one space at the very top of the garden that's not open

to guests – where there's a teeny tiny tent in residence. 'That's ours', laughs Mark. 'We hated the idea of not being able to camp here ourselves so we've got our own tent up for whenever we want to treat ourselves.' A campsite that's so good the owners camp there themselves? You won't get a better recommendation than that, not for all the donkey sheds in Sidmouth.

COOL FACTOR Never before, in the history of human camping, has so much variety been packed into 0.89 acres of garden.

WHO'S IN Tents, glampers – yes. Campervans, caravans, dogs, groups – no.

ON SITE There's a communal campfire near the bottom of the field and 6 small bring-your-own-tent pitches scattered around the side in cosy nooks and crannies beneath or behind trees. The loos, in buildings attached to the house, are very clean (2W, 1M, plus a compost loo), and you can choose between a conventional shower (1W, 1M) and the jungle shower under the trees. Kids love the numerous chickens and ducks that wander about the site, while a diablo and poi are available for any minors who live in hope of running away to join the circus some day. A room is given over to a freezer, a fridge, a washing machine, and microwave. There's also a covered kitchen/dining area with gas cookers, straw-bale seats, cutlery, crockery, pots, pans, tea, and coffee. A mobile shop stops at the campsite on Fridays from noon to 2pm, but there's no shop in Sweffling itself. There is some occasional traffic noise from the road that runs past the site.

OFF SITE Framlingham Castle (01728 724189; see www.english-heritage.org.uk) is an astonishingly fine yet little known 12th-century fortress with frequent child-friendly events. The coastal gems of Dunwich, Southwold, and Aldeburgh are within striking distance, as is the world-famous bird reserve at Minsmere (see www.rspb.org.uk) with nature trails, hides, and visitor centre. More birdwatching, as well as walks along the Alde Estuary and boat trips are all to be had at Snape Maltings (01728 688303;

www.snapemaltings.co.uk), whose concert hall is the home of the Aldeburgh Festival (01728 687110), co-founded by Benjamin Britten and held every June.

FOOD AND DRINK If you visit before Alde Garden's White Horse pub has reopened, a pleasant 8-and-a-bit-minute stroll through a meadow will take you to another White Horse (01728 663497; www.whitehorserendham. co.uk) at Rendham – there's a third White Horse close by too, nobody knows quite why – where you can get a decent bite to eat and sup some locally brewed Earl Soham ale. The extensive Friday Street Farm Shop (01728 602783; www. fridaystfarm.co.uk) at Farnham sells its own home-grown fruit and vegetables and doubles as a café.

GETTING THERE Be ye warned – satnav will take you on a rather circuitous route through Sweffling. Rather you should aim for the small town of Saxmundham on the A12. From there, take the B1119 west. Pass the White Horse in Rendham, round a sharp left- then right-hand bend, and immediately after another sharp left-hand bend, turn right at a crossroads and you're at Alde Garden.

PUBLIC TRANSPORT If you can get yourself to Saxmundham station (www.nationalexpresseastanglia.com), Marie or Mark will generously collect you and take you the 3½ miles to the site for free, if you give them some advance warning.

OPEN Easter–October.

THE DAMAGE Small tent (up to 4-man) £12 in high season/£10 in low season, per night; large tent (more than 4-man) £18/£15; wooden tent (sleeping 2) £35/£30; bell tent £45/£40; tipi £65/£55; gypsy caravan £70/£60; yurt £75/£65. There's a discount for those staying for a week.

clippesby hall

Clippesby Hall, Hall Lane, Clippesby, Norfolk, NR29 3BL   01493 367800   www.clippesby.com

Clippesby Hall in the Norfolk Broads achieves the near impossible – managing to make a large campsite feel friendly, non-commercial, peaceful, and altogether rather lovely.

Set.in the manicured grounds of John Lindsay's family manor house, the site forms its own little self-contained canvas village. The facilities are pretty extensive, with 115 pitches (many with electric hook-ups), a small outdoor swimming pool, two grass tennis courts, a football pitch, mini-golf, archery courses, two children's play areas – including a BeWILDerwood-style adventure playground – a tree house in the woods, a games room, cycle trail, bike hire, shop, café, holiday cottages, pine lodges, and even an onsite pub.

You might assume that this place is about as quiet and peaceful as a night on the hard shoulder of the A12. But somehow John and his family have managed to incorporate all these amenities into the grounds of their home, while still retaining its unique character and personality. The result is an exceptionally tasteful camping park with a relaxed, family atmosphere.

The site began life as a market garden, but campers have been coming here since the 1970s. It has gradually evolved at its own pace over the years and today the pitches are divided across several discrete camping areas, each landscaped and spacious enough to avoid any feeling of overcrowding, and named according to their individual characters. Pine Woods is a dog-free space almost entirely surrounded by conifers, The

Orchard has plenty of tree cover, while The Dell is hidden away in a quiet corner with woodland pitches just for tents. Rabbits Grove is a favourite among younger campers, and the Cedar Lawn has pitches spread out over a gently sloping sweep of lawn beneath a huge cedar, complete with rope swing. There is plenty of space between pitches and some interesting little nooks and crannies mean that even in busy periods you can still find a relatively secluded space to call your own.

Clippesby Hall is the perfect location from which to explore the Broads National Park, a network of rivers and lakes that forms Britain's largest protected wetland. Although the rivers are natural, the lakes are man-made, the result of 400 years of enthusiastic peat digging from the 12th century onwards. Hundreds of acres of peat were dug up for fuel in the absence of suitable woodland in the area. However, water soon began seeping through the porous ground, causing marshes and then lakes to appear. In a centuries-old example of how human intervention can significantly change the landscape, nature has also demonstrated its ability to adapt to a changing environment, and this collaboration of industry and nature has resulted in a stunning waterscape.

True to form, John has organised a unique way of exploring the Broads. The CanoeMan (aka Mark Wilkinson), accompanied by his two springer spaniels, Mr Darcy and Uisce, takes you directly from the site for a peaceful nature-spotting canoe trail through beautiful waterways inaccessible to

motor-powered boats. If you'd rather explore the local area by pedal power, Clippesby also hires out bikes along with circular route maps, helmets, locks, and repair kits (child seats and other accessories too).

Don't be surprised when you are personally guided to your pitch on arrival – it's all part of the service, along with the deliberate decision not to put large, obtrusive pitch markers and unnecessary signs everywhere. After all, this is John's home and garden. It's been in the family since his grandfather bought the hall back in 1945, and he doesn't want to ruin it by making it look like, well, a campsite. And that's the beauty of this unique place. It doesn't feel like a conventional, commercial campsite. It's more like camping in the delightful grounds of a stately home.

COOL FACTOR Extensive facilities combined with a peaceful, relaxed, family atmosphere.

WHO'S IN Tents, campervans, caravans, motorhomes, dogs (on leads) – yes. Groups – sometimes.

ON SITE Some 115 pitches (with and without hook-ups) spread out in separate glades (some of which have tent-only areas). Plenty of entertainment and things to do on site (see p174). The facilities blocks are dotted around the place and have modern showers, toilets, basins, and washing-up sinks with draining boards outside. There's even a family room with a bath. Plenty of staff members on site mean that everything is kept clean and well maintained. Recycling is encouraged as part of the green ethos. No campfires.

OFF SITE Your Clippesby Hall welcome pack includes a booklet all about discovering the Norfolk Broads, including ideas for days out by foot, bike, boat, or canoe. One of the best means of exploration is in a Canadian canoe with knowledgeable CanoeMan, Mark Wilkinson (01603 499177). Or, for something bigger, head for Potter Heigham – 'the Blackpool of the Broads' as Mark likes to call it – 4 miles north of the campsite, where there are boatyards hiring out all sorts of vessels by the hour or day, as well as pleasure-boat trips. The nearest beaches are around 6 miles away, at Winterton-on-Sea, Sea Palling, and Horsey, where you'll also find Horsey Windpump (01263 740241). Climb its 5 flights of steep steps for views over the coast and broadlands landscape, or walk along the canal to Horsey Mere.

FOOD AND DRINK You don't actually need to leave the site. Susie's Coffee Shop serves hot drinks and croissants for breakfast, and sandwiches and cakes throughout the day. You can order freshly baked bread or pizza to take away, and the shop sells local and fair-trade produce. Susie also sells ice cream from her summerhouse by the pool on sunny days. Campsite pub, the Muskett Arms, serves meals with locally sourced ingredients, and local real ales and ciders. If you find yourself in Woodbastwick (around 6 miles away), the Fur and Feather Inn (01603 720003) is a superb country pub with a fantastic garden for the summer. It serves Woodforde's ale, including the famous Norfolk Nog. The Woodforde Brewery is next door and offers half-hour tours on certain evenings.

GETTING THERE From the A47 between Norwich and Great Yarmouth, take the A1064 at Acle (Caister-on-Sea Road). After about a mile, take the first left at Clippesby on to the B1152 and follow the signs to Clippesby Hall.

PUBLIC TRANSPORT Take a mainline train to Norwich then the local service to Acle. From here it's a short taxi ride to the campsite.

OPEN April–October.

THE DAMAGE Prices range from £10.50 per night in low season for a tent, car, and 2 people to £30.50 in high. Extra adult £5.50; child £2.75, under-3s free; dog £3.75; hook-up £3.25.

whitwell hall

Whitwell Hall Country Centre, Whitwell, Reepham, Norfolk, NR10 4RE   01603 870875   www.freewebs.com/whitwellhall

If you get the urge to disappear off the face of the earth for a weekend but don't want to step on to a plane, then Whitwell Hall Country Centre is the place to go – although you'll have to take a few friends along with you. Because here you don't just get an individual pitch, but a whole woodland-enclosed meadow to call your own, along with a private, sheltered campfire area.

Although it's only 20 minutes from Norwich, the site feels very deep in the Norfolk countryside – especially if your route takes you along Nowhere Lane. Getting close to, and living in harmony with, nature is the aim: simple camping, cooking over an open fire, lying under the stars, and removing yourself from the trappings of modern life.

Treading lightly is also important – solar heating, rainwater harvesting, and wildlife conservation programmes are all part of the very green ethos here. Kevin Hart, who runs the site, has a wealth of wilderness camping experience and uses it to inspire the youngsters who stay here with their schools. He's camped in the Canadian backwoods, 'bivied' his way across New Zealand, and even searched for polar bears in the Arctic Circle. He is the ultimate example of how far you can get with a tent in your backpack and very little else.

Whitwell Hall aims to teach children about self-reliance in a bid to raise their confidence. It also instills a lifelong love of camping. Many of those who first came here as 10-year-olds remember that initial experience and continue to be drawn back year after year… now with their own 10-year-olds.

COOL FACTOR Back-to-nature campsite – all to yourself.
WHO'S IN? Tents, campervans (in the Paddock), dogs (by prior arrangement), groups – yes. Caravans, lone campers – no.
ON SITE Campfires allowed. Groups of campers can choose from 3 meadows: the Paddock for 4–10 tents; Kestrel for 6–13 tents; or Yew Tree for 8–50 tents. Each has an open fire 'pad' under shelter – perfect for fireside gatherings. Firewood is included. You can rent 4-person patrol tents and cooking sets. All 3 campsites have their own toilet and shower block providing simple but adequate facilities. No amplified music – it might disturb the abundant wildlife. Bats, badgers, and foxes all live here, and the centre is part of the national Red Squirrel Breeding Programme.
OFF SITE There are steam trains at Whitwell and Reepham Railway (01603 871694; www.whitwellstation.com) – almost next door to the site, and the 21-mile Marriott's Way footpath, between Norwich and Aylesham, passes nearby. The path makes its way along former railway lines so is also good for cycling. A little further afield but worth a visit is Pensthorpe Nature Reserve and Gardens (www.pensthorpe. com), near Fakenham, host to the BBC's *Springwatch*.
FOOD AND DRINK Whitwell rail station makes its own Whitwell Wobbler ale, and Reepham is endowed with 3 good pubs, including the Kings Arms (01603 870345), which has real ales, food, and jazz in the courtyard on summer Sundays.
GETTING THERE From the A140 take the A1067 towards Fakenham. Continue through Lenwade and then turn right on to Nowhere Lane. Take the third left (opposite Whitwell Common), turn right at the crossroads (signposted Reepham), and Whitwell Hall is the first entrance on the right.
OPEN All school holidays and Bank Holidays.
THE DAMAGE £17.30 per tent, per night.

deer's glade

Deer's Glade Caravan and Camping Park, White Post Road, Hanworth, Norwich, Norfolk, NR11 7HN   01263 768633
www.deersglade.co.uk

Set in a quiet woodland clearing, Deer's Glade successfully combines modern innovations with old-school camping principles. The owners, David and Heather, have taken great care and attention in creating the site, so that the hotel-style facilities – contemporary bathrooms and wi-fi access – don't come at the expense of nature and conservation. The slick showers are housed in eco-friendly wooden buildings, and the native saplings and hedges planted a few years ago are maturing into a pleasant landscaped environment. While the ground has been levelled and turfed for easy pitching, wild areas have been left around the hedges, providing a habitat for insects and birds.

The site is great for adults and children alike. Kids will make for the playground or rush to buy bags of food for the resident goats and ducks; adults can relax by the lake. From the campsite you can walk directly into the adjacent woodland, with its acres of conifer-rich foliage and resident wild deer. A tents-only camping area, Muntjac Meadow, is accessed through the woods and open in August. The deer sometimes even visit the site, but it's easier to spot them on the short amble to Gunton Park, which offers parkland walks and a large fishing lake.

Two exceptional properties in the area beg a visit. Felbrigg Hall is a remarkable 17th-century house with a delightful walled garden and orangery. And the fine Jacobean Blickling Hall is supposedly home to Anne Boleyn's headless ghost. These ancient houses hark back to an era of untold luxury. But for all their extravagance, they never had wi-fi.

COOL FACTOR Upmarket facilities in a peaceful woodland glade with occasional antlered visitors.

WHO'S IN? Everyone and everything – except generators.

ON SITE There are 100 pitches with hook-ups and 25 without for tents, caravans, and motorhomes, set out across 9 acres. Pitches with hook-ups are on either side of the gravel paths, divided by low hedges; the others are on a grassy area next to the lake. The facilities aren't as swanky in Muntjac Meadow (through the woods), but here there's a communal campfire each evening. The site shop sells basics, and locally produced meat. No noise after 11pm.

OFF SITE Felbrigg Hall (01263 837444; see www. nationaltrust.org.uk) and Blickling Hall (01263 738030) near Aylsham are both within a few miles; and the seaside towns of Cromer and Sheringham are good for sunny days.

FOOD AND DRINK There are hog roasts on the main site on summer Saturday nights. The Alby Horse Shoes Inn (01263 761378) is a traditional pub on the main road serving real ales and a locally biased menu. If you're exploring the coast, stop in at the 300-year-old Red Lion Inn (01263 825408) in Upper Sheringham; it has a Snug Bar and menu featuring locally caught fish.

GETTING THERE From Norwich, take the A140 towards Cromer; 5 miles beyond Aylsham, turn right towards Suffield Green (White Post Road), and the main site is about ½ mile along, on the right.

PUBLIC TRANSPORT Take the bus from Norwich towards Cromer, getting off at the Hanworth old post office stop, and walk down the road to the park. The nearest train stations are at North Walsham, Gunton, and Cromer.

OPEN All year. Muntjac Meadow August only.

THE DAMAGE Tent plus 2 people and a car £11.50–£15.50.

overstrand

Go Camping UK at Overstrand, Beach Close, Overstrand, Cromer, Norfolk, NR27 0PJ   01379 678711   see www.gocampinguk.co.uk

Small but perfectly located, this campsite sits atop the Norfolk cliffs with lovely views across the sea and miles of sandy beach stretching out below. Run by Go Camping UK, it's comprised of 10 'ready' tents in a line along the back of the site; and the rest of the small, flat field provides 45 unmarked pitches just for tents – not even campervans can sneak in.

Two miles along the coast from the seaside town of Cromer, which you can reach either by walking along the beach or the cliff-top path, the campsite forms a temporary summer extension to the pretty village of Overstrand. With a good pub, a well-stocked shop and post office, a café, and a children's playground next door to the site, the village meets all a camper's needs, and more besides. And while kids scramble down the cliffs to the beach from the path running along the front of the site, adults can reach it by the more sedate routes leading from the adjacent car park.

Denise and her family run the site and camp alongside you in one of their ready tents; rustling up cooked breakfasts, toasted sandwiches, and pub-type food in the evenings from the onsite Cabin Café.

COOL FACTOR For location[3], this one's hard to beat.

WHO'S IN? Tents, dogs, groups – yes. Vanners – no.

ON SITE Hot showers, toilets, and basins in one block; washing-up sinks and a washing machine (£3) in another. The café has an indoor games area with table tennis and table football, a freezer for cold packs, and an electricity supply for charging phones. No campfires.

OFF SITE The North Norfolk Coast Path (or Peddars Way) runs along the front of the site and a 40-minute walk along this takes you into the seaside town of Cromer. The National Trust's Felbrigg Hall and Sheringham Park are also nearby.

FOOD AND DRINK The White Horse (01263 579237), on Overstrand's High Street, dishes up Thornham oysters, Morston cockles, and other locally sourced fare.

GETTING THERE Take the A140 towards Cromer and, just before you reach the town, turn right at a roundabout (signposted Overstrand). Continue into Overstrand, then follow signs to the long-stay car park; the site is just past this.

PUBLIC TRANSPORT Take the train to Cromer then a taxi.

OPEN August only. www.goodintents-uk.co.uk members (£5 fee) can camp at special rates in late July and early September.

THE DAMAGE Pitch £8 per night, plus adult £3, child/dog £2. Ready tent (sleeps 5) from £206 for a weekend (3 nights).

pinewoods

Pinewoods Holiday Park, Beach Road, Wells-next-the-Sea, Norfolk, NR23 1DR   01328 710439   www.pinewoods.co.uk

Beach huts are a great British tradition. Maybe it's the fact that we can never trust the weather enough to be able to spend a whole day on the beach without shelter. Or maybe it's because most of us can't afford a home by the sea. Either way, these quirky little colourful boxes have become an endearing symbol of the British seaside. And at Pinewoods campsite, in Wells-next-the-Sea on the north Norfolk coast, you can rent one by the day, complete with deckchairs and a windbreak.

Pinewoods isn't a typical *Cool Camping* site. Owned by the Coke family – residents of the local manor house Holkham Hall – it's a big, commercial outfit with options for tenters often limited to a field by the boating lake. But come summer, the site opens up the Horse Paddock, a huge and somewhat wild area in contrast to the regimented static caravans dominating the main site. Here you can pick your own pitch and spread out among the swathes of tall grasses. And while the campsite may lack direct sea views and its own expanse of golden sands, that's where the beach huts come in – just a 10-minute walk away on a fantastic beach.

COOL FACTOR Pine-edged dunes and beach huts in reach.

WHO'S IN? Tents, dogs, groups – yes. Vanners – no.

ON SITE The Horse Paddock is a large open site with unmarked pitches for up to 300 tents. It's a bit of a trek to the facilities blocks (with loos and hot showers) on the main site, but there's a row of portaloos and running water in the field. No advance bookings, and no campfires.

OFF SITE Wells has a quay and plenty of quaint, narrow lanes to wander. One of Britain's loveliest beaches, Holkham Bay, is just up the coast, as is Holkham Hall (www.holkham. co.uk), where you'll find plenty to explore.

FOOD AND DRINK For a local pint and good-value bar food, head into Wells for the Globe Inn (01328 710206). The Victoria (01328 713230) is an exceptional gastropub at the entrance to Holkham Hall, with a regularly changing menu.

GETTING THERE From the A149 coast road, follow signs to Wells-next-the-Sea and then to the beach. Pinewoods is almost at the end of Beach Road, on the left.

PUBLIC TRANSPORT Take the train to Kings Lynn and then the popular Coasthopper bus to Wells.

OPEN March–end October. The Horse Paddock is only open in the 6-week school summer holidays.

THE DAMAGE Tent (sleeping up to 11) £11–£30; dog £3.

deepdale

Deepdale Camping, Deepdale Farm, Burnham Deepdale, Norfolk, PE31 8DD   01485 210256   www.deepdalebackpackers.co.uk

As the season of mists and mellow fruitfulness approaches, many campsites begin to close their gates. But this is just when Deepdale Camping, with its cosy tipis and yurts nestled between tent pitches, comes into its own. Which is just as well, because the word is that there's no better time to visit the north Norfolk coast than in autumn and winter, when the crowds of summer holidaymakers have dispersed and the county is a resplendent vision of russet forests and blush-coloured clouds. By day the campsite offers views over downs, marshland, and Scolt Head Island. At dusk the sky is split by inky-black arrowheads of geese, while behind Deepdale, the hazy calm of miles of marshland is broken only by abandoned boats and impressive sails. Then at night the dazzlingly starry sky can take your breath away. There's an annual programme of events on offer, with everything from writers' retreats, yoga, and relaxation to conservation weekends and singles' walking weeks. A stay here gives you the chance to savour the season and trade lazy summer camping for a wholly different and invigorating experience.

COOL FACTOR An autumn and winter wonderland.
WHO'S IN? Tents, small campervans, dogs – yes. Caravans, unsupervised under-21s, groups with more than 2 tents, tents over 6 metres – no.
ON SITE Six tipis and 2 yurts scattered among 82 tent pitches spread out across 5 paddocks. Facilities include eco-friendly hot showers, toilets, and washing-up facilities with water heated by solar panels and an oil burner back-up; onsite camping shop and the excellent and great-value Deepdale Café next door serves everything from quality English breakfasts to chunky home-made soups. No campfires.
OFF SITE Titchwell Marsh (01485 210779) is an autumnal must for watching migrating geese, lovely walks in golden-hued coastal landscapes, and warming cuppas in its café.
FOOD AND DRINK The White Horse (01485 210262), down the road has a buzzy dining room with views.
GETTING THERE The site is just off the A149 coast road, about midway between Hunstanton and Wells-next-the-Sea.
PUBLIC TRANSPORT Take the Coasthopper bus from Kings Lynn to Burnham Deepdale, alighting outside the site.
OPEN All year (advance bookings; min. 7 nights July–August).
THE DAMAGE Adult £4.50–£9; child £2.50–£5. Tipi £40–£114 (depending on size; season) per night; yurt £50–£145.

jubilee park

Jubilee Caravan Park, Stixwould Road, Woodhall Spa, Lincolnshire, LN10 6QH 01526 352448 see www.e-lindsey.gov.uk

Unusually for a campsite, this one is run by a local council and actually sits within the grounds of the town's park. So while you may not get that away-from-it-all feeling offered by rural campsites, you do have an outdoor heated swimming pool, children's playground, bowling green, cricket field, pitch and putt, tennis courts, café, cycle hire, and even a croquet lawn on your tent-step. All without the holiday park atmosphere these facilities would usually generate, as this is a quiet, low-key place.

The campsite has been here for decades – one caravanner has been returning for more than 30 years now – so the landscaping is established and mature, with a line of weeping willows lounging across the centre and tall hedges offering privacy and shelter from the very minor adjacent road. And while the lido is the big pull for many campers here, Woodhall Spa is a pretty and interesting town that deserves exploration. Full of independent shops and cafés, and with an old-fashioned cinema and tea house just across the road from the site, it also has an interesting history as an Edwardian spa town and base for the RAF 617 (Dambuster) Squadron.

COOL FACTOR Holiday park facilities minus the mayhem.
WHO'S IN? Tents, campervans, caravans, dogs, groups – yes.
ON SITE Total of 98 pitches (with and without hook-ups) spread across 5 flat camping areas, 1 for long-term caravans. The toilet/shower (2W, 2M) block is a bit on the municipal side, but it is adequate and regularly cleaned. No campfires.
OFF SITE The pool is open end May–early September pretty much all day, every day. A nostalgic visit to the Kinema in the Woods (01526 352166) includes organ music and an intermission to buy sweets and ice creams.
FOOD AND DRINK A mile or so down the road is the small pub and restaurant at Village Limits (01526 353312; www.villagelimits.co.uk) – regular winner of local food awards. Head to Just Desserts in town for ice cream treats, and the Bakery & Delicatessen for upmarket picnic fare.
GETTING THERE From the A1, take the A153 to Tattershall and then follow the B1192 to Woodhall Spa. There are signs to Jubilee Park as you enter the town.
PUBLIC TRANSPORT National Express coaches stop at Woodhall Spa en route between London and Grimsby. Local buses from Boston, Spalding, Horncastle, and Lincoln call here.
OPEN April–October.
THE DAMAGE A tent plus 2 people £8.50–£15 per night.

central

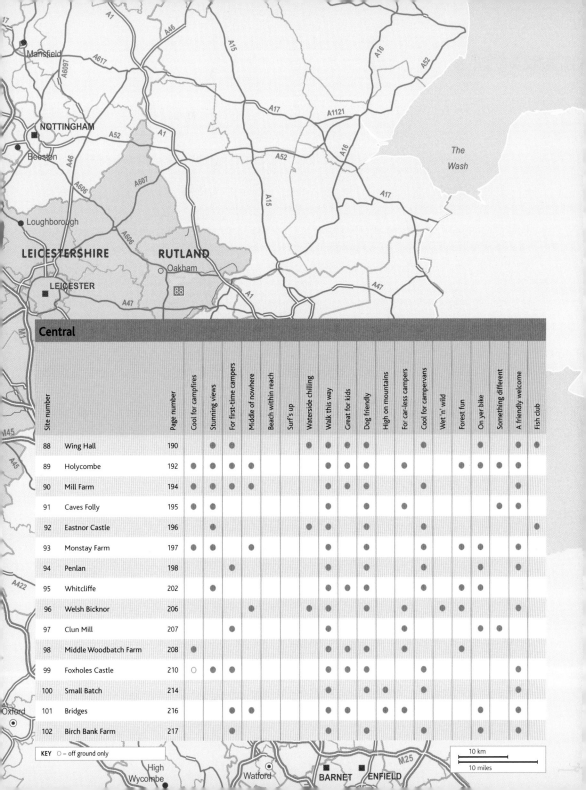

Central

Site number		Page number	Cool for campfires	Stunning views	For first-time campers	Middle of nowhere	Beach within reach	Surf's up	Waterside chilling	Walk this way	Great for kids	Dog friendly	High on mountains	For car-less campers	Cool for campervans	Wet 'n' wild	Forest fun	On yer bike	Something different	A friendly welcome	Fish club
88	Wing Hall	190		●	●				●	●	●	●			●			●		●	●
89	Holycombe	192	●	●	●	●				●	●	●		●			●	●	●	●	
90	Mill Farm	194	●	●	●	●				●	●				●					●	
91	Caves Folly	195	●	●						●		●			●				●	●	
92	Eastnor Castle	196		●					●	●		●			●						●
93	Monstay Farm	197	●	●		●				●		●					●	●		●	
94	Penlan	198			●						●							●			
95	Whitcliffe	202		●						●	●	●					●	●			
96	Welsh Bicknor	206			●					●	●				●	●	●			●	
97	Clun Mill	207			●					●					●			●	●		
98	Middle Woodbatch Farm	208	●							●	●	●								●	
99	Foxholes Castle	210	○	●	●					●	●	●			●					●	
100	Small Batch	214		●						●	●	●		●						●	
101	Bridges	216			●	●				●	●	●	●	●						●	
102	Birch Bank Farm	217		●							●								●	●	

KEY ○ – off ground only

10 km
10 miles

wing hall

Wing Hall, Wing, Oakham, Rutland, LE15 8RY   01572 737090/737283   www.winghall.co.uk

The 100 acres of garden and grassland surrounding Wing Hall make for a near-perfect camping spot. Sitting just outside the pretty Rutland village of Wing, the site overlooks a collage of woods and rolling fields of wheat, rape, and (on closer inspection) buttercups. And just a mile down the road is the lovely 3,100-acre reservoir, Rutland Water. Created by flooding in 1974, the lake and its environs now provide a haven for wildlife, and sport and leisure opportunities – with the 25-mile track around its perimeter making a super cycle route.

Robin Curley's great-great-grandfather built Wing Hall in 1891; she has lived here all her life, long before tiny Rutland regained its independence as a county. The campsite used to be a basic fiver-a-night stop, but Robin and her five children have since created something sophisticated. Son Lyndon has transformed the onsite shop into a delectable deli stocked with locally sourced organic produce, artisan breads, wines, and ales alongside the usual basics, and daughter Zia runs the Veranda Café. Enjoying one of her cream teas on the lawn, you can easily forget you're on a campsite – it feels more like the grounds of a stately home. And despite its popularity, with the number of free-range children often matching the 100 or so roaming hens, the no-music policy helps to maintain an air of peace. As night falls, parents swiftly collect up their charges in compliance with one of the few onsite rules – kids back under supervision after dark. And if splendid isolation is required, there are plenty of nooks and crannies and hideaway pitches to hole up in.

COOL FACTOR If you weren't to the manor born this is a great place to play pretend.

WHO'S IN? Tents, caravans, dogs (on leads) – yes. Young/single-sex/3 or more tents groups – by arrangement only.

ON SITE Just 20 of the 250 pitches are for caravans. Seven new showers have joined 5 older coin-operated (50p pieces) ones; 6 covered alfresco washing-up sinks; and 2 blocks of toilets complete the facilities, although there are plans for a washing machine. Fish (and birdwatch) on the 2 lakes at the bottom of the estate for a daily fee. No campfires.

OFF SITE Right next door, Art de Jardin showcases contemporary artwork on selected days between June and August. At Rutland Water, Normanton Church Museum (01572 653026) charts the history of the reservoir, and the Rutland Belle (01572 787630) cruises around the shoreline from Whitwell. The Rock Blok outdoor adventure centre (01780 460060) has a high-rope course and abseil tower.

FOOD AND DRINK The Veranda Café opens at weekends; if you want to venture further afield, the 17th-century Kings Arms (01572 737634) in Wing is a short walk away and has real ales and top-notch, local, seasonal food.

GETTING THERE From the A47 take the A6003, on the outskirts of Uppingham, towards Oakham. At Preston, turn right after the village pub, signposted Wing. Follow the road up the hill to Wing and turn right into the campsite, which is at the top.

PUBLIC TRANSPORT Train to Oakham, then either the Rutland Flyer bus towards Corby, which passes through Wing once a day in one direction and twice in the other (Mon–Sat), or a taxi (around £10).

OPEN All year.

THE DAMAGE Adult £7 per night; child (under-14) £3.50.

holycombe

Holycombe, Whichford, Shipston-on-Stour, Warwickshire, CV36 5PH   01608 684239   www.holycombe.com

Historic Warwickshire is geographically and culturally (as birthplace of the Bard) at the heart of England, boasting some of the country's most quintessentially English towns and villages. Sadly, for enthusiasts of the very British pastime of camping, it has tended to offer little in the way of *A Midsummer Night's Dream* under canvas. The village of Whichford, however, is harbouring one of the county's best-kept secrets; with its mash-up of the medieval, middle-eastern, and the mystical, Holycombe surely won't stay unknown for long.

The six-acre site is built in the grounds of a Norman castle, the legacy of which is a splendid water-filled moat harbouring carp among its bulrushes. Local mystics have it that Holycombe was a sacred Neolithic site, too, evidenced by six converging ley lines, and with a stone circle to venerate that unusual spiritual asset. The irony is that this rich heritage lay beneath a scrapyard until Sally and Andy Birtwell built their eco-home and house of healing, overlooked by an alternative campsite perfect for purists and – with furnished Bedouin, tipi, and bell tents – part-timers.

Adjoining the wildlife-filled Site of Special Interest, Whichford Wood, Holycombe has a natural beauty to match its rich history, too. It's also handily located a short walk from a classic Cotswold pub. So after a long ramble, or a pint up the road, you can light a campfire as dusk settles on the valley, and banter long into the night about whether ley lines really do exist, or ponder on what might be lurking at the bottom of that mysterious moat.

COOL FACTOR *Countryfile* meets *Time Team* with a sprinkling of *The Blair Witch Project*.

WHO'S IN? Tents, groups, families, dogs – yes. Demi-glampers and lovers of alternative therapies (treatments like acupuncture and Kinesiology are available at Holycombe House). Camper/caravans aren't catered for, but permitted.

ON SITE Campfires allowed, and wood supplied. Enhance the vibe of this extraordinary setting by camping in a Bedouin tent, one of 2 bell tents, or a majestic tipi (all equipped with futon mattresses and snug touches), and for special occasions a long-barn yurt is available. The kitchen log cabin has a fridge, sink, electric cooker, and seating. Two hot electric showers and 3 loos (2 compost, 1 flush). Light sleepers beware – nearby church bells ring every quarter-hour.

OFF SITE Holycombe adjoins Whichford Wood, where you might see Muntjac deer, polecats, or kingfishers. Buy a hand-made memento from Whichford Pottery (01608 684416).

FOOD AND DRINK Wander the ½ mile to the Norman Knight (01608 684621) for traditional ales, flagstone floors, exposed timbers, and gastropub-grub while the kids run free on the village green. Wyatts Farm Shop (01608 684835), near Greater Rollright, has a good choice of local meat and veg.

GETTING THERE Take the A3400 northbound at Chipping Norton roundabout. Follow signs for Whichford and, soon after the speed limit sign as you enter the village, take the first right down a steep lane; Holycombe is down on the right.

PUBLIC TRANSPORT Moreton-in-Marsh station is 5 miles away; a taxi to Holycombe will cost roughly £15.

OPEN All year. Bedouin, bell tents, and tipi May–September.

THE DAMAGE Adult £7.50 per night; child (3 to 16 years) £3.75, under-2s free. Bedouin/bell tent £25; tipi £40; long-barn yurt on request – all 2-night min. stay at weekends.

mill farm

Mill Farm, Barton Road, Long Compton, Shipston-on-Stour, Warwickshire, CV36 5NZ   01608 684663   herricksalmon@vodafoneemail.co.uk

Mill Farm campsite lies in the land that time forgot. You approach through a time warp of unkempt country lanes, and the farmyard and surrounding buildings are delightfully rustic. It's just a large, no-frills field in quiet scenery, and you can pitch where you want, when you want, and light a campfire where you want, when you want. Dogs, kids, and ball games are all embraced as part of the place's genuinely relaxed vibe. The family owners are welcoming and happy to help with anything you need, including photocopies of the local – very beautiful and unspoilt – dragonfly nature trail, named so for its shape. A 10-minute wander along the lane into Long Compton is a pleasant way to pass some time; pick up a paper, pop into the pub, or purchase some produce from a pavement stall.

If it's windy, pitching by the hedge gives good shelter. And lighting a fire adds to the warmth and ambience; settle near your own fire pit, or join someone else's – it's that kind of place. People come back year after year; one camper told us that it hasn't changed in the 30 years he's been visiting. And for that, we can all be very grateful.

COOL FACTOR A huge, relaxed field with campfires.

WHO'S IN? Every man and his dog are welcome.

ON SITE Campfires allowed in fire pits dotted around the field. 'Officially' 11 spacious pitches. No hook-ups. Clean loos with basins and plenty of free hot water, but no showers. Basic and clean washing-up area. Plenty of space to play ball games; lovely donkeys to stroke and chickens to watch. Friendly owners happy to freeze ice blocks.

OFF SITE The historic towns of Moreton-in-Marsh and Chipping Norton are both within 6 miles and offer a variety of historical architecture and tea, antique, and interiors shops.

FOOD AND DRINK When available you can buy fresh free-range eggs at the farm door. Honesty-box local produce is a mile away in Barton and ½ mile away in Long Compton. Moreton-in-Marsh has a choice of restaurants and a weekly market on Tuesdays, selling everything from fresh fish, veg, and bread to all kinds of home hardware.

GETTING THERE From the A3400 at Long Compton (the church on your left), take the next left into Barton Road. Mill Farm is ½ mile up the road, on the right.

PUBLIC TRANSPORT Train to Moreton-in-Marsh, then taxi.

OPEN March–October.

THE DAMAGE £7–£8 per pitch, per night.

caves folly

Caves Folly Eco Campsite, Evendine Lane, Colwall, nr Malvern, Worcestershire, WR13 6DU   01684 540631   www.cavesfolly.com

You can make your way to Caves Folly Eco Campsite by public transport and be collected, but you're positively encouraged to arrive on foot, bike, or even horseback (stabling can be arranged locally). A no-car policy is the only rule at this most laid-back and welcoming of places to stay.

You can pitch wherever you like in the lusciousness of the organic glade and wild-flower meadow. The time of year shapes what extent of labyrinth the glade will be in. Spring flowers make way for bending branches laden with fruit come autumn. The campsite is adjoined to the owner's organic nursery, so a mass of colour and scent emits from the flowerbeds and greenhouses, while the backdrop is the stunning British Camp – an Iron-Age hill fort atop the most easterly of the Malvern Hills that inspired many a poet, including WH Auden. You will awaken to the sound of wild birds and perhaps a field mouse or two. And when you doze off, it'll be to the sound of your personal campfire's crackling embers. Just don't be tempted to say 'Will my car be all right parked around the corner?' You'll be (very politely) turned away.

COOL FACTOR An eco-site surrounded by flowers and with the Malverns for a backdrop.
WHO'S IN? Tents, dogs, groups – yes. Any motors – no.
ON SITE Campfires allowed anywhere on site. Pitch wherever you want among the 2 acres – in the open field or shady glade in the orchard. Currently campers use the loo and shower attached to owner Wil's house, and the adjoining log cabin when it's empty, but new facilities are planned. Wil is very helpful and happy to freeze ice blocks and other bits.
OFF SITE The Malvern Hills offer no shortage of outdoor walks and bike trails (see www.malverntrail.co.uk). Take a bottle with you to fill with the famous water from one of the many shrine-like springs dotted around the hills – the village of Malvern Wells is a particularly good spot for them. The Malvern Theatres (01684 892277) is an arts centre featuring the latest cinema releases and contemporary plays.
FOOD AND DRINK The onsite shop has lots of in-season organic goodies. The Wellington Inn (01684 540269) serves yummy food within strolling distance. The gorgeous market town of Ledbury, 3 miles away, has some great food shops.
PUBLIC TRANSPORT Train/bus to Colwall and 5-min walk.
OPEN April–October.
THE DAMAGE From £6 per person, per night.

eastnor castle

Eastnor Castle, Ledbury, Herefordshire, HR8 1RL   01531 633160   www.eastnorcastle.com

The sign of a really good campsite is when you can crawl from your tent in the morning and find yourself gazing into the eyes of a young stag – not the bleary-eyed groom-to-be variety, but a real red deer. Camp at the top of Eastnor Castle's 23-acre camping field – right next to their deer park – and there's every chance it could happen to you.

If you time your arrival right, there are some pretty fantastic places to pitch down at the foot of the field, too, by the lakes (due to the need to rotate pitches this bit isn't always open, so ring first). On the slopes opposite, in a whirl of trees and hills, sits Eastnor Castle, a fairy-tale confection built in the early 19th century. Little wonder the park is a designated Area of Outstanding Natural Beauty.

The site is closed for five weeks each summer to host The Big Chill festival, but that should still allow plenty of good sunshine time for a thorough wander around the estate. The absolutely unmissable experience here, though, is climbing the hill through the deer park to the obelisk at the summit. It offers an even better view of the Malvern Hills than that afforded at the campsite – so take a camera along.

COOL FACTOR Red deer for neighbours, and castle views.

WHO'S IN? Tents, campervans, caravans, dogs (on leads), big groups, young groups (with an organisation) – yes.

ON SITE Little in terms of facilities on the 23-acre site – just some standpipes and a CDP. Licence to fish in the lakes £5 a day. The castle has its own gift shop and café. Those without their own loo are not allowed to stay here. No campfires.

OFF SITE The castle holds events such as open-air theatre, and is very child friendly. Campers can get a family ticket (2 adults, 3 children) for half price (£11.63).

FOOD AND DRINK Ledbury is home to swish new café-deli Cameron and Swan (01531 636791), but its pubs are trumped by the Oak Inn (01531 640954) at Staplow.

GETTING THERE Leave the M50 at junction 2 and take the A417 into Ledbury before following the Eastnor Castle signs on to the A449 (signposted Worcester and Malvern). After 1 mile turn right again on to the A438. The entrance to the castle is on the right after 1 mile.

PUBLIC TRANSPORT Train to Ledbury then a taxi ride or walk (it's only 2 miles).

OPEN Variable – call or check website.

THE DAMAGE Caravan, campervan, trailer, or family tent £6.50 per night (concessions available); small tent £3.

monstay farm

Monstay Farm, Burrington, Ludlow, Shropshire, SY8 2HE   01584 318007   www.monstayfarm.co.uk

Some say that Britain's decline as a world power is directly attributable to the dearth of campsites offering facilities for campers who want to bring their horse along. If that's so, no one can blame the owners of Monstay Farm, whose stables are ready and waiting (though will need to be pre-booked). Opened in 2009, the 100-acre sheep-and-cattle farm's campsite sports two slightly sloping fields, one with a gorgeous view west to the Cambrian Mountains, while the other looks south over a flock of sheep and Mortimer Forest. The nearby facilities are basic but clean. And the whole shebang is up a very long track and thus away from traffic noise. Kids intent on hiding-and-seeking, den-building, or just getting away from their fuddy-duddy parents for a while will delight in the woods adjacent to the site. Off-road cyclists of all ages, meanwhile, can take off on the trail that runs through the farm or head for the paths that cross Mortimer Forest. The River Teme, which flows a few miles to the north, is a hit with wild swimmers, while those who prefer the dryness of footpaths can enjoy a pleasant circular walk down to the church at Burrington.

COOL FACTOR Want to take your horse camping? Trot right up.

WHO'S IN? Tents, campervans, caravans, dogs, big groups – yes. Motorhomes, young groups – no.

ON SITE Communal fire circle and fire bowls for hire (£5), and kindling and firewood for sale. Pitches: 20 for tents, 5 for caravans; 6 electric hook-ups. Three somewhat rustic loos and 2 showers. The owners will freeze ice packs and groceries can be ordered in advance. Downside: an area next to the site strewn with farm equipment isn't all that visually appealing.

OFF SITE A mountain bike trail runs across the farm and there are more in Mortimer Forest, which is also home to bridleways and, for walkers, both the Herefordshire Trail and the new Mortimer Trail (see www.ldwa.org.uk).

FOOD AND DRINK Two really good pubs in the area: the Riverside (01568 708440) at Aymestry with posh nosh and beer garden, and the Royal George (01544 267322) at Lingen.

GETTING THERE Follow directions to Whitcliffe (see p205) and Monstay Farm is 2 miles further up the road.

PUBLIC TRANSPORT Train to Ludlow, then taxi (£6).

OPEN Easter–late October (weather dependent).

THE DAMAGE Tent: adult £5.50 per night; child (5 to 16 years) £1.50, under-5s free. Caravan: £10; hook-up £3.

The further west one ventures into Herefordshire the more it seems like a different country all of its own, lost in some distant time; the sort of place you could expect to turn a corner and bump into a buxom milkmaid shouldering a rustic yoke. It's no surprise, then, when the friendly owners at Penlan Campsite inform us that the 'modern' part of their stone and wooden farmhouse dates from the late 1600s (the rest of it being a good hundred years older).

A mere half-mile from the Welsh border and seemingly hundreds of miles from anywhere anyone might call home, Penlan Farm is a 50-acre smallholding where Peter and Margaret run a flock of sheep and a herd of cattle organically, and where an apple orchard blossoms majestically each spring. Whether the livestock appreciate the views or not is a matter for speculation. Visitors to the site, however, can hardly fail to do so. To the far right are the iconic Brecon Beacons; while next to them lurk the hulking Black Mountains, untamed by the gentler Herefordshire hills to the east. Drop down a field or two (the owners encourage their guests to go for a wander) and look to the left and there are the Malverns. On a clear day you can even pick out the village of Birdlip on the edge of the Cotswolds, some 60 miles away.

penlan

Penlan Caravan Park and Campsite, Brilley, Hay-on-Wye, Herefordshire, HR3 6JW   01497 831485   www.penlancampsite.co.uk

The campsite here first started taking customers in the 1960s, but was closed a decade later when the farm became the property of the National Trust (which also owns the exquisite Cwmmau Farm a few fields away – well worth the stroll). Peter and Margaret – both born and bred in the area – decided in 1997 to reopen the site (which doesn't belong to the Trust) and have been sharing its extraordinary peace and quiet with campers ever since. The camping area is a small, gently sloping cutlass-shaped swathe of lovingly tended greensward. The caravan pitches – eight of which are seasonal – are at the back, while campers get the pick of the front row seats and enjoy the additional advantage of the shelter afforded by a low beech hedge.

The lane that runs directly behind the site is, happily, almost exclusively the domain of infrequent tractors. It's a pity that telegraph poles cross the field below, but in summer it does mean that the wires between them are lined with swallows and pied wagtails. Look higher up and you might be lucky enough to catch a red kite riding the thermals while, closer to hand, there are various species of tit that nest in the eight boxes dotted about the site.

As evening draws on, and just as the streets of Hereford light up to create a glowing display

in the valley below, the horseshoe bats living in the farm's ancient barns take flight. Finally, as night falls, the woods behind the campsite are haunted by the calls of tawny owls. For those who enjoy looking down once in a while, the good news is that not all the local wildlife is airborne: a pond on the farm is home to great crested newts, who do most of their scurrying about on warm nights.

COOL FACTOR A tranquil piece of lovely borderland in Britain's own twilight zone.

WHO'S IN Tents, campervans, caravans, dogs (on leads) – yes. Groups – no.

ON SITE There are 12 touring pitches (of which 10 have hook-ups) and 12 more for tents. An unobtrusive hut houses immaculately clean and modern loos (1M, 2W) and 2 electric showers (1M, 1W). While there are no facilities specifically geared to the needs of disabled people, there are at least no steps on the site to negotiate. A giant Jenga set awaits children of all ages. Ice packs can be frozen in the freezer part of the fridge/freezer in the barn, where there are also tables piled high with leaflets on local attractions. The nearest shop is a Londis at Witney (3 miles), though Kington (4 miles) boasts a Co-op and a Spar. There are no campfires allowed, but the owners do have BBQs on stands that can be borrowed free of charge (don't forget to bring your own charcoal, though).

OFF SITE Hay-on-Wye, with its cafés, independent shops, whole host of second-hand bookshops, and world-famous literary festival, is just 7 miles away and well worth a day trip or two. (If you're planning to camp at Penlan during the festival do book up well in advance.) The black and white villages of Herefordshire are on the doorstep, and the official 40-mile trail around them makes for an excellent day's cycle (see www.blackandwhitehouses.co.uk). At Paddles and Pedals (01497 820604; www.canoehire.co.uk) in Hay-on-Wye you can hire a kayak or Canadian canoe and have an adventure along the River Wye (and, best of all, they'll pick you up from wherever you end up), or you can pick up a bicycle to hit the roads and do all the hard work yourself. There are also no fewer than 5 pony-trekking companies in the area (see www.hay-on-wye.co.uk).

FOOD AND DRINK The Sun Inn (01544 327677; www.thesuninnwinforton.co.uk) at Winforton comes recommended (but do reserve a table). The Erwood Station Craft Centre and Gallery (01982 560674; www.erwood-station.co.uk) at Erwood has a good café, as well as a resident wood turner. Connoisseurs of the fermented apple should head for the presses at Dunkertons Cider (01544 388653; www.dunkertons.co.uk) in Pembridge. While at New House Farm (01544 327849) in Almeley they make their own organic ice cream.

GETTING THERE Don't put the postcode into your satnav – you'll end up half a mile away and in a bit of a jam if you're coming with a caravan. From Leominster, follow the A44 west towards Rhayader until it swerves around Kington. One mile after the second roundabout, turn left (signposted Kington Town Centre, Hergest, Brilley). After ½ mile, take the second turn right (signposted Brilley). After exactly 4 miles, look out for a National Trust signpost on the left (blink and you'll miss it!). At the same junction, turn left into Apostles Lane. Penlan is the first farmhouse on the right.

OPEN Easter–end October.

THE DAMAGE Advance booking only. Tent: adult £6; child (under 12 years) £3, under-5s free. Caravan/motorhome: £14; awning £2.50; porch awning £1.50; electricity £3. Gazebo £3. Extra car £5 (first car free). Dog £1.50. A slightly higher tariff applies during Bank Holiday weekends.

whitcliffe

Whitcliffe Campsite, North Farm, Whitcliffe, Ludlow, Shropshire, SY8 2HD   01584 872026   www.northfarmludlow.co.uk

It was all very well for Dante to claim that the only perfect view is the one of the sky above our heads, but then he never climbed the hill west of Ludlow to Whitcliffe Campsite. Had he done so he might have had some serious second thoughts, for here is a panorama to rival any cloudscape you might care to imagine.

Indeed, given the right weather, a stay at Whitcliffe allows for one of the great British camping experiences: settling down in the early evening to watch as the sun, dropping below the hill at your back, lights up Ludlow's parish church in the valley at your feet. As the minutes slip by, the stone tower of St Laurence's turns from russet to gold and, at last, to jet-black.

The difficulty is in keeping one's eyes on the church, because just to the left of it is the once mighty Ludlow Castle, while behind the town the summits of Titterstone Clee and Brown Clee vie for attention. After dark, the lights of Ludlow huddle together as if for protection from these twin hulks. Or at least that's what appears to be happening, especially if you've watched the spectacle while sipping at a bottle of the Ludlow Brewing Company's excellent Boiling Well.

Several cats patrol the grounds, one of whom is very friendly should you be in the mood for a bit of feline fussing. Meanwhile, if you hear a high piercing cry from the other side of the hedge, get your camera out and stalk quietly towards it (David Attenborough-style) because it will almost certainly have come from a peacock.

But Whitcliffe isn't just about tranquil evenings and picturesque birdlife – the owners run a riding school, too, so if you book in advance you can go for a hack through Mortimer Forest which, very conveniently, is right next door (£19 per hour, minimum age five years, weight limit 101 kilograms). The forest – which is the remnant of a great Saxon wooded hunting area – is also criss-crossed with trails for walkers and mountain bikers.

A precipitous mile below (the campsite itself is quite steep but has nearly a dozen level pitches), the historic town of Ludlow is a veritable treasure trove of delights. There are the picturesque weirs, over which the mellifluous River Teme flows; the mighty hulk of the Norman-built castle; as well as St Laurence's church, the so-called Cathedral of the Marches (stlaurences.org.uk).

The town was also the first in Britain to declare itself a member of Cittaslow, a movement that aims to improve the quality of living by eschewing the breakneck speeds at which modern life is led. In Ludlow's case, this means that there's a farmers' market (9am–2pm on the second and fourth Thursdays of the month), independent shops dripping with local produce, and more festivals and fairs than might possibly be imagined in one place. These include a transport festival, a music festival, a May Fair, an arts festival (including some open-air Shakespeare plays in the castle), a food and drink festival (foodfestival.co.uk), and a medieval Christmas Fayre (see ludlow.org.uk for a calendar of events).

Ludlow Castle and the River Teme

A special treat for gourmands comes around every August in the shape of the Magnalonga Walk (magnalonga.co.uk), a seven-mile ramble with stops for delicious local food and drink en route. Poetry lovers, meanwhile, may want to pay homage at St Laurence's graveyard where, by the church's north wall, AE Housman's ashes are buried next to the stump of a cherry tree.

COOL FACTOR Where else are you going to get such a stonking grandstand view of Ludlow with riding lessons thrown in?

WHO'S IN? Tents, campervans, caravans, dogs (on leads) – yes. Groups – no.

ON SITE There are 11 level pitches, all with electric hook-ups, and an indeterminate number of sloping ones without. The camping field drops away quite steeply, so if all the level pitches are booked (and they must be booked in advance), be prepared to Velcro your sleeping mat to your groundsheet. There are 3 nice clean loos housed around the farmhouse and stables, a couple of decent (free) showers, and indoor washing-up facilities ranged around a stable yard. Ice packs can be frozen free of charge – just hand them to the owner. No campfires allowed, but bricks are provided for BBQs (and there's a £10 fine for any grass that gets burnt).

OFF SITE Mortimer Forest is right next door, and it would be a shame not to visit for a sylvan stroll or a ride either on a horse or a mountain bike (for which there are signposted trails). Bikes can be hired at Wheely Wonderful Cycling (01568 770755; www.wheelywonderfulcycling.co.uk). Ludlow Castle (01584 873355; www.ludlowcastle.com) is a terrifically well-preserved Norman fortress hosting a busy calendar of events, including medieval games and have-a-go archery. Nearby Stokesay Castle (01588 672544; see www.english-heritage.org.uk) is really just a fortified medieval manor house, but also well worth a visit. For a completely different day out near Church Stretton, the Acton Scott historic working farm (01694 781307; www.actonscott.com) – made famous as the venue for TV's

Victorian Farm and Escape in Time – offers an insight into what life on a Victorian estate might have been like.

FOOD AND DRINK For a real splash out, Mr Underhill's (01584 874431; www.mr-underhills.co.uk), on the banks of the River Teme in Ludlow, is a Michelin-starred restaurant famous for its 9-course market menu of the day. Sadly, the pubs in Ludlow do not have such a great reputation for food, but the Queens (01584 879177; www.thequeensludlow.com) is said to be the best of them. If you're feeling completely indolent, Munchies (01584 872636) will deliver pizza from noon to midnight. Alternatively, the Ludlow Food Centre (confusingly not in Ludlow but at Bromfield – 01584 856000; www.ludlowfoodcentre.co.uk) boasts 8 kitchens producing food and drink to buy, more than 80 per cent of which is sourced from Shropshire and its surrounding counties.

GETTING THERE From the B4361 that runs from north to south through Ludlow (starting off as Corve Street and becoming Old Street) head south over Ludford Bridge. Take the first right (almost immediately). This is the steeply climbing Whitcliffe Road. North Farm (aka Whitcliffe Campsite), which is signposted, is about a mile up the road on the left.

PUBLIC TRANSPORT Take a train to Ludlow, and a taxi from the station to the site should only cost a fiver.

OPEN Easter–late September.

THE DAMAGE Adult £5 per night; child (10 to 16 years) £2, (5 to 9 years) £1, under-5s free. Level pitch £2 extra (and minimum overall charge £12 per night). Awning/gazebo £1. Dog 50p.

welsh bicknor

Welsh Bicknor YHA, nr Goodrich, Ross-on-Wye, Herefordshire, HR9 6JJ   01594 860300   see www.yha.org.uk

The back of beyond. There's nothing quite like being there, but it's an experience few campsites in England can actually guarantee. That's what makes the journey to Welsh Bicknor's hostel so satisfying. Launch yourself up a steep hill from Goodrich Castle and you'll find the road eventually peters out into a treelined lane plunging down the other side into a huge loop of the River Wye. At its very end there is, at last, a pool of sunlight illuminating a patch of the hostel – a vast Victorian former rectory.

Set in 25 acres of woods and pasture, the hostel's campsite is a large field on the other side of a decorously decaying deconsecrated church, and enjoys views of the Forest of Dean. Hidden below the line of trees and bushes that gird the site, the River Wye slinks its way to the hauntingly beautiful bend at Symonds Yat, a couple of miles away. There's a stone jetty at one corner of the field giving access to the river, making it perfect for a paddle-to-your-camp trip. But if you're more the walking-boots-and-jaunty-whistle kind, the Wye Valley Walk runs through the field on its way to all manner of adventures (and Chepstow).

COOL FACTOR Just paddle up and pitch.

WHO'S IN? Everyone (and dogs), apart from caravans.

ON SITE Maximum of 30 people. No hook-ups. It's a 2-minute walk to the facilities – 2 loos (1W, 1M), 3 showers (all unisex), and a fully equipped kitchen shared with hostellers. The red-brick hostel is closed 10am–5pm, but tents can be pitched at any time. An onsite shop sells basic bits (bread, milk, toothpaste). No campfires.

OFF SITE Lovely Goodrich Castle is at the bottom of the hill (see www.english-heritage.org.uk). Canoes can be hired at Ross-on-Wye (01600 890883; www.thecanoehire.co.uk).

FOOD AND DRINK There are 2 very good pubs over the Wye, just across the old railway bridge: the Courtfield Arms (01594 860207) and the Forge Hammer (01594 860310), which doubles up as an Indian restaurant.

GETTING THERE Take the A40 then B4229 to Goodrich village, then the road that crosses eastwards above the B4229, following it up the hill to the hostel, at the very end.

PUBLIC TRANSPORT Two buses run between Monmouth and Ross-on-Wye: no. 34 stops at Goodrich Castle, and no. 35 stops near the railway bridge.

OPEN April–October.

THE DAMAGE £6–£9 per person & £3 non-YHA members.

clun mill

Clun Mill YHA, The Mill, Clun, Craven Arms, Shropshire, SY7 8NY   01588 640582   see www.yha.org.uk

As every fan of AE Housman knows, 'Clunton and Clunbury/Clungunford and Clun/Are the quietest places/Under the sun.' It's refreshing to note that, over 100 years after Shropshire's second-best poet (lest we forget, Wilfred Owen was an Oswestry lad) penned his paean to Clun and its hinterland, the village remains a somnolent backwater, apparently inoculated from the rapid pace of 21st-century life. Less than fittingly then, its youth hostel is housed in a former mill that was probably the noisiest thing in the village during Housman's time.

Today, its old cobbled stable houses comfy chairs and rings to the sound of guests telling tales of the footpath and bridleway. Outside, the hostel's petite grassy grounds provide room for tents. There's a pitch-where-you-like attitude but, by a happy coincidence, the flattest area also offers the best view: over the fields to a wooded hillside. Meanwhile, the photogenic village shakes off its somnolence with surprising frequency. In May, it hosts both a Green Man and a Booze 'n' Blues festival. August is carnival time and, if you're here in October, you can catch the Clun Valley Beer festival.

COOL FACTOR A laid-back site at a lovely old mill.

WHO'S IN? Tents, groups (no more than 20 people) – yes. Campervans, caravans, dogs (except guide dogs) – no.

ON SITE A maximum of 20 campers allowed, leaving plenty of room. There's a clean wet room with loo and shower, and a drying room. Table tennis table and bike storage in the cart house; board games in the hostel. Excellent kitchen with cooker, microwave, fridge/freezer, toaster, and kettle. Unfortunately some electricity lines pass overhead and campfires aren't allowed, but there's a BBQ outside.

OFF SITE The hostel has a folder teeming with local walks accompanied by attractive hand-drawn maps. The Norman castle at Clun is largely ruined, but eerily beautiful.

FOOD AND DRINK Clun's White Horse Inn (01588 640305) gives a discount to YHA members and does brekkies.

GETTING THERE Enter Clun on the A488. Turn east along the High Street, then second left down Ford Street. Turn right at the end, then left down Hospital Lane. Site's on the right.

PUBLIC TRANSPORT Train to Craven Arms and then the shuttle bus to Clun (April–September).

OPEN April–October.

THE DAMAGE £7 per person, per night; Fri/Sat £8 (plus £1.50 per night for non-YHA members).

middle woodbatch farm

Middle Woodbatch Farm, Woodbatch Road, Bishop's Castle, Shropshire, SY9 5JT   07989 496875   www.middlewoodbatchfarm.co.uk

Cross a 170-acre farm that takes a maximum of 10 tents at any one time with friendly owners who hold a relaxed pitch-where-you-like attitude and you've got yourself one very roomy campsite. And if you don't mind a walk to the facilities (about two thirds of a mile at the furthest point), you really can get away from everything and everyone.

A family farm since the 1930s, Middle Woodbatch is close enough to the small town of Bishop's Castle so that its two excellent pubs–cum–microbreweries are within walking distance (about a mile and a half), but just far enough away to feel completely countrified. The farm comes complete with some woodland (build those dens, kids), two top-notch wet rooms (with non-slip cushion flooring), a super-clean campers' kitchen, and an eye-easing view from most fields over the top of its neighbouring town to the distinctive bulk of the Long Mynd. There are also herds of cattle, flocks of sheep, the odd pig, and chickens moseying about.

Walkers (and, hey, amblers and shamblers too) can tumble out of their tents to attack a portion of the 139-mile Shropshire Way, which cruises right through the farm, while the Bishop's Castle Ring (aka the BC Ring), Offa's Dyke Path, and Kerry Ridgeway are but a hot buttered scone's throw away.

At the farmhouse there are three bedrooms for those in your party who prefer a B&B to an airbed & breakfast, while horses in your group can be put up in the farm's stables and put out to graze in a lush field (ready for the Blue Remembered Hills Bridleway, which also runs through the farm).

COOL FACTOR Room to breathe, and then some.

WHO'S IN? Tents, well-behaved dogs – yes. Campervans, caravans, groups – no.

ON SITE Fire bowls for every pitch (firewood £3 per bag). Just 10 pitches, 1 loo, and 2 wet rooms (showers £1 – honesty pot); a bench in the wet room can be used for baby-changing; wheelchair access for loo, but no handrails. Campers' kitchen includes fridge/freezer, microwave, toaster, washing-up sink, kettle, sockets, and info leaflets.

OFF SITE At weekends (2pm–5pm) you can get steamed up at Bishop's Castle Railway and Museum (www.bcrailway.co.uk). The town also has a small leisure centre with a swimming pool (01588 630243). Down the road at Craven Arms there's Mickey Miller's Family Playbarn (01588 673800), should the weather discourage family play outdoors.

FOOD AND DRINK The 2 microbrewery pubs in town are the Six Bells (01588 638930) with its occasional cheery theme night (Dutch dishes, Bulgarian dishes, and more) and the Three Tuns (01588 638797), which has pretensions to gastronomy. The Rocke Cottage Tea Rooms (01588 660631), is a pleasant 1920s/1930s throwback at Clungunford, serving scones, cakes, light lunches, and all manner of teas.

GETTING THERE From the A488 at Bishop's Castle turn west along the B4385 (Brampton Road) and, at the church on your left, turn left (effectively straight ahead) on to Kerry Lane. Take the fourth left on to Woodbatch Road, to the end.

PUBLIC TRANSPORT Either take the train to Church Stretton and shuttle bus (April–September) or train to Shrewsbury and bus no. 552/553, to Bishop's Castle. The owners will pick up from Bishop's Castle by arrangement.

OPEN April–September.

THE DAMAGE Adult £7; child £2.50, under-6s free.

Deli in Bishop's Castle

In a world too often characterised by blandness and uniformity, the creative touches with which Foxholes Castle campsite abound are a balm to the soul. Take the full-sized knight, for instance, who looks out over the owners' castellated roof, his raised sword defying all-comers. Then there's the metal sculpture of a fox skulking around a hedge, the Easter Island head (no campsite should be without one) popping up in the middle of a field, and the little Buddha adorning a quiet corner. These quirky bits and bobs all jumble together to give this large campsite (it covers 10 acres of a 28-acre smallholding), within kissing distance of Bishop's Castle, a very human aspect.

The site is divided into four fields, each with its own character. The top field is a tents-only affair, and has the distinct feel of a hilltop Iron-Age fort, only without the ramparts or information board. There's a slightly more sheltered half-acre field for those who prefer a cosier pitch, a touring field reserved for caravans and campervans, and a slightly out-of-the-way field, which has been largely left to meadow with just a strip around the outside mown for camping (if you're a fan of goldfinches, this is definitely the place for you – they're outnumbered only by the butterflies). And if you forget your tent, a comfy six-bed bunkhouse in the farmyard awaits.

foxholes castle

Foxholes Castle Camping, Montgomery Road, Bishop's Castle, Shropshire, SY9 5HA   01588 638924   www.foxholes-castle.co.uk

There's also a choice of view. You can have hills, hills, hills, or hills. There can be few campsites the length and breadth of England that enjoy such a vista: the foothills of the Cambrian mountain range, the famous bulk of the Long Mynd, Stiperstones – in whose Roman lead mines Wild Edric is said to be buried with his soldiers, ready to fight should England ever be endangered – and a cornucopia of other bumps, knolls, and mounds besides. With an almost 360-degree panorama, it's as near to heaven as a hillophile is ever likely to get.

Walkers are very well catered for, too, with several long-distance footpaths running close by. The Shropshire Way, meanwhile, actually runs right through the site on its giddy 139-mile loop around the county's finest scenery. For the less ambitious, the attractive small town of Bishop's Castle is a five-minute stroll away, with its artsy community and two excellent microbreweries. The only disappointment is the town's name – the eponymous castle is only a wall now, and if you want to see a bishop then you'll just have to bring your own.

Foxholes' owners, Chris and Wendy, are trying to make the site as eco-friendly as possible, and so aside from encouraging recycling, they have just built a new facilities block whose showers are heated by solar power and whose loos are flushed

by rain water. They're also on a mission to make the site as wildlife-friendly as possible, and they've certainly had a great deal of success in attracting birdlife – as a minute spent listening to the seemingly constant riot of birdsong from the trees will confirm. And while you're there, do throw a few coins into the open hand of the Buddha statue. Chris and Wendy have no idea who started this tradition or why, but every so often they scoop up all the money left there and send it off to the Air Ambulance service.

COOL FACTOR Views, views, views (and wildlife).

WHO'S IN? Tents, campervans, caravans, dogs ('must be well-behaved, but we love them'), big groups, (well-mannered) young groups – yes.

ON SITE Washing machine drums on legs are provided for campfires (it's £3 for a bag of logs). The number of pitches is somewhat variable, but there are thought to be 'up to 100'. No hook-ups. The wash-room building is brand new and immaculate inside. Designed by the owners themselves, it is fitted with solar panels providing hot water for the showers and a rain collection facility for loo flushing. There are 7 toilets (4W, 3M), 9 showers, and 3 separate wet rooms (each also with a loo – one of them kitted out for use by people with disabilities). While there's no playground, kids have plenty of room for playing games, and the top field is especially good for kite flying. Ice packs can be popped into the fridge/freezer available to campers. There's a sink for washing-up and hot water with which to do so.

OFF SITE For a small town, Bishop's Castle (www.bishopscastle.co.uk) is a happening place. Each year it plays host to a May Fair (weekend after the first May Bank Holiday); a walking festival (second week of June; www.walkingfestival.co.uk); stone-skimming championships (last Sunday in June; 01588 638818); a carnival (first Sunday in July; 01588 650446); and a beer festival (weekend after the carnival; 01588 630144) among others. If you fancy flying above them all, treat yourself to a paraglide (07774 856056; www.leavesleyaviation.com). Or merely leave the crowds behind by tackling a section of a long-distance footpath.

The Offa's Dyke Path (see www.nationaltrail.co.uk), Wild Edric's Way (see www.ldwa.org.uk), and the Kerry Ridgeway (see tourism.powys.gov.uk) are all within striking distance, the last of these doubling as a cycle route (www.ctc-maps.org.uk) if you're a pedaller rather than a plodder.

FOOD AND DRINK The Castle Hotel (01588 638403; www.the-castle-hotel.co.uk) has a reputation for excellent dishes created from locally sourced produce, and contains some wonderful gardens at the back. (See Middle Woodbatch Farm p208 for details of local pubs.) There's a farmers' market in Bishop's Castle town hall the third Saturday of every month, and an ordinary fruit and veg market there on Fridays. Sol Delicatessen (01588 638190), at the top of the High Street, is full of delicious nibbles and lush liquids with which to wash them down.

GETTING THERE Approach Bishop's Castle along the A488 that runs just to the east of the town. Turn west along the B4384 (Schoolhouse Lane) and first right up the B4385 (Bull Lane). Foxholes Castle is about half a mile along here on your left. There are lots of signs to the campsite in the vicinity so, if in doubt, follow the fox.

PUBLIC TRANSPORT Either take the train to Church Stretton and shuttle bus to Bishop's Castle (April–September; www.shropshirehillsshuttles.co.uk); or train to Shrewsbury and bus no. 552/553 to Bishop's Castle.

OPEN All year.

THE DAMAGE Adult £6 per night; child (under 13 years) £2; dog £1.

small batch

Small Batch Campsite, Ashes Valley, Little Stretton, Church Stretton, Shropshire, SY6 6PW   01694 723358
www.smallbatch-camping.webeden.co.uk

At the foot of the seven-mile hulk that is the Long Mynd, and next to a 17th-century cottage on the outskirts of the village of Little Stretton, sits a little secluded paradise for those who like to combine their camping with a bit of walking. Or even a lot of walking. 'The average walker can get a week's hiking in without once using their car', says Oscar, who has run the site with his wife Pam for over 40 years. Indeed, there's been a campsite here since the 1920s, when Oscar's grandfather William Prince was the owner.

The footpath to the Long Mynd passes right through the campsite and takes walkers alongside a stream gently up the steep-sided Ashes Hollow before suddenly depositing them close to the heavens. The view at the top is one of the great panoramas of the British countryside, and worth every step of the 300-metre climb. There are several ways back to the campsite, so no dull backtracking.

Just up the road, in tea-shop-tastic Church Stretton (where there's a café or tea room for every day of a week-and-a-half), the Shropshire Cakes and Ale Trail passes through on its search for the very best locally produced pints. There's also the Jack Mytton Way, a bridleway that forges a trail around some of the choicest bits of Shropshire. Or you can just make up your own route from the thousand-and-one footpaths that criss-cross the area.

The campsite can get a little busy at weekends in summer, so those who prefer their camping to come with a generous dose of tranquillity should aim to stay here on school nights.

COOL FACTOR The mighty Long Mynd is not on your doorstep, it *is* your doorstep.

WHO'S IN? Tents, campervans, caravans, dogs, young groups (with adult/s) – yes. Big groups – by arrangement.

ON SITE There are 30 pitches in one small, largely flat field, many of which have electric hook-ups. The showers (1W, 1M) and loos (3W, 2M) are rustic but clean. Washing-up is at an outdoor sink, and kids can play in the stream that runs across the entrance to the campsite. Trees are all around, so there's a good deal of shelter. No campfires.

OFF SITE If you've any time off from pounding around the Shropshire Hills you can always pay a visit to Bishop's Castle, Clun, Ludlow, or Shrewsbury. There's also the Acton Scott historic working farm near Church Stretton (01694 781307), which recaptures life on a Victorian estate; or the National Trust's Attingham Park (01743 708123) with its walled garden.

FOOD AND DRINK The Ragleth Inn (01694 722711) is a hop and a skip away (booking advisable). There's a farmers' market in Church Stretton every second and fourth Friday (9am–1pm), and others in Ludlow (second Thursday, 9am–2pm), Bishop's Castle (third Saturday, 9am–2pm), Craven Arms (first Saturday, 9am–2pm), and Knighton (fourth Saturday, 9.30am–1.30pm).

GETTING THERE From the A49 follow Shrewsbury/Church Stretton signs. Take the B5477 to Little Stretton, turn left at the Ragleth Inn and first right. The campsite's beyond the ford.

PUBLIC TRANSPORT Take the train to Church Stretton then bus no. 435 (Minsterley Motors; 01743 791208) to Little Stretton (alighting at the Ragleth Inn).

OPEN Easter–September.

THE DAMAGE One-person tent £10 per night; 2-person tent £12; 2 people 'in a big tent' £14; all else £14. Hook-up £2.

bridges

Bridges Long Mynd YHA, Bridges, Ratlinghope, Shrewsbury, Shropshire, SY5 0SP   01588 650656   see www.yha.org.uk

Tucked away in a valley between two huge ridges – the Long Mynd and Stiperstones – the youth hostel at the hamlet of Bridges was opened in 1931, just a year after the YHA was formed. In common with a handful of the association's hostels, an area has been set aside for campers – here it's a bijou lawn flanked by trees and topped off at one end by a retro caravan.

For first-time campers, or those who like a Plan B in place in case of rain, the great advantage of camping at a hostel is that those under canvas are welcome to use all the facilities that are available to hostellers – except the dorms, of course. Thus at Bridges, in the morning and evening (the hostel is shut during the day), campers can use the lounge, dining room, or kitchen, or even have breakfast and dinner cooked for them by the warden Angela, who grows much of the fruit and veg on site.

There's a pub just around the corner and some fabulous long-distance footpaths to try out – Wild Edric's Way and the Shropshire Way run right past the front gate – and, if you're lucky, you'll be serenaded by curlews for no extra charge.

COOL FACTOR Cosy site with fab facilities.

WHO'S IN? Tents, groups – yes. Vanners, dogs – no.

ON SITE Thirty-six pitches on 2 lawns, with 5 loos and 1 really nice shower. Slide, swings, volleyball net, table tennis, board games, and shallow brook. Tiny shop on site, map hire and map sales, bike shed. Breakfast (£5.50) at 8am – various options, including veggie; dinner (£9.50 for 3 courses) at 7pm; and packed lunches (£5). No campfires, BBQs off ground okay.

OFF SITE The Jack Mytton Way is a 'very cyclable' bridleway from Bridges to Much Wenlock; pony-trekking and horse-riding from Mynderley Stables (01694 751277).

FOOD AND DRINK Local live music pub the Horseshoe Inn (01588 650260) serves food Tues–Sat, or there's the Crown Inn (01588 650613; www.wentnor.com) at Wentnor.

GETTING THERE From the station at Church Stretton (off the A49) head west along the B4371 (Sandford Avenue), straight over the High Street and up the very steep Burway Road. Follow the sign right, to Ratlinghope, where you turn left at the T-junction, then first right. The hostel is on the left.

PUBLIC TRANSPORT Train to Church Stretton and a shuttle bus to Bridges (April–September).

OPEN All year.

THE DAMAGE £7.50 per person, per night (no credit cards).

birch bank farm

Birch Bank Farm, Stamford Lane, Christleton, Chester, Cheshire, CH3 7QD   01244 335233

Pass up a short drive, through a gate, across a small courtyard bordered with flowers, and you'll discover a tiny treat. Birch Bank Farm's campsite runs to a mere half acre, with just 14 pitches, so the words 'sprawling' and 'rammed' never get an airing here. You can plop yourself down in one of the many spots with a view of distant Beeston Castle, or hunker down under one of the apple trees. Loos and showers, meanwhile, are handily housed in a brick outbuilding right next to the farmhouse.

The farm – on which cattle graze – runs to 77 acres and has been in the same family since the farmhouse was built in 1844. The most recent dog to call the place home is a friendly young thing, and the source of no little amusement as he makes repeated dashes in vain pursuit of the many swallows who shoot about at grass level.

Cyclists have the delightful option to ride to the campsite along the Shropshire Union Canal either from Chester or Waverton, while walkers can hop on the towpath at any point from Wolverhampton to the Mersey Estuary. Just turn off at Christleton, and Robert's your mother's brother.

COOL FACTOR Small and friendly: the Ernie Wise of sites.
WHO'S IN? Tents, vanners, dogs (under control), big groups (if they book the whole site) – yes. Young groups – no.
ON SITE Fourteen pitches and 8 hook-ups. Facilities: loos (1W, 1M; and 5W, 1M in a Portakabin – with more planned); showers (1W, 1M); ice packs refrozen free of charge. There's occasional traffic noise from the road. No campfires.
OFF SITE Chester's cathedral and city walls are a day out in themselves. There are some extraordinary views from Beeston Castle (01829 260464) – 8 counties on a clear day. Kids will love the quirky Crocky Trail (01244 336161) in Waverton.
FOOD AND DRINK Christleton's Ring O' Bells (01244 335422) holds gourmet nights and has pretty tasty food on other nights too. Sheaf Farm Shop (01829 741402) near Tarvin stocks loads of local produce.
GETTING THERE From Chester take the A51 eastwards. Turn first right after Littleton. Birch Bank Farm is on the left-hand side, soon after a sharp right bend.
PUBLIC TRANSPORT Train to Chester, then bus no. 41A to Christleton village (1 mile away).
OPEN May–October.
THE DAMAGE Pitch £5 per night; adult £3; child (5 to 15 years) £2, under-5s free; electricity £2.50.

the peak district

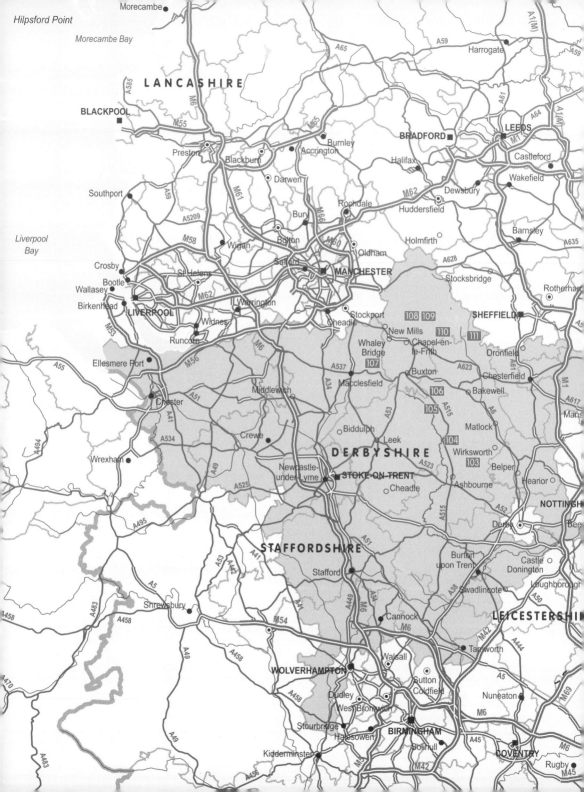

The Peak District

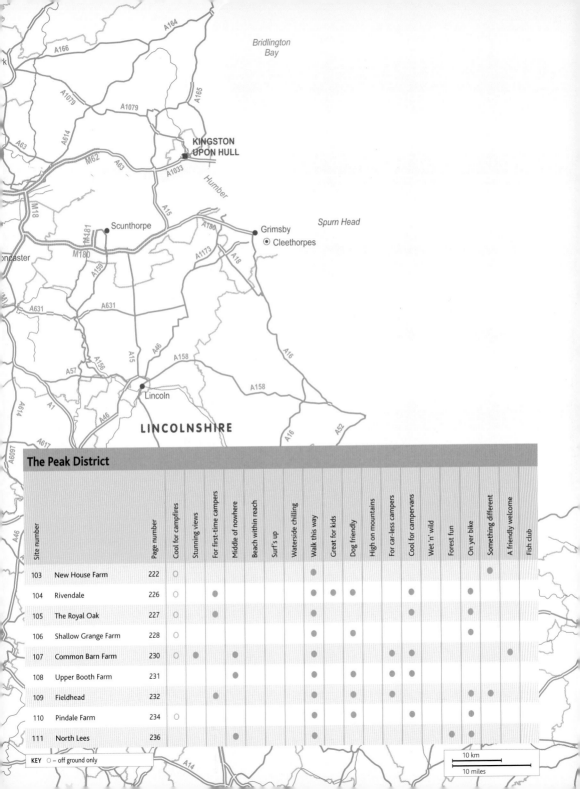

Site number		Page number	Cool for campfires	Stunning views	For first-time campers	Middle of nowhere	Beach within reach	Surf's up	Waterside chilling	Walk this way	Great for kids	Dog friendly	High on mountains	For car-less campers	Cool for campervans	Wet 'n' wild	Forest fun	On yer bike	Something different	A friendly welcome	Fish club
103	New House Farm	222	○							●										●	
104	Rivendale	226	○		●					●	●	●			●			●			
105	The Royal Oak	227	○		●					●					●			●			
106	Shallow Grange Farm	228	○							●								●			
107	Common Barn Farm	230	○	●		●				●				●	●				●		
108	Upper Booth Farm	231				●				●	●			●	●						
109	Fieldhead	232			●					●	●				●			●	●		
110	Pindale Farm	234	○							●	●				●			●			
111	North Lees	236				●											●	●			

KEY ○ – off ground only

10 km

10 miles

new house farm

New House Farm, Longrose Lane, Kniveton, Ashbourne, Derbyshire, DE6 1JL   01335 342429   www.newhousefarm.co.uk

If you like your camping raw then you'll adore this spot located on the Derbyshire Limestone (aka White Peak). Owner Bob Smail has done his level best to make limited comfort concessions to people staying on their working family farm – not because he's a sadist but because he believes it adds value, character, and authenticity to the experience. And we believe he's right.

If you're squeamish about compost toilets or think opening your tent to find yourself face to face with a snoopy sheep is a nightmarish incident on a level with *The Exorcist*, best you look elsewhere. Because New House is all about blending in with the surroundings, which just so happen to be a playground of no-holds-barred natural wonderment.

Once you've found the narrow lane that leads to the farm, it's a short drive (or walk) to Bob's delightfully ramshackle farmhouse. Fanning out from this early Georgian-era property are a number of old-school caravans (available to hire), animal sheds, and various workshops that are rented to local tradesmen (presently a blacksmith and a green-wood worker).

You'll also spot some of the site's lively menagerie. Chickens, ducks, geese, and goats roam freely; and if you hear voices speaking German or French from the direction of the cowshed, where a couple of students are busy mucking it out and laying fresh straw, don't be alarmed – they're more likely farm volunteers than guests, paying their way with some good old-fashioned elbow grease.

The camping fields lie just beyond the farm. There are three in total, all vast and undulating things; which ones are available depends on whether the cattle are munching their way through the grass or not. Our favourite is the one just above the escarpment, looking out over bucolic Peak District scenery. In all cases there are no marked pitches – just set up where you like.

Be warned that there's no electricity, shower block, or hot water, though there is a compost toilet and Bob allows campfires so long as they're raised off the ground (firewood available on site at £5 per bag). He can also sell you some of the farm's home-grown organic vegetables, fruit, eggs, and meat – either as premium cuts or pre-made sausages and burgers. And if you're really against camping at such basic levels, Bob's friend Craig has built an eco-pod for rent, complete with a hot shower, compost toilet, solar-powered electricity, and cooking facilities.

As for things to see and do, you can start right on the farm. Rumour has it that this area has been farmed since the Bronze Age, and Bob has created his very own archaeological trail (ask him for a map or join a tour) which takes you on an expedition of historical landmarks on his farm.

Half a mile along the road there's the sleepy village of Kniveton (which has a pub serving family meals, but no shops), and a bit further on lies the agreeable Georgian market town of Ashbourne, where walkers and cyclists can begin the pleasant and relatively flat Tissington Trail

that starts at Mapleton Lane and extends 13 miles into the Peak District, meeting the High Peak Trail (another old railway line) near Hartington. Stay a couple of days and a wonderful sense of how pre-Industrial Revolution England may have been starts to pervade. You may even find yourself tempted to roll up your sleeves and muck out the cowsheds – it'll improve your language skills, too.

COOL FACTOR A wild camping experience on a natural site steeped in history.

WHO'S IN Tents – yes. Campervans, dogs, groups – by arrangement. Caravans – no.

ON SITE Campfires allowed on a brazier or fire pan – freely available. Bag of wood £5. No showers or hot water, unfortunately, just a mains water tap in the main field and another in the farmyard, where you'll also find a basic compost toilet. For the eco-pod and its mod cons call Craig (07929 616282).

OFF SITE There are a few interesting museums and galleries in Ashbourne: the St John Street Gallery and Café (01335 347425; www.sjsg.co.uk) is packed with contemporary art, ceramics, and jewellery in a spacious Victorian building; at the Life in a Lens Museum (01629 583325; www.lifeinalensmuseum.co.uk) you can trace the history of popular photography from its invention in 1839 to more recent times, and take tea at their Victorian Tea Shop too. Cromford Mill (01629 823256; www.arkwrightsociety. org.uk) offers guided tours of the first water-powered cotton-spinning mill developed by Richard Arkwright in 1771, and the wholefood café in the yard serves lunches, home-made cakes, and hot drinks. Charming Chatsworth House (01246 565300; www.chatsworth.org) boasts a 1,000-acre park with regular events and entertainment, plus a farmyard and woodland adventure playground for kids. If you're in the mood for active sports, Carsington Sports and Leisure (01629 540478; www.carsingtonwater.com) offers a huge range of activities from sailing, kayaking, windsurfing, and powerboating to raft-building, orienteering, mountain biking, and climbing. For thrill-seeking kids, Alton Towers (www.altontowers.com) is just 30 minutes away, or there's Gulliver's Kingdom (01925 444888; www.gulliversfun.co.uk) in Matlock Bath – a family theme park designed to cater for families with children under 13 years.

FOOD AND DRINK No onsite 'shop' as such, but the site can sell you fantastic beef and lamb in all kinds of cuts, including BBQ-friendly steaks, burgers, and sausages. The Red Lion (01335 345554) on Kniveton's Main Street is the closest place to eat, offering decent grub, a friendly welcome, and a beer garden. For something a little more fancy try the Dining Room (01335 300666; www. thediningroomashbourne.co.uk) in Ashbourne. Arguably one of the best restaurants in the area, it serves seasonal, organic produce and offers a 7-course tasting menu. The Lamplight (01335 342279), also in Ashbourne, is a family-run restaurant serving traditional English and French cuisine, whose history dates back to the 16th century. You can also find farmers' markets in Matlock, Belper, Derby, and Ripley among other nearby market towns.

GETTING THERE In Ashbourne take the B5035 towards Matlock. After 3 miles, in Kniveton village, turn left opposite the church. After just over 350 metres turn right on a left-hand bend (not the sharp right turn). After another 350-odd metres turn right into the farmyard through the green gate.

PUBLIC TRANSPORT The nearest train station is Derby. Take bus nos. 109 or 1 to Ashbourne, then nos. 110/111/112 to Kniveton. The site is ½ mile up Longrose Lane from the bus stop at the village school.

OPEN April–September: school-holiday weekends only.

THE DAMAGE Adult £5 per night; child (school age) £2 per night.

rivendale

Rivendale Caravan Park, Buxton Road, Alsop-en-le-Dale, Ashbourne, Derbyshire, DE6 1QU   01335 310441
www.rivendalecaravanpark.co.uk

Once upon a time, Rivendale was an upland farm, before morphing (with a little help from human hands) into a massive industrial quarry. When this was closed down, nature began to reclaim the site, until the wild brambles were cleared away to finish its metamorphosis into today's campsite – a perfect balance between the man-made and the natural.

Spread over 37 acres and dotted with limestone farm buildings, this pretty and well-manicured site sits on a hillside overlooking Eaton and Alsop Dales, offering pitches for campers, as well as timber yurts and pods for glampers. Boasting numerous awards for conservation, it's a very leafy, natural site, with ponds, thousands of trees, and an abundance of flora and fauna. The grass pitches within the main camping area are generous, and enjoy a sheltered location thanks to the horseshoe-shaped quarry walls on the north, east, and west sides – and by a wooded bank on the south side. No-frills campers have the magical option of pitching in a separate 10-acre meadow amid orchids and other wild flowers, or taking an isolated pitch perched on the hillside overlooking stunning Eaton Dale.

COOL FACTOR A natural spot for every kind of camper.
WHO'S IN? Everyone welcome.
ON SITE BBQs and small (off ground) campfires allowed in the meadow. B&B, yurts, and pods; disabled facilities; loos and 4 decent showers on the camping meadow, 10 more in the reception building and under-floor heated shower block (all free). Laundry and (small) children's play area, plus café-restaurant (disabled access), well-stocked shop, and pub.
OFF SITE The Tissington Trail is 100 metres away, and there are footpaths from the site into Eaton, Alsop, Biggin, and Dove Dales. Crich Tramway Village (01773 854321) is a restored period village and home to the National Tramway Museum.
FOOD AND DRINK Rivendale's onsite pub offers food made from regional produce and local ales on draft. For something upmarket try Rowley's (01246 583880) at Baslow.
GETTING THERE Rivendale is directly off the A515 (Buxton Road) between Buxton and Ashbourne – on the left-hand side if you're travelling from Buxton.
PUBLIC TRANSPORT Bowers' bus no. 442 travels between Buxton and Ashbourne and stops nearby (ask for the stop between Biggin Church and Newton House).
OPEN Friday nearest 1 Feb–Sunday after New Year's Day.
THE DAMAGE Tent plus 2 adults £11 per night in summer.

the royal oak

The Royal Oak, Hurdlow, nr Buxton, Derbyshire, SK17 9QJ   01298 83288   www.peakpub.co.uk

The biggest challenge for those camping at the Royal Oak isn't wrestling with a sloping field (it's flat); being kept awake by traffic (no nearby main road); or finding things to do (it's slap bang in the middle of the Peak District). No, it's chomping their way through one of the award-winning pies sold at the pub. You could probably actually camp in one of these monsters – they're that big. Packed with fine ingredients, they make for a filling reward after a day's play in the Peaks, especially if washed down with one of the excellent local draught ales.

There's space for around 20 pitches (bring strong pegs for the rocky ground), and a converted stone barn with comfortable bunks if the weather's wreaking havoc. Surrounded by over 100 acres of farmland, with the 13-mile Tissington Trail passing right next to it and the Limestone Way actually cutting through some of the site, this is a great base for walkers and cyclists (a bike-hire company drops and collects bikes here). Bakewell, Ashbourne, and Buxton are all short drives away, making this an accessible and friendly place to get up close and personal with the British countryside – and its pies.

COOL FACTOR Who ate all the pies? We did.

WHO'S IN? Tents, campervans – yes. Caravans – no. Dogs, groups – by arrangement.

ON SITE Small campfires are allowed if contained and off the ground. Two camping fields with good washing-up facilities, free hot showers, and toilets in a clean barn. There's also a water tap and an outdoor washing line.

OFF SITE Monyash has a great park for kids, while Buxton, with its Pavilion Gardens (01298 23114) and charming Opera House (www.buxtonoperahouse.org.uk) has lots to offer.

FOOD AND DRINK The Royal Oak serves real ales, alarmingly large pies, and other award-winning pub grub. The best fry-up in the area is available at Old Smithy Tea Rooms (01629 810190) in Monyash. Piedaniels (01629 812687) in Bakewell serves fine French and English cuisine.

GETTING THERE Head towards Ashbourne (from Buxton) on the A515, and after 5 miles take the right-hand turn, signposted Hurdlow. The Royal Oak pub is on the right.

PUBLIC TRANSPORT The nearest station within walking/taxi distance is Buxton (6 miles). The Hartington Bus goes along the A515 and will stop on the main road, ½ mile away.

OPEN All year.

THE DAMAGE £13 per pitch, per night; £20 per large pitch.

shallow grange farm

Shallow Grange Farm, Old Coalpit Lane, Chelmorton, nr Buxton, Derbyshire, SK17 9SG   01298 23578   www.shallowgrange.com

It can be a nightmare finding a decent working sheep farm to camp on in the middle of the Peak District National Park. Luckily Shallow Grange, just south of Buxton, manages to combine both sheep (around 200 ewes, to be precise) and tents amid 110 acres of grassy farmland and rolling hills.

To stay here is to be in noble company, historically speaking – we're not still baahing on about sheep – since the Sherwood Foresters used the land as their summer camp back at the beginning of the last century. But, with those days long gone, it has been functioning as a campsite in its modern form for a couple of decades, run by Ed and Marilyn, who've worked hard to make the site a pleasant and highly eco-friendly experience. You'll find a comprehensive recycling system; renovated shower block with an underfloor heating system (and Dyson hand-dryers, no less); toilets with low-volume flushes; and solar panels to supplement the hot water temperatures. Their latest project is a 100,000-litre rainwater capture tank. The Merry Men would be jealous indeed.

The site's large camping meadow is flat, well drained, and bordered by ancient, low stone walls. It has space for 30 tents (with generously sized pitches), and there's a separate touring field for caravans, which has electric hook-ups.

It's a simple sort of site, despite the jazzy eco-facilities. There's a pond, where you can fish for perch, carp, and bream (all season; £5 per day). And, of course, the Peak District – a pretty good playground for all ages – is right on your doorstep.

COOL FACTOR An eco-friendly getaway among the Peaks.

WHO'S IN? Tents, dogs – yes. Campervans, caravans, groups – by arrangement.

ON SITE Campfires are allowed if raised off the grass. There are 30 pitches plus more (with hook-ups) in the caravan field. Showers and toilet facilities are modern, well equipped, and eco-friendly (though no baby-changing or disabled access). A freezer is available for ice packs. Pond to fish.

OFF SITE Chatsworth House (01246 565300) and Haddon Hall (01629 812855) are nearby, with Jane Austen-style interiors and gardens. Arbor Low Stone Circle – the 'Stonehenge of the Peak District' – is a Neolithic henge ringed by unspoilt countryside, with fantastic views over Derbyshire (about 5 miles south-west of Bakewell). For a proper chill-out, try the holistic Brackendale Spa (01629 540727).

FOOD AND DRINK The Church Inn (01298 85319) at Chelmorton serves quality traditional British pub lunches and home-cooked meals, while the Bulls Head (01629 812372) in Monyash offers good food in a refurbished dining room. It's a scenic drive to Longnor Fish & Chip Shop (01298 83317), or the Red Chilli (01335 343232) in Ashbourne does refined Indian and Bangladeshi food (takeaways available).

GETTING THERE The site is located off the A5270 (Old Coalpit Lane), a road accessed from the A6 and A515.

PUBLIC TRANSPORT Trains run hourly to Buxton, with connections to mainline services at Stockport and Manchester. Taxis are available outside the station. Buses will drop you off outside the farm gates on Old Coalpit Lane. Services include the TP (running between Manchester and Derby), and no. 193 (between Buxton and Tideswell).

OPEN All year.

THE DAMAGE Tent plus 2 people from £12 per night.

Rutland Arms Hotel, Bakewell

Bakewell Parish Church

common barn farm

Common Barn Farm, Smith Lane, Rainow, Macclesfield, Cheshire, SK10 5XJ   01625 574878   www.cottages-with-a-view.co.uk

If you like your skies big, your views panoramic, and think those who seek the shelter of walls and hedges should just bring longer tent pegs, then Common Barn Farm is going to be right up your street. Actually, it's up a humungous hill on the edge of the Peak District. The five-acre camping field – which starts off flat before dropping spectacularly away – commands the heights above Macclesfield and all points north-west. The facilities are basic in the extreme: a water tap and a simple aged portaloo, giving it the feel of a wild camp. Indeed, if you fancy pitching anywhere else on this 250-acre farm plunging downhill almost to Lamaload Reservoir, just ask Rona the owner, and she'll let you know which fields the sheep aren't using. It's a strictly adults-only site, too, making it a haven for any after a child-free break. Novice climbers, meanwhile, can spend all day honing their skills at the nearby craggy heights of Windgather Rocks. There's a B&B at the farmhouse and a couple of self-catering cottages, making it ideal for getting away with non-camping friends or family. Rona also runs a tea room here, so you can all meet up for a civilised cuppa and a bun.

COOL FACTOR It's as if you're camping on top of K2.
WHO'S IN? Tents, campervans, caravans – yes. Children, dogs – no. Groups – by negotiation.
ON SITE There's a fire basket available for campfires (bring your own firewood). Indeterminate number of pitches and 3 hook-ups for campervans/caravans. The facilities are as basic as they come: a tap and 1 portaloo. Ice packs can be refrozen. There's a tea shop (also sells eggs and sweets).
OFF SITE The 4½-mile circular Goyt Valley Walk around the Fernilee Reservoir makes for an untaxing leg-stretcher. Nearby attractions include Lyme Park (think Colin Firth/white shirt/lake; 01663 762023); Shining Tor – the highest point in Cheshire; and Buxton – with its pleasure gardens, cavern, and opera house it's a place that's, quite literally, 'lah-di-dah'.
FOOD AND DRINK There are 3 pubs in Rainow (accessible via the footpath from the site): the Robin Hood (01625 574060), the pricey gastro Highwayman (01625 573245), and the Rising Sun (01625 424235) – perhaps the best.
GETTING THERE From Macclesfield take the B4570 north for about 3 miles. Turn right up the steep Smith Lane, and the entrance to Common Barn Farm is on your right after ½ mile.
OPEN April–October.
THE DAMAGE £5 per person, per night.

upper booth farm

Upper Booth Farm, Upper Booth, nr Edale, Hope Valley, Derbyshire, S33 7ZJ   01433 670250   www.upperboothcamping.co.uk

What can you do when crowds of people – all total strangers – insist on traipsing through your garden? Of course, this isn't your average garden, but 970 acres of prime Derbyshire farmland in one of the most renowned valleys in the Peak District. It's also home to Robert and Sarah Helliwell, National Trust tenants and lifelong farmers. For the transient visitors, however, it's something else entirely – the main thoroughfare of the Pennine Way.

As their first port of call after the Kinder Scout Plateau, walkers are always stopping at Upper Booth Farm in need of plasters or refreshments. But the most useful service the farm provides is a place to crash for the night. The backdrop to the camping at Upper Booth is spectacular. It's genuinely difficult to see where the site ends and the open landscape of the Peaks begins. The campsite stretches across two fields – the first, smaller field is flat, sheltered, and near to the facilities. The second is a larger, undulating area of grass, open to expansive views.

The Helliwells have won awards for innovative and eco-friendly farming. And if there were an award for services to walkers, they'd win that too.

COOL FACTOR Panoramic Peak District views from this walkers' dream of a site.

WHO'S IN? Tents, small campervans, dogs – yes. Caravans, large motorhomes, unsupervised under-18s, big groups – no.

ON SITE Unmarked pitches across 2 fields. Toilets, shower, and washing-up facilities. Essentials like milk and fresh eggs are sold at the house. No campfires; BBQs off ground okay.

OFF SITE Outdoor bathing at the open-air swimming pool at Hathersage (01433 650843). The Ladybooth Equestrian Centre (01433 670205) in Edale has the horsey bases covered.

FOOD AND DRINK Pre-order one of the farm's 'Hampers for Campers', full of zero-food-miles local produce. The National Trust's Penny Pot Café (01433 670293) in Edale is a lovely place for a spot of tea.

GETTING THERE Upper Booth Farm is a mile from Edale in the Hope Valley. Follow the signs for Edale from the A625, look out for the signpost to Upper Booth a mile west of the turning for Edale village and station. Follow the road to the end.

PUBLIC TRANSPORT Edale train station is less than 2 miles from the site. Bus no. 260 from the station to Castleton will take you to Barber Booth – about a mile from the site.

OPEN February–November.

THE DAMAGE Adult £4 a night; child (under-12) £3; car £2.

fieldhead

Fieldhead Campsite, Edale, Hope Valley, Derbyshire, S33 7ZA   01433 670386   www.fieldhead-campsite.co.uk

The Peak District in England's Midlands is the busiest National Park in all Europe. While that may be a surprising statistic to some, those who have experienced its incredible diversity – from peaty bogs and vertiginous cliffs to green fields and billowing hills – will nod knowingly. And right in the middle of this lush, protected countryside is Fieldhead Campsite in Edale, a small but perfectly formed rambler's paradise with access to some of the best walking the district has to offer.

The site is made up of six intimately sized fields set at varying levels on a riverside hillock, with plenty of shelter provided by fences and hedges. The fields include one for families and another across the river for backpackers. Since there are no marked pitches, just pick an area that suits you. It's a small campsite, so nowhere is really far from the amenities block.

Fieldhead is a popular launch pad for the Pennine Way, the epic 270-mile path that starts in Edale and heads north along the Pennine Ridge, through the Yorkshire Dales and Northumberland, before finishing up at the Scottish Borders. The first leg, which stretches from Edale to Cowden, provides a good taster. Meanwhile, the quiet, countryside feel of this campsite is enhanced by the fact that cars are restricted to the car park. Slight downsides include a nearby railway line, so trains can be heard intermittently from some spots; and the insects, which can get a bit friendly around dusk. These are small gripes though, for what is a near-perfect basecamp for the Peak District area.

COOL FACTOR Fantastic walking opportunities from this small but perfectly formed campsite.

WHO'S IN? Tents, dogs (on leads) – yes. Groups – by arrangement. Campervans, caravans – no.

ON SITE The 6 fields include a separate family field and a small riverside field just for backpackers. Hot showers are 20p; there are disabled facilities, a washing-up area, and laundry in a clean and spacious block. No shop, but there's a Spar in Edale. The handy onsite information centre has masses of info on the Peaks area as well as maps for nearby hikes. Quiet time 10.30pm–7.30am. Neither campfires nor BBQs allowed.

OFF SITE Blue John and Treak Cliff (www.bluejohnstone. com), 2 Castleton caverns, are both interesting and have great veins of Blue John stone to see; Speedwell Cavern (01433 620512) is good for young children (no walking – you enter the cavern by boat). Kids will also enjoy the wildlife at Chestnut Centre (01298 814099) in Chapel-en-le-Frith.

FOOD AND DRINK For a hearty breakfast or a light snack the village has two cafés, plus the Rambler Country House (01433 670268) and the Old Nags Head (01433 670291) pubs, which both serve real ales and reasonable food. Slightly further afield, the Beehive (01298 812758) at Combs is a welcoming place to eat, with home-cooked food and cask ales. Croissants and bread are delivered to the site on Sundays.

GETTING THERE Edale is about 10 miles north-east of Buxton. Follow the signs for Edale from the A265. As you approach the village Fieldhead is on the right, just after the Rambler Inn.

PUBLIC TRANSPORT Train to Edale, then a 5-min. walk.

OPEN All year.

THE DAMAGE Adult £4.50–£6.50 (depending on season) per night; child £2.50–£4; car £1.50–£3.50.

Great Ridge, Edale

pindale farm

Pindale Farm, Pindale Road, Hope, Hope Valley, Derbyshire, S33 6RN   01433 620111   www.pindalefarm.co.uk

The stone buildings scattered around Pindale Farm lend the place a lovely, traditional olde-England feel. The site has led a varied existence, with previous incarnations including a lead mine and a working farm, and some of the buildings date back to the 14th century. The main – reportedly haunted – farmhouse pre-dates 1340 and is now home to campsite owner Alan Medhurst, who has transformed the buildings – a barn, an engine house, and a powder house used to store explosives – into bunkhouses, toilets, and shower blocks.

The fields surrounding these buildings have enough room for around 64 (unmarked) pitches, with two electric hook-ups available at the top of the main field. Tenters tend to pitch in the south-western meadow, which is large, flat, and shaded around the perimeter by sycamores, birches, and pines; it also gives pleasant views across some of Derbyshire's finest countryside. The lower sections are reserved for groups, where they are far enough away not to be intrusive, and Alan keeps a careful watch to ensure things stay peaceful after dark.

The area, right in the heart of the Peak District National Park, offers excellent recreational opportunities, including walking (there are many circular walks for all levels), horse-riding, climbing, fishing, caving, mountain biking, and hang gliding.

There are no food options on site, but as Pindale is located halfway between Hope and Castleton – each just a pleasant 20-minute walk away – you can easily access conveniences, as well as nearby sights.

COOL FACTOR Peaceful, natural camping in the Peak District's Hope Valley.

WHO'S IN? Tents, campervans, dogs – yes. Groups – by prior arrangement only. Caravans – no.

ON SITE Campfires are allowed if off the ground. There are decent washing and toilet facilities located in a couple of old stone barns (the ladies' are a bit further than the men's), as well as adequate (and free) showers in the old stables. There's a chest freezer available for cold blocks; washing machines and tumble-dryers available too (tokens can be bought from reception).

OFF SITE Shops like Hitch n Hike (01433 651013) in Hope, and Outside (01433 651936) in Hathersage, are good sources of outdoor products and information. Mountain bikes and more can be hired at 18 Bikes (01433 621111). A little different, Eyam Museum (01433 631371) profiles the fate of a local village that isolated itself during the bubonic plague outbreak of 1665.

FOOD AND DRINK The Woodbine Café (www.woodbine-hope.co.uk) in Hope does Full English breakfasts, while Hope Chest Deli (01433 620072) has quality delicatessen produce, and the Old Hall Tea Rooms (01433 620160) are good for a cuppa. For Sunday roasts try the Poacher's Arms (01433 620380), or Losehill House (01433 621219), which offers locally sourced organic food.

GETTING THERE Take the A6187 to Hope. Pindale Road is directly off this road (on the left if you're travelling westbound, right if you're coming from the other direction).

PUBLIC TRANSPORT Train to Hope then walk (a mile).

OPEN March–October (tents).

THE DAMAGE £6 per person, per night for 1-night stays, £5 a night for 2 or more nights.

north lees

North Lees Campsite, Birley Lane, Hathersage, Derbyshire, S32 1BR 01433 650838

An almost magical quietude emanates from North Lees, a somewhat idyllic Peak District National Park Authority campsite shielded within a grove of oak- and beech-lined woodland deep in the heart of *Pride and Prejudice* land.

Set across a few gently sloping fields, the site has its very own babbling brook and you can see England's largest cliff – Stanage Edge – peeking over the top of the distant treeline.

'The Edge' stretches for six miles and reaches a height of 25 metres in some places. If you're feeling dramatic, you can recreate the iconic shot from the 2005 film of *Pride and Prejudice* in which Keira Knightley's fast-witted Elizabeth Bennett stands atop The Edge, looking out over the swathes of Derbyshire. Of course, you'll have to get up there first, and the vertical route isn't all that easy. Which is why the tall face of this cliff is a Mecca for climbers, who swarm to the area in peak season to ascend the boulder-strewn ridge that juts out of the ground.

But you don't have to be an expert climber to enjoy the area. It's popular with ramblers and runners, too, who come to absorb the patchwork quilt of colours, from verdant green to scorched brown fields, managed for the red grouse.

And though the Peak District draws in an incredible 45 million day-visitors a year, the atmosphere at North Lees, protected behind the walls of this secluded woodland, feels wonderfully private – to the point where you'll feel like you're among the only few people in the park.

COOL FACTOR A lovely woodland setting alive with the sounds of the forest and close to The Edge.

WHO'S IN? Tents, groups, dogs (on leads) – yes. Campervans, caravans, unsupervised under-18s – no.

ON SITE There are onsite recycling facilities, hot showers, with male and female toilet blocks, a washing-up area, and a drying room. No campfires or BBQs.

OFF SITE Do some gliding lessons or a trial glide with the Derbyshire and Lancashire Gliding Club (01298 871270) at Camphill. Or head to Hathersage and splash around in the large heated outdoor pool (01433 650843).

FOOD AND DRINK The Scotsmans Pack (01433 650253) has a selection of microbrew ales and local fish and meat on its menu. The café (01433 651159) at the outdoor swimming pool in Hathersage has the earliest breakfast available in the area (starting from 8am), though Cintra's Tea Rooms (01433 651825) wins on the charm factor. The David Mellor cook shop and design museum in the Round Building (01433 650220) has an interesting café with a great terrace.

GETTING THERE Take the A6187 eastbound towards Hathersage. After about 2 miles, turn left up Jagger Lane and then left up Coggers Lane. Watch out for the Birley Lane turn-off about 2 miles on your right. North Lees is about 1 mile on the left.

PUBLIC TRANSPORT Get the train to Hathersage and it's approx. 1½ miles to the campsite. Call in advance for detailed directions if you're walking, or take a taxi.

OPEN All year.

THE DAMAGE Adult £5 per night; child (6 to 14 years) £3, under-5s free; full-time student £4; car £2. Prices go up by £1 over Bank Holidays, but you'll get a 50p discount if you arrive on public transport.

north west

North West

Site number		Page number	Cool for campfires	Stunning views	For first-time campers	Middle of nowhere	Beach within reach	Surf's up	Waterside chilling	Walk this way	Great for kids	Dog friendly	High on mountains	For car-less campers	Cool for campervans	Wet 'n' wild	Forest fun	On yer bike	Something different	A friendly welcome	Fish club
112	Jerusalem Farm	242							●					●							
113	Middle Beardshaw	244	S	●		●				●		●	●					●		●	
114	Wyreside Farm	246			●				●	●		●			●			●		●	
115	Knight Stainforth	247								●	●	●			●					●	
116	Gordale Scar	248		●		●				●			●						●		
117	Gibraltar Farm	250		●			●					●									
118	Swaledale	251	●			●			●	●										●	
119	Park House	252	C	●					●	●	●	●	●					●		●	

KEY S – specific areas
C – communal fire pits

10 km
10 miles

jerusalem farm

Jerusalem Farm, Jerusalem Lane, Booth, Halifax, West Yorkshire, HX2 6XB   01422 883246

Camping is all about getting closer to nature, so what better place to camp than in a nature reserve? With walks aplenty nearby, Jerusalem Farm – nestled in the picturesque Luddenden Valley, near Halifax – couldn't be better placed.

Luddenden is a steep and narrow valley, an almost-hidden gorge deep in the heart of Pennine Yorkshire. Luddenden Beck, long exploited by local mills for its fast-flowing waters, runs along the valley's base, and it is by the banks of this brook that you'll find Jerusalem Farm.

As a nature reserve, it's a pristine slice of Pennine perfection, with untouched woods on the surrounding slopes and steep valley walls. For maximum peace and tranquillity, no vehicles are allowed; cars are parked up by reception and equipment carried down to the camping fields.

Visitors are also drawn by the exceptional hill-walking to be found in this region, including the Pennine Way and the Calderdale Way, a 50-mile circular walk running through the site. You're likely to spot plenty of wildlife on a stroll, as much of this area is protected countryside and an important breeding and nesting area for distinctive birds including the curvy-beaked curlew and the splendid crested lapwing. You'll also see red grouse hopping around wherever there's an abundance of heather.

Jerusalem Farm may have basic facilities (there's only one shower) and you'll have to fight off the midges down by the gorgeous river pitches, but it's a genuinely lovely place to camp, and gives great access to a wild yet understated landscape.

COOL FACTOR Car-free, tent-only riverside camping, right on the Calderdale Way.

WHO'S IN? Tents, dogs (1 per group) – yes. Groups – by arrangement. Campervans, caravans, motorhomes – no.

ON SITE Thirty tent-only pitches spread across a couple of meadows, many near the river. Facilities stretch to toilets, a shower, kids' playground, and picnic tables. No campfires allowed, but BBQs permitted.

OFF SITE Eureka! (01422 330069; www.eureka.org.uk) in Halifax is a great museum for kids. Or, for something a bit different, hit the slopes at the Halifax Ski & Snowboard Centre (01422 340760). And racing fans can enjoy a flutter, as York Racecourse (01904 620911) is only an hour away by car.

FOOD AND DRINK There's a food shop 2 miles away, between Luddenden and Luddendenfoot, selling basics, and you can find eggs and milk at Dean House Farm, a 10-minute walk away. The closest pub grub is at the great Cat-I'th-Well (01422 244841), a 30-minute walk away. There's a takeaway at Luddendenfoot, and Halifax has a number of restaurants. Moyles (01422 845272) in Hebden Bridge is popular for its fresh, locally sourced meals.

GETTING THERE From the A646 at Luddenden Foot turn up Luddenden Lane at the takeaway shop. After ³/₄ mile turn right, towards Booth. Go through the village and, after the sharp left-hand bend, turn left into Jerusalem Lane. The campsite is on the right.

PUBLIC TRANSPORT The site is a 10-minute walk from the bus terminus at Booth. No. 574 travels to and from Halifax regularly. Or take a taxi from Sowerby Bridge or Hebden Bridge stations.

OPEN Easter–end September.

THE DAMAGE Adult £5 per night; child £3, under-5s free.

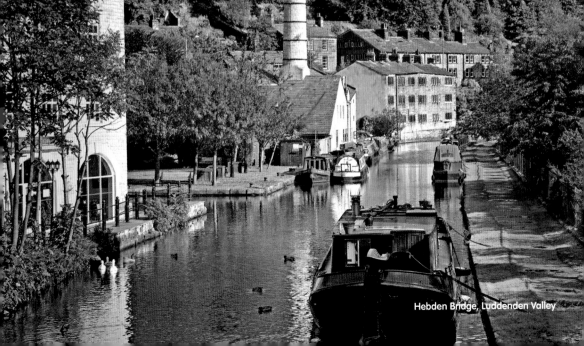

Hebden Bridge, Luddenden Valley

middle beardshaw

Middle Beardshaw Head Farm, Burnley Road, Trawden, Colne, Lancashire, BB8 8PP   01282 865257   ursulamann@hotmail.co.uk

As you wend your way through the towns of East Lancashire in search of this site, you can't help but notice all the old cotton mills and their chimneys piercing the leaden skies of Burnley and Colne. These grim relics, with their dark, gaunt-looking stone walls, resemble decaying temples from a forgotten age; left to haunt the present with their forbidding presence.

A right turn in Colne brings you into the sweet little village of Trawden and, like a curtain being flung aside, the landscape is instantly changed: gone are the 'dark Satanic mills' to be replaced by 'England's mountains green', and 'pleasant pastures seen'... Just like that, *Jerusalem* leaps to mind, and by the time Middle Beardshaw Head Farm heaves into view, a thousand voices (in your head, hopefully) are in full cry. It's as if William Blake took his final camping holiday here (in 1804) before he set about penning the iconic anthem.

This 'revelation' on the road to Burnley is a very small farm campsite, sufficient for five or six tents, and sheltered from the vastness of the windswept landscape by a screen of trees. The house would already have been old in Blake's time, and is now very ancient, with a huge view out over England's green and pleasant land. Appropriately, the facilities here are a bit rustic, while the barn housing the modern bunkhouse is an ancient leviathan of a building. Should the architecture, the culture, or the whole atmosphere of these bygone places start to wear thin, then there's also Boundary Mill, a famous temple to the God of Retail, just down the road.

COOL FACTOR   Small farm campsite set amid the contrasting scenery of East Lancashire.

WHO'S IN?   Bunkhouse: individuals and groups. Campsite: tents, and campervans (by arrangement). Dogs are welcome.

ON SITE   Campfires are permitted on the stone plinth at the top of the site, which is never more than a few steps away. There's room in the bunkhouse for up to 20 people, while the camping field has 10 pitches maximum; 2 electric hook-ups. The facilities are adequate, but a bit ramshackle and recycled, with toilets, 2 free showers, and a kitchen area with washing-up sink (which can be used by campers if the bunkhouse hasn't been exclusively booked).

OFF SITE   The original Boundary Mill mega-shop (01282 856200) is about 4 miles away. All the attractions and literary connections of Brontë country and Hebden Bridge are just over the hill in West Yorkshire.

FOOD AND DRINK   The Old Rock Café (www.oldrockcafe. co.uk) in Trawden is something of a modern legend for its 'taste of Lancashire' menu and backpacker's lunch. In Colne, and 3 miles from the campsite, are the Ivy Palace (01282 865585) – an excellent Chinese restaurant – and Carlo's Restaurant (01282 869682), lively with a real Italian feel.

GETTING THERE   From the A6068, turn on to the B6250 towards Trawden. In Trawden turn right at the church, then immediately left into Burnley Road. The campsite is a mile up, on the right.

PUBLIC TRANSPORT   Take the train to Colne, then local bus no. 21 into Trawden. From there it's a mile's walk uphill.

OPEN   All year.

THE DAMAGE   Small tent plus 2 people £5 per night; campervan/large tent and occupants £7.50. Bunkhouse £7.50 per person – must book in advance.

wyreside farm

Wyreside Farm Park, Allotment Lane, St Michael's-on-Wyre, Garstang, Lancashire, PR3 0TZ   01995 679797

Here at Wyreside, life bumbles along quietly by the peaceful waters of the River Wyre in the middle of rural Lancashire, and initially nothing looks that radical. Then you notice that the hens wandering around are a bit hippy-looking, and discover that some lay blue eggs, others green (though they taste the same as the 'normal'-looking ones) and it dawns that this is no ordinary campsite. What's more, the Badger Face Welsh Mountain sheep don't exactly belong in this level part of Lancashire – and they don't look like badgers either… Then you meet the effervescent owner, and it all becomes clear. Penny's wild about wildlife and its preservation; she's created conservation areas between the two camping fields, as well as 'butterfly bars' (Buddleia plants) to help with a healthy insect population. Should campers tire of watching weird hens, badgers masquerading as mutton, or browsing butterflies, there are plenty of distractions around here, including microlighting, parachuting, cycling the lost lanes of north Lancs, or exploring historic Lancaster or Garstang, Britain's first classified fair-trade town. And, just beyond, the Bowland Fells rear up challengingly.

COOL FACTOR A rural riverside retreat with colourful eggs.
WHO'S IN? Tents, campervans, caravans, some dogs (depending on breed, so check first) – yes. Groups – no.
ON SITE Just 12 pitches (each with hook-up), and it's not a small site, so there's plenty of room. Modern toilets and 2 free showers. The only facility lacking is a washing-up sink, but plans are afoot to take care of this. No campfires or BBQs.
OFF SITE This is an intriguing area with the Bowland Fells on the doorstep, and a seemingly undiscovered stretch of coastline on the Lune Estuary a few leisurely bike miles away.
FOOD AND DRINK The Grapes pub (01995 679229) is a 5-minute stroll away. At the Great Eccleston Fish Bar (01995 670862), 3 miles away, you can have wine with your chips. The Grade I-listed Art Deco Midland Hotel (01524 424000) in Morecambe has a posh restaurant and afternoon teas.
GETTING THERE Allotment Lane is off the southern side of the A586 (Garstang to Blackpool road), 2 miles west of the junction with the A6, and in the village of St Michael's.
PUBLIC TRANSPORT Regular Stagecoach bus no. 42 runs between St Michael's and Blackpool.
OPEN 1 March–31 October.
THE DAMAGE Tent plus 2 adults with hook-up £16 per night; extra adult £5; child £2; previously agreed dog £1.

knight stainforth

Knight Stainforth Hall, Little Stainforth, Settle, North Yorkshire, BD24 0DP   01729 822200   www.knightstainforth.co.uk

Knight Stainforth is what you could call a 'comfy' site. It's been going for over eight decades, which gives an idea of both its popularity and its owners' ability to know a thing or two about how camping should be done. The route to the site – all grassy slopes dissected with stone walls and dotted with deserted stone barns – gets you in the mood for the rural experience to come. Many use the site as a jump-off point for the Pennine Way, Cycleway, and Bridleway, and the surrounding countryside is peppered with many a foss and force. Bordering the site's edge is Stainforth Force, complete with its own fairy-tale packhorse bridge, just one of the many local features that will charm you during your stay. The site itself is a highly agreeable place; spread across two large, flat, manicured fields, it's surrounded by trees and hills, and offers decent-sized pitches that can house even supersize tents. There are a few caravans here, but they're placed in a separate area. And there's a high-end amenities block, fantastic info booth, and extensively stocked onsite shop selling maps, food, and ale (as well as locally raised beef). A comfortable site indeed…

COOL FACTOR A large, friendly site with access to plenty of activities.

WHO'S IN? Tents, campervans, dogs (no more than 2 per pitch), caravans – yes. Single-sex groups – no.

ON SITE Two large fields with a block of 8 free hot showers and toilets; a washing machine (£2) and tumble-dryer (50p). Family/disabled room; 2 washing-up areas; and well stocked shop. Games and TV room; wi-fi access. No campfires.

OFF SITE The Settle to Carlisle Railway (www.settle-carlisle. co.uk) is ranked as one of Britain's finest train journeys. Climbers should head for Castleberg Rock in Settle; and Gisburn Forest (10 miles away) has a fab mountain biking trail.

FOOD AND DRINK Settle holds farmers' markets on the second Sunday of every month. Tuck into an award-winning meal at Elaine's Tea Rooms (01729 824114) in Feizor.

GETTING THERE Take the A65 to Settle then the B6479 to Giggleswick. Turn right on to Stackhouse Lane. After about 2 miles; the site is signposted just before the crossroads.

PUBLIC TRANSPORT Train to Settle, then take Bowland bus no. B1; hop off at Stainforth.

OPEN March–October.

THE DAMAGE Tent plus 2 people £14/£17 low/high season per night; extra adult £2.50; child £1.50; dog £1; hook-up £3.

gordale scar

Gordale Scar Campsite, Gordale Farm, Malham, North Yorkshire, BD23 4DL   01729 830333

Wordsworth penned sonnets about it. James Ward painted an enormous canvas of it (now in Tate Britain). And these days you can camp in it. Gordale Scar, that gaping wound on the skin of Yorkshire's landscape, was hewn 100 metres deep through the limestone rock by successive torrents of glacial meltwater.

Sitting humbly at its mouth is Gordale Scar campsite, a site split in two by the clear waters of Gordale Beck. Out here it feels like you're at the last outpost. The road ends a mile past the campsite and is little more than the farm's driveway. And once you've pitched your tent, you'll feel miniaturised in the face of the scar's sheer cliffs.

The pathway leading to the scar's stone face (just a quarter of a mile away) passes metres from your tent, so this is an ideal spot to rest weary bones after scrabbling up and down the rock, or simply to partake in much vertical neck craning.

You'd be wise to pack your best guy ropes and industrial-strength tent pegs — or at least some spares. The breeze can pick up and the narrows of the scar direct the full force of the wind this way, so unless you want your tent to resemble the gnarled and twisted trees on the scar's cliffs, head for the shelter of some hedging or the walls.

You're not limited to the scar for your entertainment, though. The Pennine Way, Malham Cove, and wispy waterfall of Janet's Foss are a few miles from the site, so it's ideally placed to pick off some of Yorkshire's icons. Or just stay where you are and pen your own sonnet to the great scar.

COOL FACTOR Rugged and raw camping in iconic English landscape.

WHO'S IN? Tents, campervans, caravans, motorhomes, dogs – yes. Groups – by prior arrangement.

ON SITE Approx. 60 pitches; 3 hook-ups. Facilities are basic but adequate, with toilets and just 1 hot shower (10p). Fresh water is available for free, and there's a small washing-up area. No campfires but BBQs off the ground are okay.

OFF SITE If you're all walked out and fancy a change of pace, explore the monastic ruins and foodie-based diversions of nearby Bolton Abbey (01756 718009; www.boltonabbey.com), or visit Skipton Castle (01756 792442; www.skiptoncastle.co.uk), one of the best-preserved medieval castles in England.

FOOD AND DRINK The amblers' favourite is the Lister Arms (01729 830330) in Malham, a 17th-century coaching inn with decent fare and a selection of independent ales (wi-fi available). Malham's Buck Inn (01729 830317) is an upmarket option, selling local produce, real ales, and a huge choice of whiskies. More locally grown organic food can be found at the Town End Farm Shop (01729 830902) in Airton – think grass-fed beef and lamb, and local wines and microbrews.

GETTING THERE Take the road off the A65 between Gargrave and Settle to Malham. Follow signs for the tarn until the road forks, then follow the road to Gordale. The site is 2 miles up on the left.

PUBLIC TRANSPORT From Skipton take bus no. 210/211 (or sometimes 883/884) to Malham's Buck Inn and follow signs to Malham Tarn. At the fork head towards Gordale.

OPEN All year.

THE DAMAGE £3 per tent, per night, plus £3 per person; £3 per car; £1 per dog.

gibraltar farm

Gibraltar Farm Campsite, Hollins Lane, Silverdale, Lancashire, LA5 0AU   01524 701736   www.gibraltarfarm.co.uk

Morecambe Bay is a classic sweeping stretch of coast with an extended shoreline incorporating towns from Fleetwood to Barrow-in-Furness, a road trip of about 70 miles. Both beautiful and dangerous, the landscape may look like the stuff of beach dreams on a hot sunny day, with its expansive golden sands and gleaming sea in the distance, but the erratic tidal patterns hold dangers.

One of the best places from which to enjoy the sands of Morecambe Bay at a safe distance is Gibraltar Farm Campsite, near Silverdale. The camping area lies at the back of the farm, with the access road leading you through a lovely field beyond the trees, to the tent field – a large grassy area set around a rocky protrusion. You can see the capricious curls of Morecambe Bay's waves just beyond the walled perimeter.

If Morecambe Bay tires you out, then you're less than a mile away from Jenny Brown's Point, a popular viewpoint and birdwatching spot overlooking the bay. And the nearby RSPB reserve at Leighton Moss offers access to coastal lagoons, nature trails, and a visitor centre.

COOL FACTOR Farm camping with bay views.

WHO'S IN? Tents, campervans, caravans, dogs (on leads) – yes. Large young groups of under-21s – by arrangement. Groups can hire the woods for £100 per night (10 tents).

ON SITE Fifty tent pitches; 18 caravan pitches with electric hook-ups. Showers (2W, 1M), toilets (4W, 3M), disabled facilities. Washing-up area, onsite shop with home-made ice cream. Onsite sea-fishing available. BBQs high off ground allowed, only if extinguished immediately after. No campfires.

OFF SITE Wolfhouse Gallery (01524 701405) displays paintings, ceramics, and jewellery, and has a café. The Lake District is only a short scenic drive away – perfect for a picnic.

FOOD AND DRINK March down to the Woodlands Hotel (01524 701655) for excellent real ales. For BBQ inspiration, have a butchers at F & W Burrow & Son's (01524 701209).

GETTING THERE From the A6, take the B5282 to Arnside, then follow signs to Silverdale. Go through the village, then follow Hollins Lane for less than a mile; as the road turns sharply to the left, Gibraltar Farm is on the right.

PUBLIC TRANSPORT Train to Silverdale then the Silverdale Shuttle Service (Line 2) to the site.

OPEN Easter–October.

THE DAMAGE Pitch plus 2 adults and 2 children £15–£20.

swaledale

Swaledale Camping, Hoggarths Farm, Keld, Richmond, North Yorkshire, DL11 6LT   01748 886335   www.swaledalecamping.co.uk

This site is delightful in its simplicity: a working farm that breeds pedigree Swaledale sheep in a particularly isolated area of the Yorkshire Dales.

While the farm and house sit atop a steep hill, the campsite is nestled down by the River Swale. There's a large field set aside for tents, ringed by a protective stone wall, and another area right next to the river. There are no ablutions facilities, but water comes from the farm's own natural spring supply. You can buy free-range eggs when the farm's hens are laying and – the best bit – campfires are allowed.

Not only is the setting lovely, but the drive to get here, along narrow country lanes lined with old drystone walls and punctuated with placid farms and remote villages, is highly scenic too. In fact, the whole area is gorgeous. From nearby Keld you can access walks aplenty, including the 192-mile Coast to Coast hike that passes through three contrasting national parks. Or just relax near the river and enjoy the peace and quiet. You'll likely see more wildlife than people, and the glorious lack of phone reception means you won't be tempted to make any calls or download your emails.

COOL FACTOR Wild camping in the Yorkshire Dales.

WHO'S IN? Tents, campervans, caravans, well-behaved dogs – yes. Groups – by arrangement.

ON SITE Not much! Just the opportunity to buy eggs from the farm, a tap for drinking water, and a lovely river to sit by and light up your very own campfire (a limited supply of logs can be bought from the farmhouse).

OFF SITE Low Mill Outdoor Centre (01969 650432) offers adventurous outdoor activities to people of all ages. Aysgarth Falls (see www.thefalls-aysgarthfalls.com) is a spectacular triple-drop waterfall situated in a lovely wooded gorge on the River Ure – lots of well-marked walks around here, too.

FOOD AND DRINK There are no shops in Keld, but it does have a lovely lodge (01748 886259), which has a friendly bar, great views, and serves quality food made from local produce. Kirkby Stephen has the characterful Acoustic Tearoom (01768 372123) – offering live music and dinner before the show (you can bring your own wine).

GETTING THERE Like Park House (see p255), Swaledale Camping is off the B6270. Head towards Kirkby Stephen, past the turn-off for Tan Hill pub, and the site is 1 mile further.

OPEN March–October.

THE DAMAGE Small tent £3 per night; large tent £5.

park house

Park House Campsite, Keld, Swaledale, North Yorkshire, DL11 6DZ   01748 886549   www.keldbunkhouse.com

Park House is situated in the wild upper reaches of Swaledale, in the least-visited area of the Yorkshire Dales National Park, and in a place many folk consider to be the most unspoilt and emptiest chunk of scenery in northern England.

The campsite at first seems to be in a very isolated spot, and for this reason may not suit the kind of camper who requires ready-made entertainment or the bright lights of a city in the vicinity. Or any lights, in fact, with a night sky here that can be astounding. So why is there such a well-organised small campsite so far away from civilisation – besides the obvious attraction of being so far away from civilisation, of course?

It's all down to a bloke named Wainwright, who was a very successful Lake District guidebook writer. When he'd completed his Lakeland masterpieces, he decided to invent a walk right across England from St Bees in the Lake District, to Robin Hoods Bay (see pp264–267) on the North Yorkshire coast. The book, which he aptly named *A Coast to Coast Walk*, sold in lorry-loads, and the walk proved so glorious that it caught on like wildfire.

Before long, hungry, bedraggled disciples of the route were seeking sustenance and lodgings all along the walk, and a small industry was born to service the needs of these intrepid hikers. Park House, where the wild, wet, deserted moors of the North Pennines drop into the lovely upper reaches of Swaledale, is in just the right spot for exhausted trekkers to rest and recover their strength overnight, and thus a campsite (and bunkhouse) was born.

One of the blessings of this site's origins is that the facilities and services on offer here are geared towards making life easy for the lightweight backpacker. So for us wimpier campers, the provision of real meals and alcoholic refreshment in the warmth and shelter of the barn makes Park House something of a sybarite's paradise. And, despite the seeming solitude of the surroundings, a short stroll up the lane leads to the village of Keld which, besides being one of England's cutest hamlets, also accommodates a very civilised restaurant.

So while that first impression of Park House being purely a place for walkers to swap whoppers about their outdoor adventures is true, it isn't the whole story, and the real reason for bringing your camping contraption here has little to do with the hearty food or cockle-warming booze on offer, nor the interesting characters who drop in from the misty hills above. No, it's more to do with where the site is, and the scenic delights of upper Swaledale itself – especially so in early summer, when its famous meadows are ablaze with colour for a few short weeks.

The site is situated immediately next to the River Swale, and there are a couple of excellent pools in the river within a few hundred metres for that invigorating dip after a lengthy walking expedition or, in midsummer, a longer acquaintance with the smooth peaty waters of the

Keld village

Swale. Park House may be a vital servicing point on the Coast to Coast Walk, but it isn't quite as cut off as first impressions suggest, and the main appeal here is the scenic situation of this stunning little campsite, and the ease with which the scenery can be accessed straight from your little sliver of the easy life. Most of all, make sure that you bring your boots, and a will to use them. Oh yes, and the bikini too – for those temptingly cool, clear pools in the River Swale.

COOL FACTOR A tiny campsite in huge and beautiful surroundings.

WHO'S IN Tents, campervans, caravans, dogs – yes. Groups – weary walking ones only.

ON SITE With just 12 pitches normally (backpackers are never turned away), the site is small and its facilities reflect this. There are toilets, 2 free showers, clothes-drying facilities (besides the wringer), and a warm, dry barn with tables and chairs for campers' use. There are also 6 electric hook-ups for power-crazed campers. Perhaps the best facility here though is Heather, who runs the campsite. This lovely, bubbly lady from Lancashire cooks the meals, pulls the pints (well cans and bottles), and generally just makes everyone feel welcome. Campfires are not allowed in a general sense, but there is a fixed fire grate.

OFF SITE This part of Swaledale is probably the prettiest place in the Yorkshire Dales, which you'll discover upon walking to the ruined remains of 17th-century farmhouse, Crackpot Hall, and then down to Muker village. The best time for walking here is mid June, when the famous Swaledale meadows are awash with wild flowers, and turn a walk through this place into an emotional experience. Further afield, there's the impressive Richmond Castle (01748 822493) just over 15 miles away. Over a high pass into Wensleydale you'll find the Wensleydale Creamery (01969 667664; www.wensleydale.co.uk) of *Wallace and Gromit* fame. At Aysgarth (also in Wensleydale) you'll discover a lovely set of waterfalls in the River Ure, alongside the National Park Visitor Centre and a nice café. Bolton Castle (01969 623981; www.boltoncastle.co.uk) is an awesome apparition, with its own café and restaurant.

FOOD AND DRINK Heather's onsite culinary offerings include bacon, egg, or egg-and-bacon baguettes in the mornings, and for dinner beef or veggie curry, beef stew, or chip baguettes. Should you fancy a little more choice, a ½-mile stroll along the lane brings you to Keld Lodge (01748 886259; www.keldlodge.com), where good food is dished up with a great view. A bit further back down the valley (about 2 miles), in Thwaite, is Kearton Country Hotel (01748 886277; www.keartoncountryhotel.co.uk), where the food is sensational, though advance booking may be necessary. Beer fiends claim that the Old Peculier at the Farmers Arms (01748 886297; www.farmersarmsmuker.co.uk) in Muker is the best in Britain, while 4 miles from the site is the famous Tan Hill Inn (01833 628246; www.tanhillinn.co.uk), which is the highest pub in England. During the 2009/10 winter the customers were trapped here for several days after heavy snow one evening, so take spare clothes, a toothbrush, and interesting company, just to be on the safe side.

GETTING THERE The site is next to the B6270 (Kirkby Stephen to Richmond road), ½ mile west of Keld. The route over from Kirkby Stephen (accessible by the A685) in the west is a high, narrow, and exposed road. If you're coming from the east, access Richmond from the A1.

PUBLIC TRANSPORT The nearest train station is at Darlington, and bus no. X27 runs from there to Richmond, from where bus no. 30 goes to the campsite twice daily, and from the campsite to Richmond thrice daily.

OPEN All year.

THE DAMAGE Adult £6 per night; child £3; electric hook-up £3. Dogs free.

north east

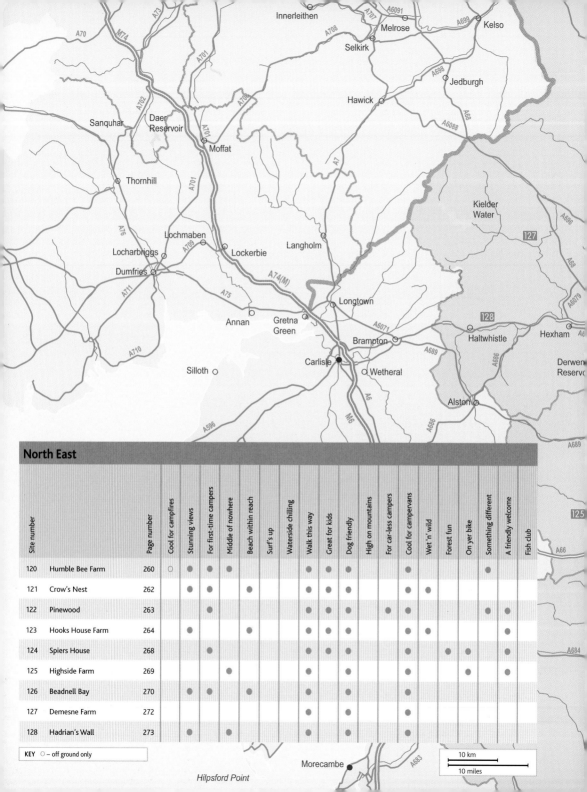

North East

Site number		Page number	Cool for campfires	Stunning views	For first-time campers	Middle of nowhere	Beach within reach	Surf's up	Waterside chilling	Walk this way	Great for kids	Dog friendly	High on mountains	For car-less campers	Cool for campervans	Wet 'n' wild	Forest fun	On yer bike	Something different	A friendly welcome	Fish club
120	Humble Bee Farm	260	○	●	●	●				●	●	●			●				●		
121	Crow's Nest	262		●	●		●			●	●	●			●	●					
122	Pinewood	263			●					●	●	●		●	●				●	●	
123	Hooks House Farm	264		●			●			●					●					●	
124	Spiers House	268			●					●	●	●					●	●		●	
125	Highside Farm	269				●				●		●						●		●	
126	Beadnell Bay	270		●	●		●			●	●	●			●						
127	Demesne Farm	272								●		●									
128	Hadrian's Wall	273		●						●	●	●									

KEY ○ – off ground only

10 km
10 miles

humble bee farm

Humble Bee Farm, Flixton, Scarborough, North Yorkshire, YO11 3UJ   01723 890437   www.humblebeefarm.co.uk

As you bounce along the bumpy farm track and Humble Bee Farm comes into view, it quickly becomes clear that this is going to be a special place to camp. Hidden away in a tranquil valley among the Yorkshire Wolds, the farm's surrounding fields are edged with the vibrant reds, blues, and yellows of bellflowers, harebells, and wild mignonette. These wild flowers have been planted to provide birdseed mix and are part of the farm's commitment to conserve wildlife and promote biodiversity; encouraging lapwings, corn buntings, skylarks, and even deer to visit the farm.

While there are no age barriers to enjoying a stay here, owners John and Julia Warters have turned part of their farm into something of a children's paradise. Two Gloucester Old Spot pigs, Bubble and Squeak, and three Shetland ponies, Mojo, Magic, and Hector, join the free-range chickens and guineafowl wandering the site and the Aylesbury ducks on the pond. There are no 'Do not feed the animals' notices here. Instead signs encourage kids to feed the ponies and pigs, with information about what they like to eat, and they can also collect eggs from the hen house. There's a children's playground, and the exciting option of camping in a wigwam.

But it's not just youngsters who enjoy this place. The quarter-acre site is set in some 320 acres of farmland, with lovely views over sweeping hills and a remote, peaceful atmosphere – despite all those kids. Signposted walks around the farm encourage campers to explore the local countryside.

COOL FACTOR A pretty and very child-friendly farm.

WHO'S IN? Tents, campervans, caravans, dogs – yes. Groups of under-21s, transit vans without prior arrangement – no.

ON SITE Campfires allowed in rented fire baskets delivered directly to your tent, complete with firelighters, kindling, and wood. Twenty pitches with hook-ups are set out on either side of a farm track; 4 heated wigwams with mod cons; and there's room for another 20 tents across a slightly sloping grassy area at the bottom of the site. Two modern facilities blocks provide toilets, showers, basins, a family/disabled bathroom, hairdryers, laundry, and a dishwashing room; the farm shop supplies basics as well as local sausages, bacon, and ice cream – and those camping essentials, marshmallows.

OFF SITE A section of the 70-mile Yorkshire Wolds Way runs alongside the site; you can follow the path for about 7 miles to Filey, with its large sandy beach and sheltered bay.

FOOD AND DRINK The Foxhound Inn (01723 890301) in Flixton is 1½ miles down the road and comes highly recommended for its huge portions of pub grub. The Filey Deli (Belle Vue Street) boasts the best cupcakes in town; at old-fashioned Bramwells Tea Room (01723 513344) you can enjoy toasted teacakes to a Doris Day soundtrack.

GETTING THERE Take the A64 (from York towards Scarborough) and, at the Staxton roundabout, take the second exit on to the A1039, signposted Filey. Just before you enter Flixton take a right-hand turn, signposted Fordon. At the top of the hill turn right, to Humble Bee Farm.

PUBLIC TRANSPORT Bus no. 118 runs from Filey via Folkton and Flixton to Scarborough 3–4 times each day.

OPEN All year.

THE DAMAGE Tent, car, plus 4 people £16–£26 per night. Wigwams (sleeping up to 5) £12.50 adult/£5 child per night.

crow's nest

Crow's Nest Caravan Park, Gristhorpe, Filey, North Yorkshire, YO14 9PS   01723 582206   www.crowsnestcaravanpark.com

Crow's Nest is a tale of two campsites. The first is a large holiday park with a bar, café, fish-and-chip shop, indoor swimming pool, and row upon row of static caravans. Not exactly *Cool Camping*. But venture a little further, and in sharp contrast you'll find a large tents-only field with panoramic views over the sea and across the Yorkshire Wolds and Vale of Pickering. A children's playground forms a handy boundary between the two very different areas.

The tent field climbs up and then slopes gently down towards the cliff-top. There's room for around 200 tents (and the odd campervan) on a pitch-where-you-like basis. As you head up the hill, you'll spy some secluded areas surrounded by hedges for small groups of tents, and the closer you get to the sea, the quieter and more peaceful the site becomes. Large family groups head for the serviced pitches near the playground, while a mixture of couples, groups, and families is spread across the rest of the site. You can take the path down the cliffs to the shingle beach at Gristhorpe Bay and, if you're lucky, you might spot members of the local seal colony that live on and around the rocks here.

COOL FACTOR Tents-only cliff-top site with sea views.
WHO'S IN? Tents, 1 or 2 campervans, dogs, groups – yes.
ON SITE Lots of space between pitches. Ablutions blocks are on the main site; but there is a covered washing-up station on the camping field. A well-stocked shop joins the other facilities on the main holiday-park site, where you can refreeze cold packs and stock up on food and drink basics. About 12 electric hook-ups near the play area. No campfires.
OFF SITE The Cleveland Way runs along the cliff-top in front of the site and takes you into Filey (around 2½ miles) in one direction, and Scarborough (5 miles) in the other.
FOOD AND DRINK The restaurant at the Copper Horse (01723 8620290) in Seamer has a theatrical theme and award-winning food. For great fish and chips, head to Inghams (01723 513320) on Belle Vue Street in Filey.
GETTING THERE The site is just off the A165 between Scarborough and Filey; 2½ miles north of Filey there's a roundabout with a Jet petrol station on the corner. Turn left here and Crow's Nest is the second caravan park on the left.
PUBLIC TRANSPORT Bus no. 121 runs between Scarborough and Hull, calling regularly at Gristhorpe.
OPEN 1 March–31 October.
THE DAMAGE Tent (inc up to 4 people) £15–£25 per night.

pinewood

Pinewood Holiday Park, Racecourse Road, Scarborough, North Yorkshire, YO12 5TG   07787 378111/01723 367278
www.pinewood-holiday-park.co.uk

Yeehah! Camp Pinewood goes one better than other tipi sites, offering cowboy shacks and bell tents, too. Here you can enjoy the Wild West theme with some home comforts in one of four 'authentic' and eight 'modern' tipis. They share one of the three camping areas along with two cowboy cavalry tents and four shacks. All tents are equipped with futons and cube beds, rugs, outside decking with picnic benches, and the luxury of electricity (so not exactly the cowboy lifestyle, but we don't mind).

There's also a flat, no-frills camping field with lots of space for just 14 pitches, boasting great views over the Yorkshire Wolds. Kids can disappear off into the wooded area at the bottom of the site, which has paths weaving around the trees, to play tag, hide-and-seek and, of course, Cowboys and Indians.

Owners Kerry and Dave have done their time in the retail trade and resolutely refuse to sell anything useful from the site shop. You'll have to make the short trip into Scarborough for stocking up on food and drink; but they'll happily sell you essential items like bows and arrows, toy guns, and a cowboy hat or two to equip you for the theme.

COOL FACTOR The east coast's answer to the Wild West.
WHO'S IN? Tents, caravans, dogs (on leads), groups (can book the whole site; campfires permitted in this case) – yes.
ON SITE Three distinct areas totalling 7 acres: tipi camp, tent field offering 14 pitches with electric hook-ups, and an adult-only caravan field. Modern shower and toilet block, alfresco washing-up sinks. Extensive recycling is part of a generally green ethos. Some traffic noise, and neighbouring fields harbour communication masts. No campfires.
OFF SITE A 2-mile footpath takes you into Scarborough. The quieter of its two beaches is North Bay, where you'll find the Sealife Centre (01723 373414) and Peasholm Park nearby.
FOOD AND DRINK For fish and chips, the Harbour View Café on Scarborough's West Pier. For a pint and hefty helping of pub grub, the Denison Arms (01723 862131) in East Ayton.
GETTING THERE The site is just off the A170 (Scarborough to Pickering road) about 1½ miles on the left before you reach Scarborough. Look for the sign at the top of the hill.
PUBLIC TRANSPORT Take the train to Scarborough and a number of local buses to Pickering run past the site.
OPEN All year.
THE DAMAGE Tent plus 2 people £14 per night. Tipis/cowboy tents/shacks from £70 per night. Dogs free.

hooks house farm

Hooks House Farm, Whitby Road, Robin Hoods Bay, North Yorkshire, YO22 4PE   01947 880283   www.hookshousefarm.co.uk

Robin Hoods Bay, near Whitby in North Yorkshire, is an area steeped in romance and intrigue. Its very name is a mystery: there's nothing to link this place with the infamous green-clad hero of Sherwood Forest, but the name stands as an inexplicable suggestion of some legendary past.

What's certain is that this was smuggler country. And if you arrive at Hooks House Farm late on a clear evening under a full moon, you'll be able to picture the scenes from long ago, as the breathtaking sight of the wide sweep of the bay is laid out beneath you in the silvery moonlight... Step back a few centuries and you'd have spotted the shadowy figures as they emerged from small wooden boats and scuttled towards the shore clutching their contraband...Throughout the 18th century, locals crippled by high taxes turned to illegal imports to make money, receiving tobacco, brandy, rum, and silk from Europe. Gangs of smugglers used a network of underground passages and secret tunnels to deliver the stash inland, making a tidy profit in the process.

Even now, the charming town of Robin Hoods Bay has the feel of an age-old smugglers' den, with unfeasibly narrow streets and tight passageways — although these days you're more likely to stumble across a second-hand bookshop than hidden contraband. Ancient fishermen's cottages cling to the near-vertical slope as the cliff drops down to a little harbour at the water's edge. In addition to this older part of town there's a newer, Victorian enclave on the flat ground at the top. The well-ordered mansions are a world apart from the cobbled jumble below.

To shed some light on the town's past, the volunteer-run museum (01947 881252), reached via the narrow cobbled pathways and steps, has a model of a smuggler's house, showing how contraband could be concealed, as well as stories of shipwrecks and historic rescues.

Although the bay is picturesque, it doesn't have a beach to tempt sunbathers. The ground is dark and rocky — more suitable for bracing walks, rockpool explorations, and fossil hunting than lazing around. But the wide sweep of this bay is stunning. And at the friendly, family-run campsite at Hooks House Farm, high up on the hill above town, you couldn't wish for a better vantage point. The first-rate views really make this site: from its grassy field sloping gently down towards the sea you can watch the tide wash in and out over the whole sweep of shoreline, or gaze across a colourful patchwork of sheep- and cow-dotted fields, woods, rolling hills, and moors.

And if you're feeling energetic, the surrounding countryside (including the Yorkshire Moors) is perfectly placed for outdoor fun. The disused railway line that runs through here on its way from Scarborough to Whitby has been transformed into a popular walking and cycling path, and forms part of the wittily named Moor-to-Sea path, a long-distance route that provides up to four days of cycling. Robin Hoods Bay also marks the eastern end of the classic Coast to Coast Walk, while the

Cleveland Way, a 110-mile National Trail between Helmsley and Filey around the North Yorkshire Moors, also makes its way along the coast here. If you're after shorter walks, try the half-mile stretch beginning with a footpath from the site down to the town, where you'll find several cosy pubs – all great venues for discussing the demise of smuggling as a lucrative career, the possibility of finding fossils on the beach, or even for speculating on how Robin Hoods Bay might have found its name.

COOL FACTOR Panoramic views over sea and moor from a peaceful, low-key site.

WHO'S IN Tents, vanners, dogs – yes. Groups – no.

ON SITE Pitches for 75 tents and 25 campervans/caravans spread out across a gently sloping field. A second field provides pitches for a few tents around the edge, but most is left as a family play area. Clean but basic facilities, with 3 showers, 5 basins, and 4 toilets in separate blocks for men and women; there's also a block with washing cubicles. A further block has 3 washing-up sinks, a kettle, a microwave, fridge and freezers; and there's recycling for paper, cardboard, plastic tins, cans, and glass. The campsite vibe is peaceful, relaxed, and low-key, with no organised entertainment and no long list of rules and regulations to adhere to. It is next to a road, but as it isn't inundated with vehicles you're more likely to be bothered by the cries of seagulls and bleatings of sheep in the nearby fields than by traffic noise. The owners, Jill and Gordon Halder, are famously attentive, ensuring that all the facilities are kept suitably clean and that visitors have everything they need. No campfires.

OFF SITE Robin Hoods Bay's narrow streets are fun to explore and the town has its own cinema at the Swell Café Bar (01947 880180; www.swell.org.uk). With original 1820s pews, it feels more like a theatre than a cinema. Whitby is only 6 miles up the coast and its abbey is a good place to start your visit. Take in the views over the town and the coast (and the tea shop) before you head down the famous 199 steps into the bustling, higgledy-piggledy streets of the old town and harbour. If you're here with kids, the harbour walls make a good spot for crabbing, while the beach awaits for kite-flying, fossil-hunting, and exploring rock pools at low tide. Several boat trips leave from the harbour; between mid September and early November the *Speksioneer* and its sister boat, the *Esk Belle II* ('The Big Yellow Boat') set off in search of minke whales that follow the shoals of North Sea herring as they swim down from the Arctic to their spawning grounds off the coast of Whitby. If you're lucky, you might also spot porpoises, dolphins, and seals, and even if you're not, you'll definitely see some beautiful coastal scenery.

FOOD AND DRINK Pubs in the town include the Dolphin (01947 880337), which has a cosy, old-world smugglers' feel; the Bay Hotel (01947 880278), where you can overlook the bay from the quayside as you enjoy a drink or meal; and the Laurel Inn (01947 880400), which has a bar carved from solid rock. Bramblewick restaurant (01947 880187; www.bramblewick.org) is a café by day and offers candle-lit dining by night, and kids will love the old-fashioned Browns sweetshop, with its traditional sweets and hand-made chocolates. The town also has a fishmonger's, and lovely fresh bread is sold at the General Store.

GETTING THERE Heading south from Whitby on the A171 take the B1447, signposted Robin Hoods Bay, and Hooks House Farm is on the right, ½ mile before the village. If you are travelling north, ignore the first couple of signs to Robin Hoods Bay and take the B1447 turning.

PUBLIC TRANSPORT Bus no. 93 runs between Scarborough and Middlesbrough, regularly stopping in Robin Hoods Bay and Whitby. It stops at the campsite gate throughout the year.

OPEN All year.

THE DAMAGE Adult £5–£7.50 (depending on season) per night; child £3; electric hook-up £3–£4.

spiers house

Spiers House, Cropton Forest, Cropton, Pickering, North Yorkshire, YO18 8ES   01751 417591   see www.forestholidays.co.uk

Spiers House campsite has been through a few changes since we last featured it in *Cool Camping*. Refurbished fully, it now boasts a fancy café and reception, a swanky loo block, and several luxury huts with hot tubs and *real* beds. Some pitches have also been taken over by Eurocamp, but don't worry – for all the cosmetic changes, the heart of the site hasn't changed. Its location, about 20 miles west of Scarborough in the North Yorkshire Moors, is still fantastic if you're looking for an active and varied holiday, especially if you're into mountain biking. Spiers House is in the middle of Cropton Forest, so you get immediate access to miles of hassle-free, traffic-free (but not effort-free!) cycling. Up on the moors above Rosedale is perhaps the best off-road biking route in Britain; rangers run organised tours for the uninitiated. There's also a full range of hiking tours, such as the Bird Walk, which leaves at dawn for a morning-chorus concert by your feathery neighbours. There are casual tours, too, and a steam railway, chugging between Pickering and Grosmont. It may have had a facelift, but Spiers House remains the fantastic adventure hub it has always been.

COOL FACTOR Fantastic off-road biking opportunities all around. Beautifully situated for a hassle-free holiday.

WHO'S IN? Everyone.

ON SITE Decent toilets, hot showers, family room, disabled facilities, laundry, washing-up sinks, and children's play area. Onsite shop sells food, maps, gas refills, and a few camping accessories. No campfires.

OFF SITE A steam-train journey along the North Yorkshire Moors Railway (01751 472508) makes a lovely day out, and the bright lights of Scarborough are also within easy reach. Castle Howard (01653 648444) is impressive, too.

FOOD AND DRINK In Cropton, you'll find the excellent New Inn (01751 417330), with fabulous food and its own microbrewery. If it's fruit you're after, try the PYO service at Cedar Barn (01751 475614), about 8 miles away.

GETTING THERE From the A170 (Thirsk to Scarborough road) at Wrelton, take the minor road towards Rosedale Abbey. The site's signposted, a mile after Cropton village.

PUBLIC TRANSPORT In high season only – the Moorbus service (from Pickering), drops 2 miles from the site.

OPEN All year.

THE DAMAGE Tent plus 2 people £11.50–£17.50 (seasonal; min. stay 2/3 nights in high). Adult £5–£6.50; child £2.50–£4.

highside farm

Highside Farm, Bowbank, Middleton-in-Teesdale, County Durham, DL12 0NT   01833 640135   www.highsidefarm.co.uk

Sitting atop the North Pennines, Highside Farm's smallholding has only five pitches, so its miniature size almost guarantees you'll have plenty of peace and quiet. And if that isn't enough to whet your appetite, the extensive views from your tent across the valley to Lunedale and Teesdale surely will.

Talking of appetite, the site's owners, Richard and Stephanie, also run a working farm specialising in raising Teeswater sheep and Shorthorn cattle. And what the farm sows, you can reap. All the farm-produced meat is available for your campsite stove and dining pleasure. And, when the chickens aren't on strike, there are fresh eggs to be had, too. But if cooking sounds like far too much effort, you can place an order for breakfast the next day – anything from bacon sandwiches to a Full English can be rustled up.

Richard and Stephanie have succeeded in creating a campsite true to what they love about camping. No security barriers, packed-out camping fields, or rules and regulations; just good views, a rural setting, nice walks, and that back-to-nature feeling. With a sprinkling of good local food on top.

COOL FACTOR Miniature rural site with tasty farm treats.

WHO'S IN? Campervans, caravans, dogs – yes. Groups, no.

ON SITE A maximum of 10 allowed on site. The single hot shower and solitary WC sit inside a traditional farm building along with a washing-up sink; an additional loo is on the site. There are 2 hook-ups (£2.50). No campfires, but BBQs okay.

OFF SITE The Pennine Way is a short stroll away, or you can head to High Force, Britain's largest waterfall. Staindrop's Raby Castle (01833 660202; www.rabycastle.com) has a fantastic art collection and lavish grounds.

FOOD AND DRINK In addition to the seasonal offerings at Highside Farm, grab yourself some local Cotherstone cheese, named after a village in Teesdale. It's available from the Middleton-in-Teesdale farmers' market (the first Sunday of the month) or from Armitages (01833 640226) in Middleton-in-Teesdale. The Rose and Crown (01833 650213) in Romaldkirk is only a 10-minute drive from the campsite, boasting high-quality service and meals you wish you had at home.

GETTING THERE Take the A685 towards Brough, then the B6276. The site is 2 miles away from Middleton-in-Teesdale, on your right.

OPEN May–September.

THE DAMAGE £8 per person, per night; under-4s half price.

beadnell bay

Beadnell Bay, Beadnell, Chathill, Northumberland, NE67 5BX   01665 720586   see www.campingandcaravanningclub.co.uk

Time itself seems to operate in an entirely different dimension in this north-eastern oasis of tranquillity and beauty. Or is it just that this remote coastal strip remains as it has been for hundreds of years, and that the only real signs of development are a collection of amazing fortresses built nearly 1,000 years ago?

Beadnell Bay campsite, situated right next to the sea, is about two miles south of Seahouses. Despite being quite possibly the smallest seaside resort in the world, it still boasts a couple of pubs, a few chippies, and a working fishing harbour with boats running out to visit the famous Farne Islands – home of birds, but nothing (and nobody) else.

One of the best ways to discover the quiet, level back roads of Beadnell Bay is by bike. Pedal along the coast road in awe as you cruise north from Seahouses to Bamburgh Castle, eventually reaching the Holy Island of Lindisfarne. However, if walking is more your style, discover the real thrill of this coast by rambling down to the empty Embleton Bay, where you can gaze southwards to the atmospheric ruins of Dunstanburgh Castle.

The site itself would be best described as unremarkable – a flat featureless field providing not a scrap of shelter to stop the occasionally wicked east wind from pummelling your tent. But all this is unimportant – did you come here to sit and ponder how glamorous the toilet block is? No. Chances are you'll be too busy falling under the spell of the empty coastline, and the history that still trembles through the air.

COOL FACTOR A stunningly timeless stretch of deserted coastline.

WHO'S IN? Tents, campervans, dogs – yes. Caravans – no.

ON SITE Single, exposed field with 150 pitches. Decent facilities with toilets, free hot showers, disabled toilet and shower, washing-up sinks, laundry; gas refills at reception; freezer; wi-fi. No campfires.

OFF SITE If you've done all the castles including Bamburgh (01668 214515; www.bamburghcastle.com), Alnwick (01665 510777; www.alnwickcastle.com) – famously used as a Hogwarts set in the *Harry Potter* films – and Dunstanburgh (01665 576231), then see what's on at the Alnwick Playhouse (01665 510785; www.alnwickplayhouse.co.uk).

FOOD AND DRINK Head to Swallow Fish (01665 721052; www.swallowfish.co.uk) in Seahouses for BBQ supplies of local seafood, including crab and sea bass, as well as their famous smoked fish (usually someone on hand to show you around the smokehouse, too). For something a little pricey but worth it, try the Tree House at Alnwick Garden (01665 511852). Or breakfast like a king on Craster kippers from L Robson & Sons (01665 576223). The Ship Inn (01665 576262) at Low Newton-by-the-Sea is worth the journey – a lovely pub with a menu rich in local seafood.

GETTING THERE From the A1, 5 miles north of Alnwick, take the B6347 east then the B1340 to Beadnell. The site is on the left after a bend to the north of Beadnell.

PUBLIC TRANSPORT Train to Morpeth or Alnwick then bus no. 501, which stops 300 metres from the site.

OPEN April–October.

THE DAMAGE Adult £5.10–£8.25 per night (depending on season); child £2.55–£2.77. An additional £7.10 fee for non-members.

Bamburgh Castle

demesne farm

Demesne Farm Campsite, Bellingham, Hexham, Northumberland, NE48 2BS   01434 220258   www.demesnefarmcampsite.co.uk

Demesne Farm's patch of flat green sits on the outskirts of the sleepy, blink-and-you'll-miss-it village of Bellingham. In fact, it's the location of this rural retreat coupled with having the Pennine Way right on the doorstep that make it so popular. Demesne Farm is first and foremost a haven for walkers and cyclists who, after a long day spent tackling the Pennines, need a pastoral pillow on which to rest their weary heads. The campsite isn't large – just one field given over to campers – but it feels bigger as it looks out over a wide expanse of rural England that glows golden as the sun falls. And to those weary walkers, it's heaven. Over the busy summer months an overflow field is opened to maintain the harmonious balance at Demesne Farm. And what a farm it is; real rustic characteristics and smells alongside the resident animals. You'll notice that they're completely unperturbed by the presence of campers – especially the inquisitive brood of chickens. They'll scrabble around your guy ropes and take a peck out of everything in reach, but it's these feathered touches that make Demesne Farm such a firm favourite of all who visit there.

COOL FACTOR Comfort on the Pennine Way's doorstep.

WHO'S IN? Tents, campervans, caravans, motorhomes, dogs (on leads) – yes. Single-sex/multiple family groups – no.

ON SITE Approx. 30 pitches; 2 blocks (1W, 1M) with hot showers (50p for 6 minutes). Washing-up facilities and CDP. Quiet time 10.30pm–7.30am. BBQs allowed off the ground if cleared immediately afterwards. No campfires.

OFF SITE The closest and main attraction is Kielder Water & Forest Park (01434 220616) – the largest man-made lake and planted forest in Northern Europe. Wander the historic streets of Hexham and Bellingham.

FOOD AND DRINK The picks of the pub crop are the Black Bull (01434 220226) and the Rose & Crown (01434 220202). Nearby Hexham's farmers' market has a BBQ-tastic selection of fresh organic meat and veg.

GETTING THERE Take the A6079 to Chollerford and join the B6320 to Bellingham. In Bellingham, turn right at Lloyds TSB bank and the campsite is 100 metres down, on the right.

PUBLIC TRANSPORT From Hexham train station jump on bus no. 880 to Bellingham.

OPEN May–October/November.

THE DAMAGE Tent plus 1 or 2 people and a car £8/£12 per night. Extra adult £5; child (4 to 15 years) £3, under-3s free.

hadrian's wall

Hadrian's Wall Campsite, Melkridge Tilery, nr Haltwhistle, Northumberland, NE49 9PG   01434 320495   www.hadrianswallcampsite.co.uk

The 73 miles of Emperor Hadrian's monumental, Pict-proof stone wall is Northumberland's most famous landmark. Though its military barracks are long gone, the ruins of this historic structure remain impressively atmospheric. It's easy to imagine how the soldiers must have felt, keeping watch at the very outpost of the civilised world. The wall is now a World Heritage Site, but you can still camp just a mile or so from one of the most dramatic sections at Hadrian's Wall Campsite.

The site is terraced on four levels, with top level 'Everest' commanding impressive views and the perfect sunset vantage point. In the summer months, an extra 'wild camping' field is opened up, with oodles of space for large families. Weary backpackers can also rejoice: there's a strip dedicated entirely to your aching bones – no need to book, just stagger up on the day. The campsite is well located for walks along Hadrian's Wall Path, an 84-mile National Trail shadowing the line of the wall. The site-owners will even arrange transport to or from your start/finish points, leaving you free to enjoy your linear walk and the wall. Just keep an eye out for those Picts.

COOL FACTOR A mere mile away from Hadrian's Wall.

WHO'S IN? Tents, campervans, caravans, dogs, groups – yes.

ON SITE Terraced pitches; 7 hot showers, toilets, laundry, and hook-ups. Disabled access and facilities. Basic groceries sold. Bunk barn sleeping 10. No campfires or disposable BBQs.

OFF SITE The Housesteads Roman Fort and Museum (01434 344363) is just down the road.

FOOD AND DRINK Herding Hill Farm (01434 320668) in Haltwhistle has a farm shop and café selling its own-produced goodies. The Milecastle Inn (01434 321372), a mile to the west, has wooden beams covered in nick-nacks, an open fire, and a resident ghost.

GETTING THERE Just east of Haltwhistle, from the B6318 (Military Road), take the turning to Melkridge. The site is just 300 metres on the left. From the A69, 1 mile east of Haltwhistle, there's a staggered crossroads at Melkridge village. Take the turning opposite the village and continue for 2 miles.

PUBLIC TRANSPORT Ask nicely and the owners might collect you from Haltwhistle station or a nearby bus stop.

OPEN All year.

THE DAMAGE Backpacker £8; tent and car £8; caravan/trailer tent £12.50, plus £2 per person, per night. Bunk barn £15 per person, per night.

cumbria and the lakes

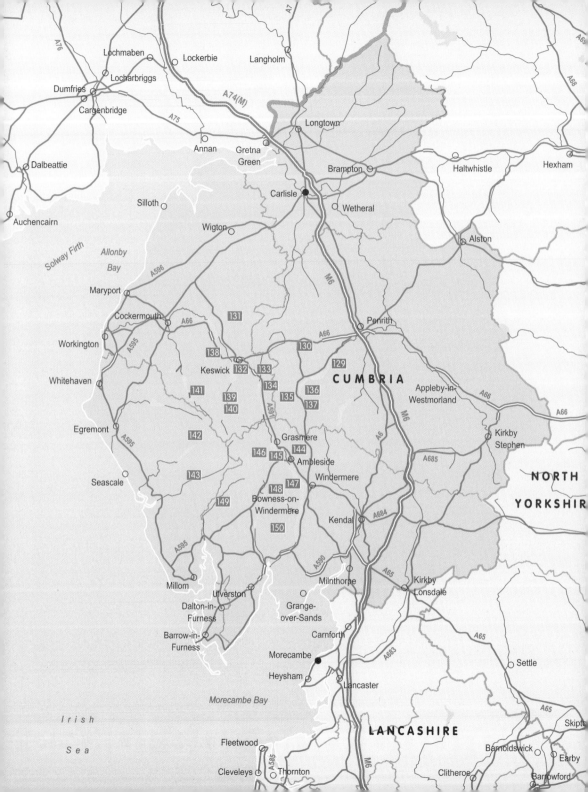

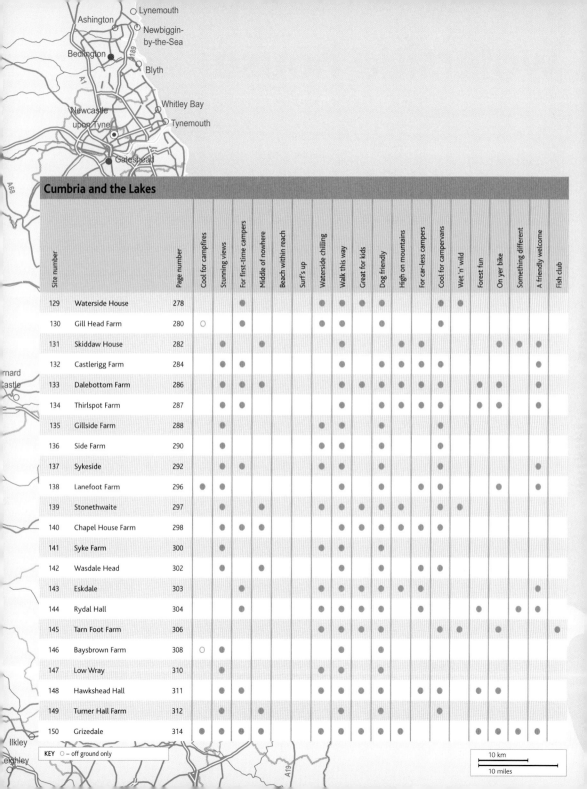

Cumbria and the Lakes

Site number		Page number	Cool for campfires	Stunning views	For first-time campers	Middle of nowhere	Beach within reach	Surf's up	Waterside chilling	Walk this way	Great for kids	Dog friendly	High on mountains	For car-less campers	Cool for campervans	Wet 'n' wild	Forest fun	On yer bike	Something different	A friendly welcome	Fish club
129	Waterside House	278			●				●	●	●	●			●	●					
130	Gill Head Farm	280	○		●				●	●		●			●						
131	Skiddaw House	282		●		●				●			●	●				●	●	●	
132	Castlerigg Farm	284		●	●					●	●	●			●					●	
133	Dalebottom Farm	286		●	●					●	●	●	●		●		●	●			
134	Thirlspot Farm	287		●						●	●	●			●						
135	Gillside Farm	288		●						●		●			●						
136	Side Farm	290		●					●	●					●						
137	Sykeside	292		●						●										●	
138	Lanefoot Farm	296	●							●					●			●		●	
139	Stonethwaite	297		●		●				●		●			●	●					
140	Chapel House Farm	298		●	●	●				●	●	●									
141	Syke Farm	300		●					●	●		●									
142	Wasdale Head	302		●		●				●					●	●					
143	Eskdale	303			●				●	●	●	●			●					●	
144	Rydal Hall	304			●				●	●	●	●		●			●		●	●	
145	Tarn Foot Farm	306		●					●	●	●	●			●			●			●
146	Baysbrown Farm	308	○	●						●											
147	Low Wray	310		●					●	●		●									
148	Hawkshead Hall	311		●	●					●	●	●			●		●	●			
149	Turner Hall Farm	312		●		●				●		●			●						
150	Grizedale	314	●	●	●	●			●	●	●	●	●				●	●	●	●	

10 km

10 miles

waterside house

Waterside House Campsite, Howtown Road, Pooley Bridge, Penrith, Cumbria, CA10 2NA   01768 486332
www.watersidefarm-campsite.co.uk

Ullswater isn't exactly lacking in campsites. It has all kinds, from large and loud commercial parks to quieter farms and hidden spots. But Waterside House is one of our favourites; there's something easy-going yet professional about the place that makes you feel relaxed and in safe hands.

Undoubtedly this has something to do with it being a family-run site, handed down through several generations to current tenants Joan and Colin Lowis and their son Mark. Not only that, but, as the name suggests, Waterside is snuggled right up against the lake's shore. Pitch on the grass to the left of reception and your morning views will be of the surrounding fells (including the ancient woodland at the foot of Barton Fell), foregrounded by the gently bobbing moored boats and curious swans and ducks.

The lakeside pitches continue, on the other side of the reception block, with picnic tables and a children's play area. There's also a second field for campers who don't want to be right on the water, which tends to cater more for families and larger, activities-based young groups.

Since Waterside is a working farm, the atmosphere is pleasingly rural. You might even experience, depending on the season, activities such as lambing and shearing. Then again, there's every chance you'll be hiring one of Waterside's rowboats or sea cycles to enjoy the lake, heading off for lunch in pretty Pooley Bridge (there's a lakeshore footpath from the site), or borrowing a mountain bike to explore the surrounding terrain.

COOL FACTOR Lakeside bliss in a rousingly rural setting.

WHO'S IN? Tents, campervans, caravans, dogs – yes. Groups – supervised only.

ON SITE Some of the 90 pitches have electric hook-ups and there's a children's play area near the water. The shower and toilet facilities are a bit old-fashioned, but there's plenty of hot water, and hairdryers. Another block has a washing machine (£3 in tokens), dryer (50p), and coffee machine. A well-stocked shop does gas and bottle exchange; freezer for ice packs; phone; volleyball and table tennis. You can even store your boat and use the launch. No campfires, but BBQs are fine.

OFF SITE Aside from all the lake-based activities on offer (try a steamer ride with Ullswater Steamers; book with the site), there's Dalemain House (01768 486450) to visit, with its wonderful garden and various events on throughout summer. For the kids: Eden Ostrich World (01768 881771) has ostriches, wallabies, guinea pigs, and even spiders.

FOOD AND DRINK The Howtown Hotel (01768 486514) has great food, an old-fashioned ambience, and friendly staff (dress smartly). The Martindale (01768 868111) is less formal and sells local produce.

GETTING THERE Take the A592 for Ullswater and Pooley Bridge. Turn left at the lake; go straight on, over the river and through Pooley Bridge. Take the first right, towards Howtown, and Waterside House is the second campsite on the right.

PUBLIC TRANSPORT Penrith station is 5½ miles from the site. The bus from Penrith to Patterdale will drop you off at Pooley Bridge, but a taxi is the only way to get right to the door.

OPEN March–October.

THE DAMAGE Tent plus 2 people and a car £14–£22 (depending on season) per night.

gill head farm

Gill Head Farm, Troutbeck, Matterdale, Penrith, Cumbria, CA11 0ST   01768 779652   www.gillheadfarm.co.uk

Gill Head is a lovely little working hill farm that's been run by the same family for generations. Ensconced within the Lake District National Park, yet far removed from the tourist hordes, it offers space for tents and caravans, as well as B&B rooms and six rather funky timber camping pods.

The main camping meadow is wide and flat with space for around 50 pitches (the 21 hardstanding caravan pitches are in a separate field), offering campers grand views to the mighty Blencathra – known locally as 'Saddleback', a ridge of six separate fell tops – and Northern Fells, stretching right down the valley to Keswick.

In keeping with the splendid, spacious setting, the site has a laid-back, natural feel to it. There are fields, and streams to paddle in, an organised play area for children, and decent facilities that include a modern and spacious shower, toilet, and laundry block. There's even a log cabin (with TV lounge and sheltered BBQ area) for communal get-togethers and wet-weather relaxation.

Beyond lie the Lakes and a wealth of hiking, biking, gill scrambling, and water-based activities, and the owners have been thoughtful enough to arrange regular onsite activities, games, and even bushcraft courses (run by local firm Reach Beyond Adventure). Those 'who don't want to feel like they're on a campsite', as the owners put it, can ask to pitch in the 'hidden' field, which comes with its own waterfall and steep, wooded banks. You'll have to walk further to the shower block, but it's a small price to pay for such pleasant, leafy isolation.

COOL FACTOR Relaxed site within easy reach of the Lakes.

WHO'S IN? Tents, caravans, campervans, dogs – yes. Groups – by arrangement.

ON SITE Campfires off the ground are allowed. Modern, spacious toilet/shower (5W, 4M) block; undercover BBQ and dining/recreation area; comprehensive play area for kids; dog-walking trails; lock up for bikes; shop offering basics and takeaway breakfasts. Onsite activities and bushcraft courses.

OFF SITE The surrounding area has some of the best walking in the Lakes – ask on site for info and routes. Ullswater (www.ullswater.co.uk) is a short drive away and, being England's second largest lake, has a huge range of activities and water sports to offer, including sailing, kayaking, and fishing trips. The Rheged Centre (01768 868000) in Penrith has shops, a giant cinema, and kids' activities. Rookin House Equestrian Centre (01768 483561) is an adventure venue with everything from shooting and archery to riding lessons and trekking.

FOOD AND DRINK The refurbished Troutbeck Inn (01768 483635) is within walking distance, with pricey but delicious food. The Mill Inn (01768 779632) in calm, unspoiled Mungrisdale serves good food based on traditional Cumbrian fare. Veggies love the Lakeland Pedlar Café (01768 774492), an organic wholefood vegetarian café with beautiful views.

GETTING THERE Take the A66 towards Keswick. At the Troutbeck Inn T-junction take the A5091, signposted Ullswater. After 100 metres turn right for Gill Head Farm.

PUBLIC TRANSPORT Train to Penrith or Keswick then bus no. X4 or X5 (every hour between Penrith and Keswick) to the Troutbeck Inn and walk the ¼ mile to the site.

OPEN March–November.

THE DAMAGE £7.50–£8.50 (depending on season) per person, per night; camping pod £30–£40; hook-up £1.

skiddaw house

Skiddaw House YHA, Bassenthwaite, Keswick, Cumbria, CA12 4QX   07747 174293   www.skiddawhouse.co.uk

Welcome to the highest hostel in Britain – 470 metres up on a high pass in the northern Lake District, only accessible on foot or (at a pinch) by bicycle. Skiddaw House is an isolated 200-year-old former shooting lodge and sometime shepherd's bothy. Its campsite, a two-minute walk away, is diminutive in the extreme – a tiny patch of grass inside the ruins of what may have been a stable (no one really knows). However, the walls, such as they are, do give a bit of protection from the wind. Happily they don't block out the views, though, which are astonishing. Campers can enjoy an uninterrupted gawp all the way down a long valley jealously guarded by the hills of Great Calva and Blencathra. The nearest neighbours are over two miles away, which explains why Skiddaw House is off-grid. Electricity comes from a generator, cooking gas from cylinders, and water arrives straight off the fell (you should boil it, really, but lots of people don't).

Inside the hostel there's a lounge with a piano, library, and a stock of board games; while a large kitchen/diner sports an eclectic collection of cooking utensils and, the pièce de résistance, three different Daniel O'Donnell mugs, including the rare 'On Tour' number. If Daniel did ever make it here he'd have come along one of three branches of the Cumbria Way – from the road near Bassenthwaite (3 miles – passing Britain's best-named trio of hills: Little Cockup, Cockup, and Great Cockup), the car park near Applethwaite (3 miles), or Nether Row (8 miles). You choose – getting here's part of the fun.

COOL FACTOR No mobile signal – the definition of heaven in the 21st century.

WHO'S IN? Tents, big groups, young groups – yes. Campervans, caravans, dogs – no.

ON SITE There's a maximum of 30 campers allowed, but it's unlikely that's ever been reached. Campers can use the rustic hostel loos (1W, 1M), excitingly drafty shower, and kitchen/dining room. There are board games in the lounge and a library that includes children's books. No freezer or fridge, but there is a cool room. A shop sells basic foodstuffs, mainly in tins. Unfortunately the hostel is closed between 10am and 5pm. No campfires allowed.

OFF SITE Walking and mountain biking are the orders of the day here. You can head off along the Cumbria Way (www.thecumbriaway.info) in 3 directions (the route splits here), though some of the cycling is quite tough going south. The delights of Keswick are a 6½-mile hike/pedal away.

FOOD AND DRINK Although there are no pubs within easy striking range of Skiddaw, the Horse and Farrier (01768 779688) at Threlkeld, and the Sun Inn (01768 776439) in Bassenthwaite are worth stopping off at on the way in or out. Market days in Keswick are Thursday and Saturday.

GETTING THERE Don't use the postcode in your satnav or Google Map – both will take you to Peter House Farm, 3 miles away. The OS grid reference for Skiddaw House is NY 287 291 – follow the red diamonds of the Cumbria Way to the hostel.

PUBLIC TRANSPORT Train to Penrith then Stagecoach bus no. X4 or X5 to Threlkeld (5 miles) or Keswick (6 miles). Walking boots at the ready for the rest of the journey.

OPEN March–October.

THE DAMAGE £7 per person, per night (plus £1.50 for non-YHA members).

castlerigg farm

Castlerigg Farm Camping Site, Castlerigg, Keswick, Cumbria, CA12 4TE   01768 772479   www.castleriggfarm.com

Keswick is undoubtedly the tourism focal point in the northern half of the Lake District, and there are a good number of campsites to be found within reach of the bright lights of Hiking City. Some are big corporate places, others club sites bursting at the seams, and most require booking years in advance to get a pitch in the peak periods.

Camping should be about spontaneity, chucking the tent in the boot, or strapping it to the rucksack, and taking off when it suits. But if it's a weekend or the school holidays, where on Planet Lakeland can you find an uncommercial campsite within walking distance of Keswick's diversions that doesn't need booking months in advance?

This is where Castlerigg Farm, sitting atop its hill with a huge view out over Keswick, comes riding to your tenting rescue. There's probably enough space for the entire camping fraternity to stay here and look upon the fells, but by design, they don't pack them in tight. What you get here is a cast-iron guarantee of noiseless nights, complete P&Q, and a fantastic night sky.

The site's lofty location may be a bit of a deterrent to those in need of the bright lights (25 minutes down to town – 45 back up), but this does mean that the hills are just a few steps from the campsite, and for many this is the better deal. In much less time than it takes to descend to the chaos of Keswick, those few steps along the lane will take the soul and soles to some of the loveliest Lakeland views, and is it not better for the spirit to be soaring nearer the sky than the shops?

COOL FACTOR Guaranteed undisturbed nights.

WHO'S IN? Tents, campervans, caravans, dogs – yes. Groups – no.

ON SITE Eighty pitches, of which 24 have hook-ups. The modern and spotless facilities block has loos and showers (6 altogether, 50p metered). There's also a laundry; washing-up sinks; small shop; onsite café. Ice packs can be frozen, phones recharged, and the laptop refreshed. Strictly no noise after 10.30pm. No campfires, but BBQs off the ground are okay.

OFF SITE This is a place where the car can be left motionless for the duration. Besides the obvious allure of walking the fells straight from the site, there is so much else to do nearby. Firstly, the splendid old Keswick Launch Company (01768 772263), which runs a scheduled service gliding around Derwentwater. At Honister Slate Mine (01768 777230) there's a dizzying Via Ferrata and underground tours.

FOOD AND DRINK The site's own Hayloft Café serves breakfast, lunch, packed lunches, and evening meals – all containing local seasonal ingredients. Keswick is awash with decent food, but highly recommended is the Mill Inn (01768 779632; www.the-millinn.co.uk) in Mungrisdale, where only the view can distract you from the delicious food.

GETTING THERE Castlerigg Farm is signposted off the A591 at the top of the hill travelling out of Keswick towards Ambleside.

PUBLIC TRANSPORT The Stagecoach bus no. 555 (Lancaster–Kendal–Keswick) stops at the end of the lane, about 300 metres from the site. All of the places mentioned above are easily accessible by bus or bike.

OPEN March–November.

THE DAMAGE Tent plus 2 adults £12–£15 (depending on season) per night; extra adult £5–£6.20; child £2.90–£3.50.

dalebottom farm

Dalebottom Farm, Naddle, Keswick, Cumbria, CA12 4TF   01768 772176   www.dalebottomfarm.co.uk

Dalebottom's name describes it perfectly in a purely physical sense (it's at the valley bottom), but is oh so inadequate when you throw open your tent flaps of a morning and gaze out at the surroundings. In fact, the effect is just as efficacious if performed in the evening, or any time of day, as this simple farm campsite is encircled by nothing but natural Cumbrian beauty; most of it poking skywards.

The farm lies in the small and fairly reclusive Naddle Valley, a few miles from Keswick, not far from Thirlmere, and just off the main Lakeland thoroughfare. A handy spot for exploring the national park, then, and perfect for carless campers who can get about on a green mixture of public transport and Shanks's pony. The transport is supplied in the form of regular bus no. 555, which threads its way right through the Lakes. It'll drop you and your rucksack in any number of places for a lovely return ramble through, on, above, or below the endlessly dramatic and colourful scenery. If even that seems a bit too carbon-heavy, you can just wander from the site into the landscape for a week or more without falling into a familiar footprint.

COOL FACTOR Ditch the car and step out into the immediately astounding surroundings.

WHO'S IN? Tents, vanners, dogs – yes. Groups – no.

ON SITE The main camping field is huge but never gets full, which is just as well as the facilities wouldn't cope. These include toilets; 4 showers (20p pieces); 2 washing-up sinks; 8 hook-ups. The small farmhouse shop sells daily essentials. Ice packs can be refrozen, too, should the Lakeland summer be sweltering. No campfires, but BBQs off the ground allowed.

OFF SITE See Castlerigg Farm (p284) for easily accessible Derwentwater activities. The Quarry and Mining Museum (01768 779747) at Threlkeld is a pleasant walk from the site, with underground tours and a steam train.

FOOD AND DRINK The nearest eateries are 2 miles down the road towards Ambleside: the Kings Head (01768 772393) and the Dale Head Hall Hotel (01768 772478), both at Thirlspot – see opposite.

GETTING THERE Dalebottom Farm is just off the A591 between Ambleside and Keswick, 3 miles south of Keswick.

PUBLIC TRANSPORT The Stagecoach bus no. 555, from Lancaster to Keswick, passes the site.

OPEN March–October (tents)/end November (campervans).

THE DAMAGE Adult £7 per night; child £3.50.

thirlspot farm

Thirlspot Farm, Thirlmere, Keswick, Cumbria, CA12 4TW 01768 772551 (no advance bookings taken)

Another nigh-on perfect little Lake District site. Not perfect in terms of efficiency, immaculate coiffure, or all-singing all-dancing facilities; perfect in that simple feeling of well-being, which seeps into the soul on your arrival. This might have something to do with the mountainous backdrop that manages to wield an emotional power over us. One such pile of potential life-enhancing rock stands tall and proud right behind Thirlspot Farm. It's called Helvellyn, and there are several different ways to its summit from the campsite, each challenging, but each life-affirming in many ways.

But can one mountain really be sufficient for a well-balanced holiday? Or reason to call this a nigh-on perfect campsite? Some of us think so, but in case you have any lingering doubts, just take a look at the amazing OS Explorer OL5 map, and discover all the other life-validatory, blister-inducing opportunities on offer from Thirlspot. Oh, and did we mention that the King's Head, one of the Lake District's finest traditional coaching inns, is directly next door to the campsite? So Thirlspot might actually be a bit better than nigh-on perfect...

COOL FACTOR Be humbled by the scenery.

WHO'S IN? Tents, campervans, dogs (if under control; this is a sheep farm), motorcycling groups – yes. Caravans – no.

ON SITE Just 25 pitches in total. A minor downside to this stunning situation is the proximity to the main road on one side, so traffic noise may be a concern. The simple, rustic facilities are in one of the old stone outbuildings, with toilets, 4 free showers (2W, 2M). No washing-up sinks; no advance bookings; no campfires – but BBQs off the ground are okay.

OFF SITE The cycle path around Thirlmere is just across the road, and the Mining Museum (see opposite) is a scenic and peaceful 5-mile overland pedal along St-John's-in-the-Vale.

FOOD AND DRINK The adjacent King's Head (01768 772393) is undoubtedly good, but not friendly on the wallet. Across the road, the Dale Head Hall Hotel (01768 772478) has posh nosh, proper wine, and a fantastic view, but is also pricey. Campsite-owner Steve Gaskell suggests the Salutation Inn (01768 779614) at Threlkeld – an authentic Lakeland pub.

GETTING THERE The site is on the east side of the A591, 5 miles south of Keswick.

PUBLIC TRANSPORT As opposite.

OPEN Early March–mid November.

THE DAMAGE Adult £6 per night; child £3; car £2; dog £1.

gillside farm

Gillside Farm, Glenridding, Penrith, Cumbria, CA11 0QQ   01768 482346   www.gillsidecaravanandcampingsite.co.uk

The phrase 'location, location, location' definitely rings true at Gillside Farm, a site sitting pretty up in the Ullswater Valley. You can relish one of the finest views in the Lakes standing here, in the shadow of Helvellyn, and looking out across the reaches of the valley. You're free to set up camp wherever you like; you can even sleep within earshot of the moss-lined beck that tinkers eagerly past the field. The site's split into two, with canvas campers in one field overlooking the valley, and the caravans across the road under tree cover.

For the aspiring Wainwright in you, Gillside Farm is ideally placed to tick off some must-do treks. The track up to Helvellyn and Striding Edge runs right alongside the farm – great for access, but as a camper, you may want to avoid this busy walkers' A-road by pitching further up the hill, nearer the welcome protection of the lichen-mottled walls. You'll be rewarded with near-panoramic views into the Ullswater Valley. But if the call of the fells falls on deaf ears, then this pathway also leads you into town and towards less-strenuous activities around the lake's edge. Time a trip down to Ullswater right and you can get the boat out to Howtown or Pooley Bridge and walk back to Glenridding on the path along the shoreline. Whatever your plans, consult the invaluable five-day weather report in the farm window.

With its picturesque views and easy access to water and walking, Gillside Farm is, at least in camping terms, a gem as precious as the local granite once was – although thankfully not as costly.

COOL FACTOR Low-key camping with outstanding views.
WHO'S IN? Tents, campervans, caravans, dogs – yes. Groups – no.
ON SITE Unmarked pitches spread across one tent field. Hot showers (20p), toilet block, and wash-room. Basic provisions, fresh milk, and eggs are available from the farmhouse shop, and cooked breakfasts are served from a hut on the track. Rabbits and sheep roam around the site, unfazed by the temporary squatters – just be careful where you stash your food. The pathway by the site's edge can be an intrusion. No campfires.
OFF SITE Uncover the Lakes' mining heritage at Threlkeld Quarry and Mining Museum (01768 779747) near Keswick. Or how about a night at the movies? The Rheged Centre (01768 868000; www.rheged.com) in Penrith has a state-of-the-art cinema with 7 IMAX-style gigantic screens showing movies every day.
FOOD AND DRINK The Travellers Rest (01768 482298), with views out to Ullswater, is a nice place to end the day. It serves a selection of cask ales, and the Travellers Mixed Grill will satisfy any post-hike appetite. Every third Tuesday Penrith hosts a farmers' market (01768 817817) with oodles of mouth-watering local specialities on offer.
GETTING THERE Take the A591 to Windermere. Then follow the A592 over the Kirkstone Pass to Glenridding. Turn left on to Greenside Road and then follow the brown signs.
PUBLIC TRANSPORT From Penrith take bus no. 108 to Glenridding town centre. The site is up Greenside Road and is well signposted.
OPEN March–October.
THE DAMAGE Adult £7 per night; child (5 to 16 years) £3; pitch £1; vehicle £1.

side farm

Side Farm Campsite, Patterdale, Penrith, Cumbria, CA11 0NP   01768 482337

Side Farm Campsite just might be one of the most perfectly scenically situated campsites on the planet. It can be found on the eastern side of the Lake District, comfortably sandwiched between the steep slopes of Place Fell and the sylvan shores of Ullswater – the second largest, but most enchanting, of the region's lakes. The view across it happens to be one of the most compelling and beautiful sights in England, and to simply be able to open your tent every morning and look out at this astonishing vista is reason enough to stay a substantial while at Side Farm.

The family-run, working farm site is decent and friendly enough so, for many, sitting by the tent with a book, a beer – or both – and soaking up the magnificence of the surroundings is enough entertainment. However, others might have something different in mind: lake larking. Indeed, you will see many turning up with canoes, dinghies, and other petite water vessels with the aim of paddling and sailing the alluring Ullswater. The lake comes with a 10mph speed limit, so it's safe for novice waterborne craft-masters. If you like keeping your toes dry, the walks from Howtown to Patterdale and Place Fell to Sandwick are equal if not superior in their breathtaking capabilities. Maybe you'll be tempted by the slopes of Helvellyn; all the routes up this monster are inspiring, but the one that everybody should do at least once is the dance across the top of Striding Edge. Then you can return back to the flat, safe bounds of Side Farm – the simple site with one hell(vellyn) of a view.

COOL FACTOR Scenically perfect lakeside campsite with a phenomenal selection of nearby walks.

WHO'S IN? Tents, campervans, small motorhomes, dogs – yes. Caravans, large groups (unless pre-arranged) – no.

ON SITE There are roughly 70 pitches spread out across the lakeside grass. Facilities-wise, there's one clean toilet block and 2 shower blocks (each with 2W, 2M). You can get a great cuppa at the onsite tea room. BBQs allowed off the ground. No campfires.

OFF SITE A variety of lake cruises are offered by Ullswater Steamers (01768 482229; www.ullswater-steamers.co.uk). A cinema and a national mountaineering exhibition can be found at Rheged (01768 868000; www.rheged.com). And of course there are plenty of walks in the area, as well as a lake offering bountiful opportunities for water fun.

FOOD AND DRINK The Patterdale Hotel is less than ½ mile away and offers mouth-watering dinners using fresh, seasonal, Cumbrian produce (01768 482231; www.patterdalehotel.co.uk). But if you're looking for something tasty to slap on the barbie, then look no further than the mini-market in Glenridding, which sells local meats. While you're there, if all that market madness leaves you thirsty, grab a pint at the Travellers Rest pub (01768 482298).

GETTING THERE From junction 40 of the M6 take the A66 west, then the A592 along the shore of Ullswater, through Glenridding centre, then turn left into a track to Side Farm – just after the church on the right.

PUBLIC TRANSPORT Take a train to Penrith, from where you can catch a bus (no. 108) to Patterdale and then it's a short walk to the site.

OPEN March–October.

THE DAMAGE Adult £7 per night; child £3; car £2.

sykeside

Sykeside Camping Park, Brotherswater, Patterdale, Cumbria, CA11 0NZ   01768 482239   www.sykeside.co.uk

Sykeside is one of those campsites that are all about the views. Situated in the midst and mists of the Lake District's Dovedale Valley and surrounded by the fells of Dove Crag, Hart Crag, and Fairfield, it offers glorious mountain vistas wherever you decide to pitch – and the Lakes themselves are enticingly close by.

Innumerable campers have been spilling into Sykeside's friendly embrace for over 35 years now. The current owners have been running the place for more than a decade, and know a thing or two about how to make things run efficiently. The campsite is fastidiously cared for, with neatly trimmed and well-nourished grass, but still manages to emit a reassuringly natural, outdoorsy vibe. Tent pitches are unmarked so campers can choose their very own patch of grass on which to throw their canvas when they arrive.

The best place to pitch is on the terrace on the left-hand side of the site. As it's higher up it gives better views and stays relatively dry all year round (it's the only part of the site open to tents in the winter months), and as you can't take cars up the bank it's often quieter there in summer. (A word of warning, though: it's very occasionally reserved for the use of a school group.)

The onsite facilities are superb. It's true that the bunkhouses and showers could do with a bit of a makeover, but there's a well-stocked shop (summer only) at reception, and a bar (weekends only), as well as the onsite Brotherswater Inn – a quintessential Lake District pub that offers decent grub, draught beer, and accommodation for any non-tenters. Then for the kids there's the use of an entire spare field (except during lambing season) allowing plenty of space for running around and football games.

The location is a boon for walkers, with some excellent routes starting straight from the site: from easy strolls around Brothers Water – a relatively little lake for this district's standards, and favourite of Dorothy Wordsworth, no less – to more challenging ascents up the likes of Fairfield, Helvellyn, and High Street. It's easy to pick up the Fairfield Horseshoe ridge walk, ramble to Priest's Hole cave, or amble on to Ambleside.

In fact, about 40 peaks in the Eastern and far-Eastern fell ranges are feasibly within reach, depending on how far you fancy stretching your legs on any given day – and on the weather, of course. If you do leave, be sure to keep your food somewhere safe. There may not be any bears around, but the local badgers are stealthy and prone to breaking into tents to steal your stash of Jaffa Cakes if you aren't careful.

The nearby area is also full of activity options. You can walk to the top of the Kirkstone Pass and enjoy a pint or an afternoon tea at the agreeable inn there or catch a steamer from Glenridding (four miles away) to Howtown or Pooley Bridge, then stroll back along the shores of Ullswater lake. And if you'd prefer to do your exploration from a sedentary position, hire a rowing boat on Ullswater and spend an afternoon fishing or picnicking.

Brothers Water

With polite, helpful staff making sure the site remains quiet after 11pm, a complete lack of mobile signal (though the pub does offer a very slow wi-fi connection), and a host of wildlife and nature right on your doorstep, Sykeside provides another fantastic get-away-from-it-all camping experience among the plethora of wonders that make up the Lake District.

COOL FACTOR Panoramic mountain views and great hiking action right in the middle of the Lakes.

WHO'S IN Tents, campervans, caravans, motorhomes, dogs, big groups (Duke of Edinburgh only) – yes.

ON SITE There's space for 80 tents, 19 motorhomes, and 5 caravans. The toilet and shower (5W, 6M) facilities are slightly run down but clean (hot water can be scarce when the site is full); shaving sockets and power points are available in the shower block. There's also a laundry room, dishwashing area (with freezer for ice packs), and well-stocked shop at reception (open summer only) selling groceries, camping equipment, maps, and guides. As well as the onsite Brotherswater Inn, there's the cosy Barn End bar (open at weekends throughout summer) for meals and drinks in the evening. Play facilities for kids are limited to an empty field. No campfires.

OFF SITE Boat trips with Ullswater Steamers (01768 482229) from Glenridding (a 10-minute drive) are available all year round: you can take a boat halfway around Ullswater, then walk back to your car. If you'd prefer a more adventurous trip, Glenridding Sailing Centre (01768 482541; www.glenriddingsailingcentre.co.uk) offers a range of sailing tuition and boat hire. On dry land, a 30-minute drive away, Castlerigg Stone Circle (see www.visitcumbria.com) is a sight to rival Stonehenge. Keswick has the surprisingly excellent Cumberland Pencil Museum (www.pencilmuseum.co.uk) and a very good museum and art gallery (www.keswickmuseum.webs.com) for rainy days. You can also spot ospreys nearby, at Bassenthwaite (www.ospreywatch.co.uk).

FOOD AND DRINK The Brotherswater Inn serves generous portions of hearty pub grub along with a full range of beers and lagers. The Glass House (01539 432137; www.theglasshouserestaurant.co.uk) in Ambleside, 6 miles away, is located in an atmospheric listed building and serves great lunches and dinners, superb wines, European beers, home-made flavoured vodkas, over 60 malt whiskies (some of which are very rare), and a collection of vintage Armagnac dating back to 1900. The tea room at Cote How Organic (01539 432765), at Rydal, is definitely worth a visit for a cream tea and to stock up on local organic food.

GETTING THERE If you're travelling from the south, take the A591 Kendal bypass to Windermere. Just past Windermere turn right on to the A592 towards the Kirkstone Pass and Ullswater. Head over the pass and down the other side and you'll see the Brotherswater Inn on the left. Turn into the pub car park – then drive through for the campsite. If you're coming from the north, take the A66 towards Keswick. After ¼ mile turn left, on to the A592 towards Windermere and the Kirkstone Pass; pass Ullswater, and the entrance to the campsite is about 2 miles beyond Patterdale, on the right-hand side of the road, before the Brotherswater Inn. If you miss this entrance, turn into the pub car park and go on through to the site.

PUBLIC TRANSPORT The nearest train stations are Windermere (12 miles) and Penrith (18 miles), where you can pick up the Kirkstone Rambler (bus no. 517, runs at weekends from Easter until October, and every day during the school summer holidays) to Glenridding.

OPEN All year except Christmas Day.

THE DAMAGE Tent plus 2 people and a car £13–£22.50 (depending on season) per night.

lanefoot farm

Lanefoot Farm, Thornthwaite, Keswick, Cumbria, CA12 5RZ   01768 778097   see www.stayinthornthwaite.co.uk

There's a pitch to suit all tastes at Lanefoot Farm. Love views? Park yourself in the big open field with a stonking vista of Skiddaw. Taking the kids? Head for the cosy family field. Seen the weather forecast and fancy a bit of shelter? Pop into the back garden of the farmhouse and find yourself a quiet spot among the trees.

Wonderfully amiable owners Gareth and Helen took over this campsite, in its little corner near Keswick, a few years ago and injected it with new life (and some free-range chickens). The facilities are the sort you'd be happy to eat your dinner off, there's a little shop on site, chickens roaming free, and a friendly atmosphere.

Cyclists are well catered for – the site is bang on the C2C route and there are mountain bike trails aplenty in the nearby Whinlatter Forest. And if you've turned up to discover you've forgotten to pack your tent (we've all done it) there's a shepherd's hut, with four mattresses, for hire.

Finally, for pub quiz devotees: nearby Bassenthwaite Lake is home to the vendace, Britain's rarest fish. Next question please, landlord.

COOL FACTOR Brill views, and a shelter too.

WHO'S IN? Tents, campervans, caravans, dogs (on leads), big groups (not stag/hen), young groups (activities) – yes.

ON SITE Campfires: £5.50 for a wheel rim, wood, and kindling. Pitches: 60 tents, 12 caravans; 15 hook-ups. Good clean loos (3W, 3M) and 3 bright showers, washing-up area, drying room, huge wall maps, and info. Ice packs (20p), and tiny shop sells basics and meats. There is some traffic noise.

OFF SITE Walks include Grizedale Pike and Skiddaw. Mountain bikers have the mountainous Whinlatter Forest trails (see www.forestry.gov.uk); birders have the hide on Bassenthwaite Lake and the osprey-viewing platform.

FOOD AND DRINK Try a mini pub/hotel crawl in Braithwaite: the Royal Oak (01768 778533), Coledale Inn (01768 778272), and Middle Ruddings (01768 778436).

GETTING THERE From Keswick take the A66 west. Take a left turn northwards ½ mile after the B5292 turning for Braithwaite. Lanefoot Farm is on the left, after ½ mile.

PUBLIC TRANSPORT Train to Penrith then bus no. X5 to just beyond Thornthwaite, then a couple of minutes' walk.

OPEN Easter–October.

THE DAMAGE Adult £7.50–£8.50 per night; child £3.50. Shepherd's hut (sleeping 4 very snugly indeed) £30 per night.

stonethwaite

Stonethwaite Campsite, Stonethwaite, Borrowdale, Cumbria, CA12 5XG   01768 777234

Head south down Borrowdale and you'll notice the valley growing narrower and narrower until the road hits the little village of Stonethwaite and simply gives up. From here a stony track heads bravely on a further half-mile to the campsite before it too is defeated – here the valley closes up completely and only footpaths prevail.

Its location, right at the head of Borrowdale, gives the National Trust's Stonethwaite campsite a real pioneering feel. It's stretched along several hundred metres of Stonethwaite Beck, the sort of wide, shallow river beloved of gold prospectors (though there's none here, we're sorry to report, so leave your pan and sieve at home and bring a toy sailing boat instead). This means that if you camp at the very far end it is a bit of a yomp to the loos. And there are no showers but, hey, there's a river.

For the energetic who enjoy leaping from stone to stone up steep hills and over high fells there are footpaths aplenty – bring a good map and work out a circular walk. Or, if that sounds like hard work, there's an entirely flat half-mile amble down to the cosy Langstrath Country Inn.

COOL FACTOR There's a river and some mountains and not much else.

WHO'S IN? Everyone, except for groups.

ON SITE An indeterminate number of pitches on this sprawling site. A stone-built no-frills loo and washing-up sink (with a shelter) outside comprise facilities. No campfires.

OFF SITE The Cumbria Way (www.thecumbriaway.info) slides by on the other side of the Stonethwaite Beck and is reached by a convenient bridge just to the south. Or you can go underground at Honister Slate Mine (01768 777230; www.honister-slate-mine.co.uk) and look at some slate.

FOOD AND DRINK The Langstrath Country Inn (01768 777239) in Stonethwaite boasts a range of local cask ales, large stock of wines and whiskies, and some excellent dishes (including veggie and vegan options). There's a lovely cheese delicatessen in Keswick called The Cheese Delicatessen.

GETTING THERE From Keswick, follow signs for the B5289. After 7 miles turn left into Stonethwaite village. At the end of the village a track leads to the campsite.

PUBLIC TRANSPORT Bus no. 79 (aka the Borrowdale Rambler) runs from Keswick to Stonethwaite (10 mins away).

OPEN All year.

THE DAMAGE Adult £5 per night; child £3, under-5s free.

chapel house farm

Chapel House Farm, Stonethwaite, Borrowdale, Keswick, Cumbria, CA12 5XG   01768 777602

Chapel House Farm's campsite is an uncomplicated place consisting of a single open field where the Stonethwaite and Derwent Valleys join forces to form Borrowdale, and like anywhere in this valley, the view is astonishing.

Cars aren't allowed on site, creating not only a safer and more relaxed setting, but adding to that notion that camping is somehow a return to the simple life by removing automotive reminders of modern times. And once the car has been banished, there really is no need to use it again; there's a bus stop outside the site, with regular services (open-topped in summer) travelling up and down Borrowdale to Keswick and all its rainy-day leisure activities, and even over the Honister Pass to Buttermere.

It's impossible to visit the Lake District and not take advantage of the many fell-walking opportunities, and Borrowdale is indeed ringed by the high fells, but this wooded sylvan valley also offers many miles of stress-free river- and lake-side strolling.

Chapel House Farm is very popular with young families, too, and on any sunny summer's day the nearby Stonethwaite Beck, and a place called Black Moss Pot (a dramatic little gorge) in Langstrath Beck, are alive to the sound of children of all ages splashing about in the shallow water or swimming in the big, deep river pools. All in all, this is straightforward camping, with almost too many activity options, in one of the most appealing locations in the Lake District.

COOL FACTOR Beautiful location with gorgeous natural swimming pools nearby.

WHO'S IN? Tents, campervans, (limited number of) caravans, dogs – yes. Supervised groups (outdoor activities mainly) – by prior arrangement.

ON SITE About 70 pitches, with the cars and campervans restricted to the parking area. The facilities (7 toilets, 4 showers, 3 outside washing-up sinks) are really quite crude; only the showers (50p) have hot water, but they normally suffice. There's a new camping barn. No campfires, but BBQs are acceptable if off the ground.

OFF SITE Buses (or your boots even) allow easy access to Keswick (15-minute bus journey), where all sorts of activities await (see p295). There are walks aplenty all around and adrenaline junkies are catered for at the Keswick Climbing Wall (01768 772000) and Adventure Centre (01768 775687).

FOOD AND DRINK There are dozens of good eating places in Keswick, but you've got two within easy walking distance that will cater for most tastes. The Langstrath Country Inn (01768 777239) provides top-rate food (including local Herdwick lamb), carefully prepared, and at appropriate prices. And the Scafell Hotel (01768 777208) in Rosthwaite has both a restaurant menu and bar food.

GETTING THERE From junction 40 off the M6 follow the A66 west to Keswick, then the B5289 along Borrowdale. The site is 7 miles from Keswick, on the right.

PUBLIC TRANSPORT Regular hourly bus service all year between Keswick and Seatoller. In summer there are extra services every half hour, including one to Buttermere.

OPEN Flexible, but pretty much all year. Be warned: Bank Holiday weekends can be chaotically busy.

THE DAMAGE Adult £6; child £3 per night.

syke farm

Syke Farm, Buttermere, Cumbria, CA13 9XA   01768 770222 (no advance bookings taken)

Anyone who played King of the Castle as a child is going to love Syke Farm. While the pitches on the banks of Mill Beck are exquisite, there's something extra special about bagging a bit of space on the summit of one of the tiny hillocks. Wherever you camp, though, you're guaranteed a view of High Snockrigg, the hill that rises steeply above the site like a doting maiden aunt over a pram.

In one corner of the site there's a huddle of stone-built loos and showers, and a separate stone hut called Charlie's Shelter, which contains a table and benches, a sink for washing-up, and another loo and shower. Priority is given to Duke of Edinburgh Award parties (though surely they're meant to be out in the wilds being all self-reliant?) so remember to bring along a disguise that will make you look both 15 and constantly on the verge of being irredeemably lost.

For a bit of gentle exercise, campers can either walk along Mill Beck to Crummock Water or mosey through the tiny village of Buttermere – with its two excellent hotel bars and brace of tea rooms – to its namesake lake. This luscious body of water was Alfred Wainwright's favourite, and it's easy to see why. One of the smaller lakes, it's girded by wooded hills. A stroll all the way around takes 90 minutes or so, depending on whether you're a forced-march sort of walker or someone dedicated to putting the 'amble' into 'ramble'. And should any King of the Castle games have produced some dirty rascals, you can always wash them off in the lake.

COOL FACTOR Wild camping... but with creature comforts...

WHO'S IN? Tents, dogs – yes. Campervans, caravans, groups (except Duke of Edinburgh) – no.

ON SITE A variable number of pitches (this is not one of your manicured car park-like sites). A small, stone, rather cheerless hut housing 2 loos (1W, 1M) and 2 showers (1W, 1M; 50p for 6 minutes), with another nicer shower/loo in Charlie's Shelter. The car park, although on the other side of the river, is still a bit of an eyesore. No campfires.

OFF SITE Once you've walked around Buttermere Lake and conquered Scafell Pike, Pillar, and Haystacks, try Honister Slate Mine's Via Ferrata (01768 777714; see www.honister-slate-mine.co.uk) – a route once used by miners up a rock face, on which the climber is safely attached to a cable.

FOOD AND DRINK The Fish Inn (01768 770253) and the Bridge Hotel (01768 770252) have public bars and beer gardens, and are both a 2-minute walk away. Buttermere's 2 tea rooms are Croft House Café and – famed for its ice creams – Syke Farm Tea Room (despite its name, not run by this site).

GETTING THERE Take the B5289 from Keswick over the Honister Pass (or, if cycling, the back-road Newlands Pass – still a bit of a lung-buster) and past the church into Buttermere village. Turn left for Syke Farm (check in first at the farmhouse, then follow signs to the car park to reach the campsite).

PUBLIC TRANSPORT There's a bus service called the Honister Rambler that runs from Keswick bus station to Buttermere between April and October.

OPEN All year.

THE DAMAGE £7 per person, per night (£1 discount for anyone arriving without a motorised vehicle).

wasdale head

Wasdale Campsite, Wasdale Head, Seascale, Cumbria, CA20 1EX   01539 463862   see www.ntlakescampsites.org.uk

England's highest mountains may not be on the scale of the Alps or the Himalayas, but they are majestic in their own understated way. They also have the advantage of being readily accessible and, in most seasons, relatively easy to conquer with the help of a pair of decent walking boots, clement weather, and a thermos of hot tea.

Several of the country's highest mountains are clustered around the northern end of Wastwater in the Lakes, where the National Trust thoughtfully sited a camping ground at Wasdale Head. From here, you can lie in a sleeping bag, head poking out of your tent and, as the dawn mists clear, survey the encircling slopes to plan your assault on them. Wasdale Head is a handy base for England's tallest mountain, Scafell Pike. Here you'll find the start of a steep, but straightforward ascent up the rock-strewn mountain. While back at basecamp, there's a small shop for walking maps, friendly advice, and plasters. Three small fields scattered with trees provide plenty of flat grass for pitching, and with cars restricted to the parking areas it's a peaceful site. A high point on England's campsite circuit.

COOL FACTOR Wilderness location with breathtaking views of the high fells.

WHO'S IN? Tents, campervans, dogs (on leads at all times) – yes. Caravans, groups – no.

ON SITE About 120 pitches with 6 hook-ups on hardstanding. Timed barrier system in place for arrivals (8–11am; 5–8pm). A small shop selling basic food and camping accessories. Hot showers (20p), flush toilets, disabled facilities, washing machines and dryers (token operated). No campfires, no disposable BBQs.

OFF SITE Visit the Roman port of Ravenglass, or nearby Muncaster Castle (01229 717614; www.muncaster.co.uk).

FOOD AND DRINK Buy meat direct from the farmer at Wasdale Head Hall Farm (01946 726245). Or treat yourself to some tea-room goodies at the traditional Muncaster Watermill (01229 717232).

GETTING THERE Approaching from the south on the A595, turn right at Holmrook for Santon Bridge and follow the signs up to Wasdale Head. Approaching from the north, turn left at Gosforth.

OPEN All year.

THE DAMAGE Tent, plus adult and car £8–£21 per night. Extra adult £5; child £2.50; dog £1.50. Hook-up £3.

eskdale

Eskdale Camping, Boot, Holmrook, Cumbria, CA19 1TH   01946 723253 (no calls after 8pm)   see www.campingandcaravanningclub.co.uk

Arrive here from the east on foot or bicycle and you'll have had the pleasure of conquering both the Wrynose and Hardknott passes, the latter of which is claimed by locals to be the steepest and highest road in Britain. After such a challenge, there's nothing like discovering that your campsite has cracking showers and a small shop selling wine and local beer. What's more, if you've jettisoned your tent halfway up one of the hills, you can book yourself into one of the new wooden pods.

Eskdale is unusual among Camping and Caravanning Club (C&CC) sites in that the emphasis is very much on tents, which habitually outnumber campervans here by some margin. Aquaphiles will enjoy the fact that the little Eel Beck runs through the site, and should also take a walk to the low waterfall just a minute away. Tiny Boot village somehow runs to two pubs within stumbling distance and its own annual beer festival. It also serves as the terminus for the Ravenglass and Eskdale Railway, a mini narrow gauge affair that's actually extremely useful; it chugs to Ravenglass, where you can change on to a 'proper' train.

COOL FACTOR First-rate facilities in a cracking location.
WHO'S IN? Tents, small campervans, dogs, (activities-based, not stag/hen) groups – yes. Large campervans, caravans – no.
ON SITE Pitches: 80 tents; 12 campervans; 35 hook-ups; 10 pods; camping barn. Facilities: modern loos (5W, 3M); family/disabled room (1 loo, 2 showers, baby-changer); and showers (3W, 3M); 6 washing-up sinks; washing machine (£3), dryer (£1); drying room; and washing line. Swings, trampoline, adventure playground, 2-acre wood. Ice packs – BYO or hire, both 50p. Shop/off licence sells basics. No campfires.
OFF SITE Scafell Pike and the Old Man of Coniston are on your doorstep. There's Muncaster Castle and Whitehaven's innovative Beacon museum/gallery (01946 592302) too.
FOOD AND DRINK The Woolpack Inn (01946 723230) is arguably the best pub in the area. Beer festival in June.
GETTING THERE Don't use satnav. From the A595 take a turn to Santon Bridge, from there follow signs to Eskdale Green. First left after the village; site's on the left after 2 miles.
PUBLIC TRANSPORT Train to Ravenglass then on to the Ravenglass and Eskdale Railway to Boot.
OPEN March–January.
THE DAMAGE £7.50–£9 (seasonal) per person, per night. Additional non-member fee £7. Camping pod £41 per night.

rydal hall

Rydal Hall, Rydal, Ambleside, Cumbria, LA22 9LX   01539 432050   www.rydalhall.org

William Wordsworth, a man with an eye for a view, loved the hamlet of Rydal so much he took up residence there. His next-door neighbours, the Le Fleming family, owned Rydal Hall and lived the life of contemplative ease one associates with the landed gentry. It's fitting, then, that their home is now a retreat centre, and much of the ample estate is one of the most cultured campsites in England.

Perched on a hill above Rydal Water, the 16th-century mansion (all right, most of it dates from the late 19th century) boasts 34 acres of woodland, a formal Edwardian garden, a 'quiet garden' for peaceful contemplation, a waterfall with a posh hut from which to view it, numerous pieces of sculpture, a croquet lawn, and a tea shop – all of which are open to campers. Glampers are also catered for, there being yurts (run separately from the campsite) and pods dotted about the grounds.

Should you tire of wandering the estate, a 30-second saunter will take you to Rydal Mount, Wordsworth's home for the last 37 years of his life, which is now a museum dedicated to the poet. However, for properly exploring the immediate area, you should bring your walking boots and hit the Coffin Trail. The three-mile path runs right through the site on its way to Grasmere in the north and Ambleside in the south, following the route that coffins were carried along for burial in medieval times. If that sounds a tad too morbid, try the Lake Walk, which connects Grasmere and Ambleside again, but broadly follows the western side of the waterways that join the two.

COOL FACTOR Camping in the grounds of a stately home? I'll have some of that.

WHO'S IN? Tents, dogs (on leads), groups (mixed-sex and activities-based) – yes. Vanners, single-sex groups – no.

ON SITE Just one campfire pitch, but it can be booked beforehand. A maximum of 100 campers are allowed on site, so overcrowding is never a problem. The loos (3W, 2M) and showers (1W, 1M) are augmented from Easter to August by portaloos (including 4 showers), but there's a new (and one hopes rather shinier) toilet block in the pipeline. There's an adventure playground in the woods; a croquet lawn by the house (mallets and balls available to hire); and Rydal Water is a 5-minute walk away, if anyone fancies a dip.

OFF SITE Free leaflet about the Coffin Trail is available on site, and Rydal Mount and its tea room (01539 433002; www.rydalmount.co.uk) are worth a stanza of any poem.

FOOD AND DRINK A tea shop on the grounds has tables by the river (open daily, 10am–5pm). Sadly, Ambleside isn't piled high with pubs you wish were your local. The Wateredge Inn (01539 432332), though fastidiously characterless, does at least have a beer garden on the shores of Windermere. Ambleside's two art-house cinema-restaurants (one of which is vegetarian) are great, however (www.fellinisambleside.com and www.zeffirellis.com).

GETTING THERE Easy one, this. Get yourself on to the A591, from Keswick to Kendal. Rydal is on this road just north of Ambleside. The turning for Rydal Hall is off to the east, just south of the Glen Rothay Hotel and Badger Bar.

PUBLIC TRANSPORT Train to Windermere or Lancaster and bus no. 555 (www.stagecoachbus.com) to Rydal.

OPEN All year.

THE DAMAGE Adult £6.50 p/n; under-18 £4.50; car £3.

Rydal Beck runs through the estate

tarn foot farm

Tarn Foot Farm, Loughrigg, Ambleside, Cumbria, LA22 9HF   01539 432596

A tarn, as anyone schooled in the niceties of topography will tell you, is a lake or pool formed by a glacier. Cumbrians, however, play fast and loose with this definition and are wont to call almost any pond found in the hills a tarn. It's a relief, then, to discover that Loughrigg Tarn – 'Diana's Looking Glass' according to Wordsworth – is a proper glaciated lake, albeit a small one.

So quiet it's hard to believe it's just a short hop away from busy Ambleside, Tarn Foot is an old-fashioned camping gem. Perched on a hill, most of the farm is home to cattle and sheep (bring your spotter's guide – there are Herdwicks, Swaledales, and Cheviots here, among others). Pass along a short track from the ancient-looking farmyard, however, and you'll find one large bumpy field given over to tents (and the occasional campervan).

There are views of fields and woods all around, and space for children to run about and fly kites (quite successfully too, at this height), but the main attraction here is just out of sight. Cross a stile by an old oak tree and tumble down the field beyond and you'll reach the farm's eponymous tarn. The water is chilly, even in summer – so bring along a sense of adventure as well as your swimming gear – but very refreshing, and popular not only with bathers but canoeists and kayakers too.

The facilities are minimal – two loos and an outdoor sink – but campers seem to like it that way. The only downside is that it's a 'families- and couples-only' site, so lone backpackers and groups must seek their tarn-based pleasures elsewhere.

COOL FACTOR Grab those swimming togs.

WHO'S IN? Tents, campervans, dogs – yes. Caravans, groups, lone campers – no.

ON SITE There are 40 pitches, 2 rustic loos in lean-tos by the farmhouse, an outdoor washing-up sink, but no showers. Fishing licences for the tarn (which does sometimes suffer from being a bit algaefied) can be purchased from the owners. No campfires.

OFF SITE Ramblers, Sunday cyclists, and mountain bikers will want to head for Grizedale Forest (see www.forestry. gov.uk) with its many walking routes (and one suitable for wheelchairs), cycle paths to suit all abilities, and forest sculptures. Bikes can be hired locally (01229 860369; www.grizedalemountainbikes.co.uk). Ambleside runs to 2 excellent restaurant-cinemas (www.fellinisambleside.com and www.zeffirellis.com), while Lake Windermere plays host to all sorts of aquatic activities.

FOOD AND DRINK The Drunken Duck Inn (01539 436347; www.drunkenduckinn.co.uk), at tiny Barngates, has its own microbrewery and posh-nosh restaurant (eat first and just go for a drink if you're economising). Lucy's of Ambleside (01539 432288; www.lucysofambleside.co.uk) has a café/restaurant and deli that stocks regional foods.

GETTING THERE From Ambleside, head west on the A593, taking the first right after Clappersgate. After $^1/_3$ mile, take the narrow, sharply rising road on your right. The entrance to Tarn Foot Farm is almost immediately on the left.

PUBLIC TRANSPORT Train to Windermere or Lancaster and bus no. 555 to Ambleside. Then take no. 516 to Skelwith Bridge and walk up the steep hill for ¼ mile to the campsite.

OPEN All year.

THE DAMAGE £3 per person, per night; £1 per car.

baysbrown farm

Baysbrown Farm Campsite, Great Langdale, Ambleside, Cumbria, LA22 9JZ   01539 437150   www.baysbrownfarm.com

Tourist traffic jams can be a bit of a problem in beautiful places, especially when the place is as enchanting as the Lake District. Fortunately, there is some respite from the lake-lovers' mayhem in the lake-less valley of Great Langdale. And sitting serenely in the heart of it is Baysbrown Farm, which nuzzles up against a steep fell on one side while the other overlooks three generously sized camping fields that gently slope down to the valley's river.

The entire site lies beneath the humbling rocks of Crinkle Crags, Bowfell, and the Langdale Pikes, that all seem to swallow up your tent, the farmhouse, and the distant village, giving a sense of scale rarely found in the Lakes. Peering out each morning at the mist-shrouded peaks is worth the entrance money alone.

You and your tent will be at the centre of an 800-acre farm. Baahs float over the lichen-drenched walls from the resident flock of sheep and chickens run amok around your guy ropes, much to the kids' delight. Life is so much simpler here – as is the camping style. The site doesn't have any designated pitches; just rock up and find your corner of tranquillity. Then, when you're done, just walk up to the farmhouse to announce your arrival through the ever-open kitchen door and hand over your fee. There's no such thing as booking in advance here; it's not that kind of place.

Just like all Lake District sites, Baysbrown won't leave you short of things to do; grab a bike, put your boots on, or lie on the grass and stare at the peaks, thankful you're not stuck in traffic for the Lakes.

COOL FACTOR Blissful Lake District chilling, minus the lake and the congested roads.

WHO'S IN? Tents, small motorhomes/campervans/caravans (narrow site entrance with hump bridge so anything large or low won't fit), dogs – yes. Large, loud groups – no.

ON SITE Campfires and BBQs off the ground allowed. Approx. 200 first-come, first-served pitches. A big facilities block with toilets and free hot showers (5W, 4M). Separate toilet-only block (9W, 8M). Battery charging at the farm. Basic recycling facilities. Chickens and some sheep nearby. No noise after 11pm.

OFF SITE Indulge the kids (or take a nostalgic trip back to childhood stories) at the World of Beatrix Potter (08445 041233; www.hop-skip-jump.com) in nearby Bowness. Windermere and Ambleside are a 20-minute drive away, each have a host of tea rooms, shops, and museums. For free, outdoors, on-your-doorstep fun, walk the Cumbria Way.

FOOD AND DRINK Find flagstone floors, open fires, and real ales at Wainwrights' Inn (01539 438088; see www.langdale.co.uk). The Drunken Duck Inn (01539 436347; www.drunkenduckinn.co.uk) near Ambleside boasts a gastronomic menu and sensational views.

GETTING THERE Take the A591 to Ambleside then follow the B5343 to Chapel Stile. The campsite is signposted a mile past Wainwrights' Inn. If using satnav, use postcode LA22 9JR to arrive opposite the campsite entrance.

PUBLIC TRANSPORT From Ambleside train station the Langdale Rambler bus no. 516 will get you to Chapel Stile, from where it's a ¼ mile walk to the site.

OPEN March–October.

THE DAMAGE Adult £4–£6 per night; child £2–£5, under-5s free. No credit/debit card facilities.

low wray

Low Wray Campsite, Low Wray, nr Ambleside, Cumbria, LA22 0JA   01539 463862   see www.ntlakescampsites.org.uk

A night or two camping at this lakeside location is, quite frankly, unforgettable. Low Wray National Trust Campsite sits on the quieter western shore of Lake Windermere, and if the weather holds to give a decent sunrise over the lake, it can feel like the most relaxing place on earth.

As you'd expect from a National Trust site, it's well organised with good facilities. There are two main areas for camping; one set back from the lake in a clearing surrounded by trees, another right on the shore with a scattering of trees and expansive views across the water. The latter is the best place to pitch, despite a surcharge (which varies according to location: £7.50–£10) and longer walk from the car.

Aside from the great location next to England's largest lake and the possibilities for sailing, kayaking, and fishing, the campsite is well positioned to take in some of the Lake District's 'dry' attractions. There are plenty of opportunities for walking and off-road cycling, with paths leading directly from the campsite. Not forgetting that this is also Beatrix Potter country, so there's a plethora of Peter Rabbit-related activities to enjoy.

COOL FACTOR Unforgettable lakeside camping.
WHO'S IN? Tents, small campervans, dogs – yes. Caravans, groups – no.
ON SITE About 120 pitches; no hardstanding. New reception and shop; laundry (tokens from shop); kids' playground; showers; disabled facilities; boat launch (non-powered craft only). Timed barrier in place for arrivals. Midges can be vicious – take repellent. No campfires; BBQs off the ground okay.
OFF SITE Visit Beatrix Potter's former home at Hill Top (01539 436269) in Near Sawrey, with its delightfully haphazard cottage garden. The Beatrix Potter Gallery (01539 436355) in Hawkshead houses her original paintings.
FOOD AND DRINK Wander around Ambleside and visit the foodie-fantastic world of Lucy's (01539 432288) or head to the restaurant at the Drunken Duck Inn (01539 436347).
GETTING THERE From Ambleside, take the A593 to Clappersgate then turn left on to the B5286. Turn left again at the sign for Wray; the site is on the left, less than a mile away.
PUBLIC TRANSPORT Coniston Rambler bus no. 505 from Ambleside to Windermere drops you within a mile of the site.
OPEN Easter–October.
THE DAMAGE Tent, plus adult, plus car £8–£21 per night. Extra adult £5; child £2.50; dog £1.50. Book online (£5).

hawkshead hall

Hawkshead Hall Campsite, Hawkshead, Ambleside, Cumbria, LA22 0NN   01539 436221   www.hawksheadhall-campsite.com

In a small and very compact space the Lake District scenery varies from the savage to the serene, with wilderness giving way to the quaint. The area immediately around Hawkshead, and Hawkshead Hall Campsite, falls fair and square on to the serene and quaint side – the green and extremely cute Lake District of Beatrix Potter, as opposed to the high hills of Wainwright.

Two spacious, open fields comprise the campsite, whose facilities are enthusiastically maintained, and whose views are smooth and free from any rocky heights that might obscure the sun and spoil your tan. Those high hills also bring rain, and it is said that this part of the Lake District is much drier than the mountainous lands to the north. The walking here is gentle, and Hawkshead village is a lovely half-mile stroll along a traffic-free track. The village – and its huge clothes shop – besides having all sorts of historical links with Lakeland's literate nobility, is also agreeably charming. This is the Lake District for the family holiday, and for those in need of total mind or body relaxation… Or both.

COOL FACTOR Easy-going site in gentle scenery.

WHO'S IN? Tents, campervans, caravans, dogs – yes. Big groups, lone backpackers – no (families and couples only).

ON SITE The site is spread over 2 very large fields, and even at full capacity (150 pitches) there's plenty of room. A limited number of electric hook-ups are available. The facilities (toilets, 6 free showers, washing-up sinks) are housed in a clean Portakabin in the farmyard. No campfires.

OFF SITE Head to Hawkshead village for a mosey around. Renowned beauty spot Tarn Hows is a glorious 2-mile walk from the site, and John Ruskin's stately home (01539 441396) lies over the other side of Grizedale Forest.

FOOD AND DRINK A good selection of eateries in the village. Sawrey House (01539 436387) has a classy restaurant at night, and Mrs Tiggy-Winkle's Tea Room in the day.

GETTING THERE Take the ferry from Bowness across Windermere, then follow the B5285 through Sawrey and Hawkshead. The site is on the right, just beyond the village.

PUBLIC TRANSPORT Regular bus no. 505 from Ambleside to Coniston passes the site.

OPEN Mid March–mid October.

THE DAMAGE Tent plus 2 people £14.50 per night; extra adult £2.50; child (5 to 15 years) £1, under-5s free.

turner hall farm

Turner Hall Farm, Seathwaite, Broughton-in-Furness, Cumbria, LA20 6EE   01229 716420   www.duddonvalley.co.uk

If you're looking for a truly remote wilderness camping experience, pitch up at Turner Hall Farm in the Lake District's lesser-visited Duddon Valley.

The most spectacular way to arrive is over the Wrynose Pass, a tortuous zigzag of a road making for an exhilarating journey that matches some of the best Lake District walks, view for view. Even if you take the longer, winding road via Broughton Mills you have to stop to open and close gates, an action loaded with the symbolism of leaving civilisation behind.

Turner Hall Farm is tucked into the folds of the fells between the mountains of Scafell Pike to the north-west, and the Old Man of Coniston to the south-east. It's a basic campsite set up for walkers and climbers, the attraction being its location and outlook rather than the facilities. But the surrounding fells provide an unforgettable backdrop that makes for a fine, inspiring vista.

It's a raw, boulder-strewn, long-grassed site, with private corners for sheltered pitching in among the crags and drystone walls. Weathered and worn, beaten and torn, the site merges seamlessly into the rugged landscape. It's all pretty low-key for a campsite: just turn up, pitch your tent, and someone will be round to collect your money in the morning, or if you're an early-bird-type walker, just drop by the house.

Turner Hall Farm may be as off the beaten track as you can get, but thankfully you don't need a 4x4 to get there. Just remember to close the gates behind you as you leave civilisation.

COOL FACTOR A glorious wilderness among rocky crags and famous fells.

WHO'S IN? Tents, campervans, dogs, groups – yes. Caravans – no.

ON SITE Modern, clean facilities – separate toilet blocks and hot water for showers (£1 for 4 minutes) and washing-up; filtered drinking water. A post office and general store (01229 716255) with its own small gallery can be found 3 miles away in Ulpha. The campsite owner recommends you bring midge repellent, sunscreen, and waterproofs – it's not unusual to need all three in one trip. No campfires.

OFF SITE We suggest you grab some car-free time while you can and just walk, walk, walk. Do make sure you come with all your supplies. If four legs are more your style, go horse riding at Murthwaite Green Trekking Centre (01229 770876; www.murthwaitegreen.co.uk) in Silecroft. Muncaster Castle (01229 717614) near Ravenglass is allegedly one of Britain's most haunted castles.

FOOD AND DRINK Broughton-in-Furness has a butcher's and greengrocer's, both of which stock local and organic foods. The Newfield Inn (01229 716208; www.newfieldinn. co.uk), 10 minutes' walk down the road in Seathwaite, has real ale, a real fire, and real hearty food. It's open all day, so if the weather turns treacherous, you can hole up here.

GETTING THERE From Great Langdale continue over the high-gradient Wrynose Pass, following signs for Seathwaite. Turner Hall Farm is signposted on the left. The alternative route is via Broughton Mills from the A593. Continue through Seathwaite, and you'll see the campsite signposted on your right.

OPEN April–October.

THE DAMAGE Adult £5 per night; child £2; car £1; dog £1.

grizedale

Grizedale Camping Site, Bowkerstead Farm, Satterthwaite, Ulverston, Cumbria, LA12 8LL   01229 860208   www.grizedale-camping.co.uk

If ever a campsite precisely fitted the criteria to be labelled as the perfect *Cool Camping* site, then this is it. Well we think it is, or at least might very well be... if there *were* actually precise criteria for a *Cool Camping* campsite. So how did we come to this illogical conclusion? A good question, and it involves unquantifiable notional nonsense like atmosphere, vibes, emotions, nags, *Shrek*, and a bit of hobbit-ness. Then there's the old chestnut of a cracking location, and this is perhaps that most important box to be ticked before any campsite gets a certificate of worth from Tent HQ.

Taking location first, and any campsite in the Lake District has a head start over the rest, with this area's unique combination of rugged natural scenery enclosing picture-postcard valleys. But oddly, Grizedale, the location of this textbook *Cool Camping* site, isn't like anywhere else in the Lake District, and is largely covered in trees; fairly boring-looking trees at that. But we'll get back up in the arboreal canopy later, after a better look at the campsite which, handily enough, is the only one in all of Grizedale.

The camping part of the site lies in a lovely open field with a soothing view of the wooded hills all around, bestowing upon the place a feeling of snug enclosure, as the protective treescapes shut out the rest of the world completely. And we do mean completely, which is good, as there's nothing remotely urban for miles in any direction. You can almost feel the tranquillity rippling right the way through your soul here, especially when you're

sitting by an open fire on one of those balmy summer evenings we wish we had more often.

The section of the site devoted to a yurt and handful of timber pods is existentially opposite; they can be found hiding within the steep wooded hills at the back of the farm, where the atmosphere – though no less idyllic – has an intimate, odd, and almost *Lord of the Rings* sort of feel to it. If not *The Lord of the Rings* then maybe *Shrek*...or *Men in Tights* perhaps... but basically, that of a mystical forest. The more you see of Grizedale campsite the less average it becomes, and it probably won't come as a total surprise that should you not wish to part company with your nag during your camping holiday, why, you can bring him or her along with you, as a nice comfy bed and daily supply of fodder will be theirs for the entirety of your sojourn here. (Obviously the nag we refer to is of the equine variety, just in case there are any family misunderstandings.)

There's a pub nearby, and besides plenty of bridleways for your favourite horsey friend to clip-clop along, there are miles and miles of paths in the woods where the imagination can be let loose completely. Bizarre timber sculptures are dotted about nearby Grizedale Forest and could easily have been carved by hobbits. But these are all just sideshows in the forest, for the real action is either way-up in the tree canopy as part of the Go Ape high wire course, or getting down and very dirty cycling along the purpose-built ATB tracks on the forest floor.

So there you have it – Grizedale makes the perfect *Cool Camping* site for active folk who like a good dose of adrenaline served alongside their camping. Or those who'd just prefer to sit back in the glorious, soothing, and slightly mystical surroundings, and think about being active, or ponder on which film set the site most resembles. What's certain is that it has Baggins of appeal.

COOL FACTOR A quirky hideaway near all that outdoor action in Grizedale Forest.

WHO'S IN Tents, small campervans, horses, dogs – yes. Large human groups – no.

ON SITE Campfires are allowed and encouraged (as long as you purchase the wood from the farm and don't go scavenging in the forest). There are 50 tent pitches on the lower field. The facilities are housed in a barn at the farm, and are decent enough, but a fair hike from the main camping field, though much closer to the yurt and the camping pods. Four free showers in all (2W, 2M), with baby-changing in the ladies' half of the block, and a washing-up sink available to all genders. The 'horse holiday' available is purely a facility to stable a camper's own horse at the farm.

OFF SITE There aren't a lot of tourist attractions near this back-of-beyond campsite, but those that are here are stunningly different and very exciting. There is obviously the usual kind of Lake District walking available straight from the site, though it's a deal woodier than elsewhere in these parts, but as mentioned Go Ape's (www.goape.co.uk) high wires criss-cross the forest canopy, and an extreme mountain biking course called the North Face Trail (01229 860373; see www.forestry.gov.uk) zips along the woodland floor. Both adventures are designed for those with nerves (and muscles) of steel. If you aren't quite ready for the nerve-jangling, death-defying ATB course, there are miles and miles of forest tracks to cycle along, with gradients to suit all tastes and legs. All the other more traditional attractions of South Lakeland are also accessible by bike, with the Lakeside and Haverthwaite Railway (01539 531594; www.lakesiderailway.co.uk), Windermere Lake Cruises (01539 443360; www.windermere-lakecruises.co.uk), and the Lakes Aquarium (01539 530153; www.lakesaquarium.co.uk) all a pleasant stress- and precipice-free 7-mile pedal away. And another mile (or quick ferry ride across the lake) brings Fell Foot Park (01539 531273) in range, where you can sip tea by the lake or hire a traditional rowing boat.

FOOD AND DRINK The roads into Grizedale are, in a vehicle, nearly as scary as the high wires or extreme biking trails, so many folk won't be going far in the car once settled here. If the stove packs up, the fire goes out, or the camp chef goes on strike, the local pub in Satterthwaite, the Eagles Head (01229 860237; www.eagleshead.co.uk) can cater to just about every taste. The beers (Eagles Head Ale and Grized Ale) are exclusive, and there are regular changes of guest beers from local microbreweries. Should you decide to risk the road, the Kings Arms (01539 436372) in Hawkshead does simple food very well.

GETTING THERE From junction 36 off the M6 follow the A590 towards Barrow-in-Furness for 15 miles. Soon after passing the Lakeside and Haverthwaite Railway you turn right into a lane to Rusland and Satterthwaite, then follow signs for Grizedale Forest. The site is on the right.

PUBLIC TRANSPORT The nearest bus stop is on the A590, 7 miles from site, so you're better off using local taxis for getting around in the vicinity – or even your bikes. The nicest way by public transport is to take the train to Windermere, bus (or walk) to Bowness, steamer to Lakeside, then either walk, bike, or get a taxi from there. An expeditionary holiday.

OPEN All year.

THE DAMAGE Adult £7 per night; child £3. Yurt (sleeping up to 8) £50–£55 per night (depending on weeknight/weekend) and camping pods (sleeping up to 4; minimum 2-night stay) £25 per night – advance booking necessary.

index

Cool Camping: England (3rd edition)
Series Concept and Series Editor: Jonathan Knight
Researched, written, and photographed by: Jonathan Knight,
Sophie Dawson, Keith Didcock, Xenia Gregoriadis, Justin Kirby,
Paul Marsden, Mirio Mella, Andrea Oates, Sam Pow, Sue Smith,
Andy Stothert, Paul Sullivan, Alexandra Tilley Loughrey,
Richard Waters, Dixe Wills, and Jeremy Yuill.
Managing Editor: Sophie Dawson
Design: Roz Keane, Nicola Erdpresser
Styling and cover design: Kenny Grant
Proofreaders: Leanne Bryan, Claire Wedderburn-Maxwell
Editorial Assistants: Amy Sheldrake, Harriet Yeomans
Marketing: Shelley Bowdler

Published by: Punk Publishing, 3 The Yard, Pegasus Place,
London, SE11 5SD

Distributed by: Portfolio Books, 2nd Floor, Westminster House,
Kew Road, Richmond, Surrey, TW9 2ND

All photographs © Jonathan Knight/Sophie Dawson/
Jackie di Stefano/Keith Didcock/Rob Ditcher/Andrea Oates/
Sam Pow/Andy Stothert/Paul Sullivan/Alexandra Tilley
Loughrey/Richard Waters/Dixe Wills/Xenia Gregoriadis/Justin
Kirby/Paul Marsden/Mirio Mella/Sue Smith/Jeremy Yuill
except the following (all reproduced with permission):
p14–15 © iStockphoto.com/Alan Lagadu; p17 © iStockphoto.
com/David Bukach; p89 bottom © Westermill Farm; p153 top
© Dernwood Farm; p193 top ©Holycombe Campsite; p269 ©
Highside Farm; p281 © Gill Head Farm.

Front cover: Turner Hall Farm © Andy Stothert.

First extract on p147 from *Winnie the Pooh* by AA Milne. Text ©
The Trustees of the Pooh Properties 1926. Published by Egmont
UK Ltd London and used with permission. Second extract on p147
from *Pooh's Little Instruction Book* inspired by AA Milne, written by
Joan Powers. Text © The Trustees of the Pooh Properties 1995.
Used with permission of Egmont UK Ltd London.

Map p9 © MAPS IN MINUTES™/Collins Bartholomew (2011).
Regional maps pp16, 26–27, 86–87, 124–125, 168–169, 188–189,
220–221, 240–241, 258–259, 276–277 created with © www.
collinsbartholomew.com data 2010. Reproduced with permission.
Regional mapping supplied by Lovell Johns www.lovelljohns.com.

The publishers and authors have done their best to ensure
the accuracy of all information in *Cool Camping: England*,
however, they can accept no responsibility for any injury, loss
or inconvenience sustained by anyone as a result of information
contained in this book.

Punk Publishing takes its environmental responsibilities seriously.
This book has been printed on paper made from renewable
sources and we continue to work with our printers to reduce our
overall environmental impact.

A BIG THANK YOU! Thanks to everyone who has emailed with
feedback, comments, and suggestions. It's good to see so many
people at one with the *Cool Camping* ethos. In particular, thanks to
the following readers for telling us about their favourite places to
camp: Jennie Bird, Karen Dion, Cara Doddrell, Selina Fitzpatrick,
Simon Ford, Amy and Lars Franke, Felicity Gregory, Mark and
Flo Harris, Sophie Lewis, Bridie Lou, Lisa and Edgar Lovett, Lisa
Mabbley, Gill Marshall, Jodi Mullen, Daniel Nahabedian, Joanna
Reilly, Claire Richards, Julie Richardson, Michelle Roberts,
Marnie Rose, Nichola Stephenson, and Sarah Winter.

HAPPY CAMPERS?

We hope you've enjoyed reading *Cool Camping: England* and that it's inspired you to get out there.

The campsites featured in this book are a personal selection chosen by the Cool Camping team. We have visited hundreds of campsites across England to find this selection, and we hope you like them as much as we do. However, it hasn't been possible to visit every single English campsite. So, if you know of a special place that you think should be included, we'd like to hear about it. Send an email telling us the name and location of the site, some contact details and why it's special. We'll credit all useful contributions in the next edition of the book, and senders of the best emails will receive a complimentary copy. Thanks and see you out there!

england@coolcamping.co.uk